REFERENCE HANDBOOK of grammar & usage

Prepared by the Editorial Staff

SCOTT, FORESMAN AND COMPANY

Design / Robert Amft

INTRODUCTION

Some students would say that they have no need for a book that answers questions about language. "I never have any questions," they say. Oh, no? Read through the following paragraphs. Each describes a situation that leads to a question about language. Is it possible that the no-question students never find themselves in such situations? What about you? Do you ever have questions like these?

? During an interview with the admissions officer of the college you hope to attend, you explain how you have been rehabilitating a used car you recently bought. You end by saying, "The car runs good now." Suddenly you wonder: Should you have said *well* rather than *good*?

? In a letter to a former teacher, you are quoting an amusing conversation you overheard. The final sentence is a question. Where should you put the question mark—inside or outside the closing quotation marks?

? An article you are editing for a student magazine seems excellent except for one sentence: "Lots of students will come forward to voice their opposition to the proposed changes in grade-level assignment." The phrase *Lots of* seems to stick out. Is it too informal for a serious article like this?

? Listening to a TV news interview, you hear a high government official say, "Hopefully, we have the problem solved." The word *hopefully* reminds you of a newspaper column you read a while back, in which the writer deplored a frequent misuse of the word. You no longer remember any of his examples, but you think this might be the use he was condemning. Did the official misuse the word?

? In reading over the first draft of a history report, you come to the sentence "The President hoped to gradually win the support of Congress." The split infinitive—*to gradually win*—immediately catches your eye. You try moving the word *gradually* to a different spot in the sentence. But when you do, the sentence does not seem to you to read as smoothly or as clearly. Must you change it anyway?

? An opposing debater uses the word *data* and pronounces the first *a* like the *a* in *age*. You have always pronounced it like the *a* in *hat*. You conclude that you have been mispronouncing the word. Yet you are puzzled. Why hadn't you noticed before now that others were pronouncing *data* differently? And how come none of your supercritical friends ever corrected your pronunciation?

? At the beginning of a school-board meeting you attend, the members get into a discussion of some new programs. Suddenly one member explodes, "*Underachiever! Low achiever! Exceptional child! Educationally handicapped! Deprived!* We will never take a realistic look at these problems and programs until we stop talking in euphemisms." When the chairman stops the discussion there, pointing out that the programs were not scheduled to be discussed at this particular meeting, you are left with

1

two questions: What is a euphemism? Why did the member think the terms he mentioned were euphemisms?

? At a party, you witness this exchange between two recently introduced guests:

Guest 1 [after a few minutes of conversation]:   You're from the East, aren't you?

Guest 2:   Yes, I am. How did you know?

Guest 1:   From your dialect. The way you pronounced − −

Guest 2:   Dialect! What dialect? I speak perfectly good English.

Guest 1:   I didn't say you didn't. All I said was− −

Guest 2:   I do *not* speak a dialect.

Guest 1 [to the back of departing Guest 2]: Yes you do. Everyone speaks a dialect.

Does everyone speak a dialect?

Of course you have questions like these. Everybody does. And when they come up, this Reference Handbook can help you with the answers. There are almost nine hundred entries, alphabetically arranged to make finding answers easy. The entries fall roughly into four groups:

1) Grammatical items like **Adjective, Preposition, Objective complement, Case, Restrictive and nonrestrictive, Antecedent, Complex sentence, Misplaced modifiers.** The Handbook defines these items and gives examples of them, but does not discuss them at length, since you are already familiar with them from a previous, thorough study of grammar.

2) Particular words and constructions like **good, well; lot of, lots of; who, whom, whose; due to; between you and me; like, as; It's me; bring, take; reason is because.** The Handbook describes their standing in actual usage today, so that you can decide for yourself whether or not a particular construction is appropriate for you to use in a given situation.

3) Topics of universal interest, such as **Divided usage, American and British usage, Propaganda, Defining words, Outline form, Synonym, Loaded words, Fallacies in reasoning, Euphemism, Deadwood, Counter words.** In discussing these, the Handbook emphasizes what is likely to be most interesting and most helpful to students.

4) Entries that have to do with the mechanics of writing—for example, **Spelling, Capital letters, Abbreviations, Indention, Underlining, Footnotes, Plurals of nouns, Bibliography,** and the various punctuation marks (**Comma, Colon, Exclamation mark, Dash, Quotation marks, Parentheses,** etc.).

Suggestion: Before looking up any specific item, you will find it a good idea to read the entries **Levels of English usage** and **Dialect.** They will give you the background for understanding the Handbook's realistic approach to usage, reflecting how language is actually used, not how someone thinks it should be used.

Though your teacher may ask the class as a whole to read and discuss certain entries, the Handbook is primarily intended to be a private reference book—outside, as well as inside, school. You should get help from it when writing letters or papers, or preparing talks. You should use it to check on new terms and constructions that you read or hear, and want to use. Perhaps most important of all is to browse through the book, reading any articles that arouse your curiosity. Getting well acquainted with this Handbook should help you gain confidence in your use of current English.

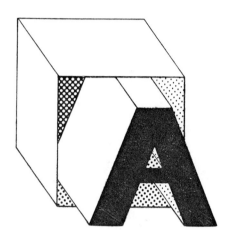

a, an   *A* and *an* are called "indefinite articles"; they function as noun markers, or noun determiners, signaling that a noun is to follow.

   1 The choice between *a* and *an* depends on the beginning *sound*, not the beginning *letter*, of the following word. *A* is used before a consonant sound:

a diploma	a W	a eulogy
a hullabaloo	a union	a one-track mind

An is used before a vowel sound:

an icicle	an S	an igloo
an omen	an underdog	an honest answer

   2 The repetition of *a* or *an* before each item of a series helps make the items more distinct. "An armchair, a table, and a footstool were all that survived the fire" is more emphatic than "An armchair, table, and footstool were all that survived the fire."

   (See also **Articles** and **Noun markers**.)

Abbreviations   Abbreviations are appropriately used in lists, footnotes, and technical writing. With certain exceptions, discussed below, they are not appropriate in ordinary writing.

   1 *Mr., Mrs., Messrs., Mmes.,* and *Dr.* are always abbreviated when used as titles before names; *St.* (Saint) often is. *Esq., Jr., Sr.* are usually abbreviated when they follow a name, as are *A.B.*, *B.S.*, *Ph.D.*, and other academic degrees:

Mr. Peter Preston, Jr.	Philip Russo, B.E., Ed.D.
Mr. Carl F. Davies, Sr.	Mmes. Garren and Kent
Gilbert O. Holcombe, Esq.	Dr. Viens
St. Anthony	Raoul F. Viens, D.D.S.

WRONG: The Sr. member of the firm consulted a Dr.
RIGHT: The senior member of the firm consulted a doctor.
RIGHT: Dr. Schulte was called in by Mr. Gorden, Sr.

2 In formal writing, titles such as *Reverend, Honorable, President, Professor,* and *Senator* are not abbreviated. In informal writing, they are abbreviated — but generally only when they come before initials or a given name:

FORMAL	INFORMAL
Reverend Paul E. Larsen	Rev. Paul E. Larsen
Professor Harold Eaton	Prof. Harold Eaton
Senator Aubrey B. Taylor	Sen. Aubrey B. Taylor

In newspapers and some magazines, however, where space is limited, the abbreviation is used alone with a surname: Rev. Larsen, Sen. Taylor. (See also **Reverend.**)

3 Certain indications of time — A.D., B.C., *a.m., p.m.* — are always abbreviated when used with figures:

670 A.D. (*or* A.D. 670)   44 B.C.   10:25 a.m.   8:15 p.m.

4 A few rather formal Latin expressions are almost always abbreviated:

cf.	*confer*	compare
e.g.	*exempli gratia*	for example
et al.	*et alii*	and others
etc.	*et cetera*	and so forth
i.e.	*id est*	that is
N.B. (*or* n.b.)	*nota bene*	note well
viz.	*videlicet*	namely
vs.	*versus*	against

In informal writing, the English equivalents of these Latin phrases are usually more appropriate.

5 Periods are used after abbreviations, except in the following instances:

a) There is a growing tendency to omit periods with the abbreviations of names of government agencies and organizations commonly referred to by their initials: *FBI, FEPC, NASA, SEC, AMA, NBC, MP.*

b) Periods are generally not used with scientific and technical abbreviations, which are regarded more as symbols than as abbreviations: *SOS,*

4

KDKA (in radio); *DDT, CH₄, C₉H₈O₄* (in chemistry); *cosec, tan* (in mathematics); *ft-lb, cgs, rpm* (in physics; used after figures).

    c) When an abbreviation comes at the end of a sentence that is punctuated with a period, only one mark is used:

A bus leaves at 10:30 a.m. and at 8:20 p.m.
But: Did you tell her that the plane leaves at 11:45 p.m.?

ability   After *ability*, use *to* and an infinitive:

But does Dan have the ability *to think* under pressure? [Not: the ability *of thinking*.]

Often the idea can be more simply expressed by using *can*:

But can Dan think under pressure?

    A noun following *ability* is preceded by *in*:

Ellen showed an even greater ability *in* science. [Not: ability *for* science.]

able   Using *able* and a passive infinitive instead of *can* or *could* results in awkward sentences:

AWKWARD: Everyone knows that Mike is not able to be hurried.
BETTER: Everyone knows that Mike cannot be hurried.

above   The use of *above* as a noun or adjective to refer to preceding material is appropriate in legal or business writing and in reference works:

The above is a summary of Dr. Brown's theory.
The above sentiments seem quite dated to today's youth.

    In other writing this use of *above* is avoided by many people, and the material is identified in some other way: "The statistics just quoted . . ," "The summary given in the preceding paragraph . . .," and so on.

absolutely   In informal English *absolutely* is used to mean "positively" or "unquestionably":

He is absolutely the stingiest man alive.

In conversation it is common as an overly emphatic, rather pompous "yes":

"Are you sure Ray will keep his promise?" "Absolutely."

    In most writing (except for dialogue) *absolutely* should be used only in its original meaning, "completely; unconditionally":

Your argument is absolutely logical, but your facts are wrong.
Mr. Davis is absolutely determined to sue the landlord.

5

Absolute phrases   Phrases that have no expressed *grammatical* connection with the rest of the sentence, though they are, of course, related to it in meaning:

The walks shoveled, Jerry came to the back door for his dollar.
An hour later, *letter in hand,* Sarah headed for the mailbox.
There stood Ralph, *his eyes sparkling with excitement.*

Absolute phrases offer a writer an effective means of adding narrative and descriptive details in a minimum number of words. Such phrases, considered modifiers of the whole sentence, are always set off by commas. (See also **Participial phrase.**)

Abstract and concrete words   Concrete words are words that name persons, places, and things that can be seen and touched: *infant, George, Paris, ravine, lion, bicycle, penny.* The referents of these words actually exist in the real world. Abstract words are words that name feelings, ideas, and actions — things that we cannot see or touch: *fear, honesty, courtesy, selfishness, laziness, greed, affection.* The referents of these words do not actually exist — as specific physical objects — in the real world.

Accent   In words of more than a single syllable, one syllable is accented — or stressed — harder than the others. This increased emphasis is called the *primary,* or *main,* accent. Some dictionaries indicate this primary stress by a heavy slant mark placed after the accented syllable: /sāf'tē/, /rō man'tik/. Other dictionaries use a "high-set" straight mark placed before the accented syllable: /'sāf-tē/, /rō-'mant-ik/.
Sometimes words of two or more syllables also have another syllable stressed, but with about half the force given to the primary accent. This lighter stress is called the *secondary* accent. It is indicated in some dictionaries by a light slant mark placed after the syllable: /dôg'kärt'/, /klam'-bāk'/, /mak'ə rō'nē/. In other dictionaries this secondary accent is indicated by a "low-set" straight mark placed before the syllable: /'dȯg-ˌkärt/, /'klam-ˌbāk/, /ˌmak-ə-'rō-nē/.

Accent marks   In formal writing, French words that have been added to English keep the accent marks used in their original French spelling. For example:

ACUTE ACCENT: blasé   exposé   fiancée   résumé
CIRCUMFLEX ACCENT: fête   tête-à-tête   rôle   crêpe
GRAVE ACCENT: suède   à la carte

In writing that is not formal, the accent marks are usually dropped unless they are needed to indicate the pronunciation. In *résumé* and *exposé,* for example, they are clearly useful in showing that these are words of three syllables, not two. But *suede* and *role* and *crepe* can be pronounced correctly without the aid of the marks.

accept, except   The similarity in sound causes these words to be confused. *Accept* means "take or receive; consent to receive; say *yes* to." It is always a verb:

Lem accepted the trophy on behalf of the team.
Who would accept such a flimsy excuse?
So far ten people have accepted our invitation.

Except is most commonly used as a preposition meaning "but":

Every room except the kitchen was repainted.

In formal English *except* is also used as a verb meaning "take out; leave out; exclude; exempt; excuse":

Mothers of small children are generally excepted from jury duty.

accompany   When *accompanied* means "escorted" or "attended," the preposition *by* is used:

The producer was accompanied by three members of his staff.

When it means "supplemented," *with* is used:

He accompanied his handshake with a pat on the shoulder.

Remember to keep the *y* when you add the ending *-ing*: *accompany, accompanying.*

Accusative case   See **Objective case.**

acoustics   When *acoustics* means "the qualities of a room or hall that determine how well sounds can be heard in it," it is considered plural and takes a plural verb:

We were told that the acoustics in Penn Hall *were* bad.

When its meaning is "the science of sound," it takes a singular verb (like the science of *mathematics*):

Is acoustics *being taught* there this semester?

Acronym   A word formed from the initial letters or syllables of other words:

AID   (from *A*gency for *I*nternational *D*evelopment)
Alcoa   (from *Al*uminum *Co*mpany of *A*merica)
CARE   (from *C*ooperative for *A*merican *R*emittances to *E*urope)
Gestapo   (from *Ge*heime *Staat*s *Po*lizei, secret state police)
NASA   (from *N*ational *A*eronautics and *S*pace *A*dministration)
radar   (from *ra*dio *d*etecting *a*nd *r*anging)
scuba   (from *s*elf-*c*ontained *u*nderwater *b*reathing *a*pparatus)
Zip code   (from *Z*one *I*mprovement *P*lan code)

Some acronyms like *radar, scuba,* and *Zip code* provide a convenient name for a new device or system. Others are mainly abbreviations of company or organization names, which may or may not suggest the purpose of the organization, as *AID* and *CARE* do. But acronyms differ from abbreviations in that they are words rather than a series of letters which can be pronounced only as letters, like *U.S.M.C.* or *KLM*.

(Compare **Blend.**)

act   When *act* means "seem or pretend to be" or "behave as though one were," it is a linking verb and is followed by an adjective, not an adverb:

She acts stupid, so everyone thinks she is stupid.
Tell Ed not to act so foolish when Mr. Hill is around.

Active and passive voice   1 A verb is said to be in the active voice when its subject is the doer of the action, and in the passive voice when its subject is the receiver of the action. A passive verb is a form of the verb *be* plus the past participle: *is written, was written, had been written, will be written,* etc. (Other forms are active.)

ACTIVE: A ten-year-old boy wrote the prizewinning slogan.
PASSIVE: The prizewinning slogan was written by a ten-year-old boy.

2 Passive verbs are useful and effective when the doer of the action is unknown, unimportant, or obvious, or when special emphasis is wanted for the receiver of the action:

Red paint had been splashed on all the walls.   [Doer unknown.]
Guns should be kept out of the reach of children.   [Doer unimportant.]
Evans was reelected last November.   [Doer obvious.]
Every building on the block was flattened by the cyclone.   [Emphasis wanted for the receiver of the action.]

Except for situations like these, however, active verbs are generally preferable. They are not only more natural, but much more direct and forceful:

AWKWARD: Whenever an error was found by Mr. Crabbe, the entire letter had to be retyped by Jenny.
MORE DIRECT: Whenever Mr. Crabbe found an error, Jenny had to retype the entire letter.

ad   *Ad* is the short, or clipped, form of *advertisement*. Since it is not an abbreviation, it is not followed by a period. The abbreviation is *adv.* or *advt.*

Ad is not usually appropriate in formal style but is used elsewhere. (See **Clipped words.**)

Adage   See **Epigram.**

adapt   When *adapt* means "adjust," it is followed by *to*:

They found it hard to adapt themselves to this strict discipline.

When it means "modify or alter for a different use," it is followed by *for* or *from*:

The author herself will adapt her stories for TV.
The movie was adapted from a chapter in *Destiny Bay*.

Addresses   When an address appears in a list or in a sentence, commas are used to set off the various parts (the house number and street, the city, the state and Zip code):

John Laird, 11019 Oakwood Terrace, Silver Spring, Maryland 20901
Mrs. Darrell Walker, 2833 Foster Avenue, Pine Valley Arizona 85999, is in charge of the contest entries.

(For the forms of addresses in letters and on envelopes, see **Letters**, sections 1, 2, and 5.)

Adjective   An adjective modifies a noun or pronoun; that is, it makes the meaning of the noun or pronoun more exact by describing or limiting it: an *arrogant* waiter, *orange* slacks, *most* newspapers, *Italian* opera, a *complaining* tenant, *that useless* vase.

1 Types. There are two general types of adjectives:

a) *Descriptive adjectives* modify nouns by telling a quality, a characteristic, or a condition of the persons or things named: a *stout* woman, *sweet* pickles, *black* and *white* flags, *mysterious* signals, a *golden* apple, a *soft-cooked* egg, the *brass* ring, a *dripping* faucet, the *forgotten* man. (Notice that *brass*, often used as a noun, is here used as an adjective; and that *dripping* and *forgotten*, parts of verbs, are here used as adjectives.)

b) *Limiting adjectives* point out the persons or things in some way or indicate number or quantity: *these* bills, *this* pencil, *that* clerk, *my two* ties, *some* students, *thirteen* guests, a *double* dose.

Proper adjectives are derived from proper nouns. Sometimes they are used as limiting adjectives (telling which ones are meant): the *Victorian* years, *Spanish* citizens, *Japanese* products. Sometimes they are used as descriptive adjectives (telling what kind): *Victorian* propriety, *Spanish* flair, *Japanese* courtesy. A number of proper adjectives have been used so often in a descriptive sense that they have become simple descriptive adjectives, written without a capital letter: *cashmere* sweaters, a *bowdlerized* book, *turkish* towels, *madras* jacket.

2 Position of adjectives. (a) Adjectives ordinarily stand immediately before the word they modify:

a *gray* sky	the *overseasoned, undercooked* stew	*several* boys
a *flat* tire	*two grouchy-looking old* men	a *certain* person

b) In some instances, adjectives are placed after the nouns they modify:

In the distance, they saw the woods, *dark* and *forbidding*. [For greater emphasis.]
Her father, *purple* with rage, pointed to the crumpled fender. [Adjective is modified by other words.]
The court *martial* is scheduled for the last week in May. [Adjective is part of a special compound word.]

c) When used as predicate complements, adjectives follow the verb—either a form of the verb *be* or of some other linking verb (*feel, seem, become, sound, taste*, etc.):

I was *afraid* too.
The boys felt *silly*.
His suspicions seem *ridiculous*.
Then the clerk became *insolent*.

(See **Linking verb.**)

3 Effective use of adjectives. "Think twice before you use an adjective," Carl Sandburg is said to have advised a writer. In following his advice, keep three points in mind. First, the adjectives you use should add to the meaning of your statements, should make your word pictures more exact. Unless they do, they are excess baggage and are better omitted. For example, in the sentence "Before he was twenty, he was the author of a successful best seller," the adjective *successful* adds nothing to the meaning; all best sellers are by definition "successful."

Second, vague, general adjectives like *good, bad, awful*, and *nice* should be avoided, especially in writing. Such adjectives, sometimes called *counter words*, seldom convey exact meanings; they merely express approval or disapproval. Describing a person as *nice*, for example, tells only that you like him, but not why you find him likable. Is it because he is *friendly, generous, amusing, honest, impartial, courteous, candid,* or *thoughtful*? Adjectives like these are needed to make descriptions meaningful and exact.

Third, avoid overloading your writing with useless, repetitious modifiers, as in "He had great big enormous hands." Using three adjectives here merely clutters up the picture; *great* and *big* add nothing once you have said *enormous*. Remember that it is not the number of adjectives you use, but their exactness, that makes writing effective.

4 Comparison. For a discussion of the use of adjectives in making comparisons, including adjectives like *unique, perfect, round, square, impossible*, see **Comparison of adjectives and adverbs** and **Faulty comparisons.**

Adjective clause A group of words containing a subject and verb that does the work of an adjective—that is, it modifies a noun or pronoun in

the sentence. An adjective clause is usually introduced by a relative pro
noun (*who, which, that*) or a relative adverb (*when, where, why*):

The player *who caught the pass* was injured.   [Modifies *player*, the antecedent of *who*.]
Blocking my way was a big sedan *that had three flat tires*.   [Modifies *se-
dan*, the antecedent of *that*.]
Mr. Carter made his fortune at a time *when there were no income taxes to
pay*.   [Modifies *time*, the antecedent of *when*.]

Often no introductory word is used:

The statistics *he quoted* were impressive — and misleading.   [Instead of:
that he quoted or *which he quoted*.]

(For help with punctuation, see **Comma**, section 5.)

Adjective phrases   Prepositional, participial, and infinitive phrases are
often used as adjectives, modifying a noun or pronoun in their sentences:

PREPOSITIONAL: Thick clouds *of smoke* billowed out.   [Modifies *clouds*;
tells what kind.]
PARTICIPIAL: The man *eating the hot dog* is our minister.   [Modifies *man*;
tells which one.]
PARTICIPIAL: Don't take the magazines *piled on the kitchen table*.   [Modi-
fies *magazines*; tells which ones.]
INFINITIVE: By then it was time *to leave*.   [Modifies *time*; tells what time
it was — time for leaving.]

adlib   From the Latin *ad libitum*, meaning "without restriction." *Adlib* is
used as a verb meaning "to make up as one goes along" or "to depart
from a written or memorized speech," as an adjective meaning "spoken or
composed extemporaneously," and as a noun meaning "something
adlibbed":

Instead of reading the statement he had prepared, the senator adlibbed.
The senator later regretted his adlib statement.
The program ran overtime because of the guest comedian's adlibs.

adult   Pronounced either /ə dult'/ or /ad'ult/.

Adverb   1 Uses. (a) Most adverbs are used to modify a verb, an adjective, an adverb, or a whole clause or sentence:

VERB MODIFIERS: Pete spoke *angrily*.   [Tells how he spoke.]
Pete slid *down*.   [Tells where he slid.]
Pete came *later*.   [Tells when he came.]
ADJECTIVE MODIFIERS: She is *unusually* fat.   [How fat?]
It was *very* expensive.   [How expensive?]

11

ADVERB MODIFIERS: He draws *extremely* well.   [How well?]
                    She speaks *very* slowly.   [How slowly?]
SENTENCE MODIFIERS: *Luckily*, I had another key.
                      Unfortunately, everyone distrusts him.

b) *Conjunctive adverbs* serve a double purpose — to join two clauses or sentences and also to indicate how the ideas in the two are related:

Huckleberry Finn has been widely read as an adventure story; *therefore* many people mistakenly think it is nothing more.

(See **Conjunctive adverbs.**)

c) *Interrogative adverbs* are used to introduce questions:

Why didn't you explain?
Where should we go to get good chili?
How did he break his arm?

2 Types. Adverbs can be conveniently classified by meaning:
a) Adverbs of manner — tell how:

neatly   clumsily   fluently   expertly   well   carelessly

b) Adverbs of time — tell when:

later   afterwards   beforehand   first   last   next

c) Adverbs of place and direction — tell where:

upstairs   forward   there   north   above   up   down

d) Adverbs of degree and measure — tell how much or to what extent:

nearly	very	entirely	surely	extremely
almost	less	much	quite	completely

(See **Intensifier.**)

3 Forms. Most adverbs are adjectives or participles plus the ending *-ly* (*swiftly, quietly, selfishly, resignedly, simperingly*). But the *-ly* ending is not a sure sign that a word is an adverb; there are dozens of common adjectives that have an *-ly* ending: *friendly, homely, manly, cowardly, leisurely.* And a large number of adverbs have developed from Old English forms without a special ending to distinguish them: *now, quite, since, then, there, where,* etc.

A number of adverbs have two forms, one ending in *-ly* and one that is the same as the adjective form:

cheaply — cheap	highly — high	secondly — second
closely — close	lately — late	sharply — sharp
deeply — deep	loudly — loud	slowly — slow
fairly — fair	nearly — near	smoothly — smooth
firstly — first	quickly — quick	tightly — tight
hardly — hard	rightly — right	wrongly — wrong

12

Some of these pairs are used interchangeably: *Drive slowly* or *Drive slow, Don't talk so loudly* or *Don't talk so loud*. (Formal English is likely to use the *-ly* form of such words; informal English is likely to use the shorter form.) But others cannot be used interchangeably, since the two forms have quite different meanings:

He came *near*.   But: It is *nearly* finished.
Kay tried *hard*.   But: She *hardly* noticed us.
I aimed too *high*.   But: Bill spoke *highly* of you.

4 Position. For the position of adverbs like *only, just, almost, even, hardly, nearly, scarcely* (in sentences like "He only ate one egg"), see **only.**

5 Effective use. Adverbs, like adjectives, should be used for a definite purpose—to make the meaning more exact, to give the reader a more vivid picture. Adverbs, like all words you use, should also be appropriate to the tone of your writing as a whole. For a specific suggestion concerning appropriateness, see **Conjunctive adverbs,** section 2.

6 Comparison. See **Comparison of adjectives and adverbs** and **Faulty comparisons.**

Adverb clause   A group of words containing a subject and verb that does the work of an adverb—that is, it serves as a modifier answering such questions as Why? How? When? Where? Under what condition? Adverb clauses are introduced by a subordinating conjunction:

Larry left **because** *he had already seen the second feature twice.*   [Tells why he left.]
Don strutted around **as if** *he owned the place.*   [Tells how he strutted.]
I ducked out of sight **whenever** *he came in.*   [Tells when I ducked.]
If *she isn't careful*, she will outsmart herself.   [Tells under what condition she will outsmart herself.]

An adverb clause at the beginning of a sentence is usually set off by a comma unless it is very short and there is no danger of misreading. (For further help with punctuation, see **Comma,** sections 4a and 5.)

Adverbial nouns   Nouns often serve as adverbs, telling how far, how long, how often, how much, when, and so on. But even though they do the work of adverbs, they are still considered nouns because they can be modified by adjectives and can have either a singular or plural form. (Some grammarians call these adverbial nouns simply "adverbials.")

I must have hiked ten *miles*.   [Tells how far; is modified by the adjective *ten*.]
The meeting lasted several *hours*.   [Tells how long; is modified by the adjective *several*.]
The festival begins the last *week* in May.   [Tells when; is modified by the adjective *last* and the phrase *in May*.]

13

Adverb phrases   Prepositional phrases and infinitive phrases are often used as adverb modifiers, answering such questions as How? When? Where? Why?

PREPOSITIONAL: He walked *with a limp.*   [Tells how.]
Call me *after lunch.*   [Tells when.]
I met them *at the gym.*   [Tells where.]
INFINITIVE: We arrived early *to get seats in the front row.*   [Tells why.]

advertisement   Pronounced /ad'vər tīz'mənt/ or /ad vėr'tis mənt/.

adviser, advisor   *Adviser* has been the more common spelling, but the *-or* form, because of its similarity to *advisory*, is being increasingly used.

-ae-, -oe-   The digraphs *-ae-* and *-oe-*, found in words that come from Greek and Latin, are both pronounced as if they were written *e* (a "long *e*" as in *equal* or a "short *e*" as in *echo*). Today the tendency is to simplify the spelling of such words to match their pronunciation:

ORIGINAL	SIMPLIFIED
aesthetic	esthetic
amoeba	ameba
anaemic	anemic
encyclopaedia	encyclopedia
mediaeval	medieval
Mount Aetna	Mount Etna
oesophagus	esophagus
subpoena	subpena

Very formal and technical writings generally keep the digraphs. And the digraph is always kept in Latin and Greek proper names (*Caesar, Oedipus*) and in Latin plurals (*antennae, larvae*).

Dictionaries frequently give both spellings. To find which is preferred for a particular word, consult a dictionary.

affect, effect   The similarity in sound causes these words to be confused. *Affect* is always a verb; it is most frequently used to mean either "to influence" or "to pretend to have or feel":

I refused to let her grouchiness affect me.
Sam affected indifference, though in truth he was greatly concerned.

Effect is used chiefly as a noun meaning "result" or "consequence":

His threats had no effect on the people upstairs.

In formal English *effect* is also used as a verb meaning "to bring about or make happen":

Father Ives effected a reconciliation between the two families.

14

afflicted   Followed by *with*, not *by*:

The valley was afflicted first with famine, then with cholera.

afterward, afterwards   Both forms are used in the United States, *afterward* being slightly more common. In England only *afterwards* is used.

again, against   Usually pronounced /ə gen'/ and /ə genst'/ by Americans. In British usage, /ə gān'/ and /ə gānst'/ are general.

aggravate   In formal English *aggravate* means "increase or make worse":

His flattery only aggravated my dislike for him.

In informal speech it is used to mean "annoy" or "irritate":

That whining voice of hers aggravates people.

agree   The preposition to be used with *agree* depends on the meaning intended:

Nora agreed *with* Len that the play was amateurish.   [Had the same opinion as.]
We tried to persuade them to agree *to* Keith's proposal.   [Consent to.]
Two weeks passed, and they still couldn't agree *on* a name for the baby. [Come to a common decision about.]
"You can have your gourmet food; it just doesn't agree *with* me," he sputtered.   [Have a good effect on; suit.]
Rob's story agrees *with* Harold's.   [Corresponds with.]

Agreement   In grammar, when we say that two words "agree," we mean that they are the same in person, number, case, or gender. In the sentence "Don't Jerry work in Waukegan?" the subject and verb do not agree. The subject *Jerry* is singular, and the verb *Don't* is plural. If the verb is changed to the singular form *Doesn't*, then the two words agree: "Doesn't Jerry work in Waukegan?"

   1 A verb agrees with its subject in person and number:

I *am* always the last one to know.   [First person singular verb *am* agrees with first person singular subject *I*.]

   a) Phrases or clauses coming between the subject and the verb do not affect the subject-verb agreement. A singular subject requires a singular verb, and a plural subject a plural verb:

A long list of telephone numbers *was* the only clue they had.   [Third person singular verb *was* agrees with third person singular subject *list*.]
All the words in the column at the right *are* of Spanish origin.   [Plural verb *are* agrees with plural subject *words*.]

(See **together with**.)

15

b) Compound subjects joined by *and* take a plural verb unless the parts of the subject mean only one person or are thought of as one thing:

The owner and the editor *determine* the policy of the paper.　[Two people.]
The owner and editor, Mr. Mochel, *writes* the editorials.　[One person.]
Macaroni and cheese *tastes* best when it's hot.
The stress and strain *was beginning* to undermine his health.

c) When the parts of a compound subject are joined by *or, nor, either . . or,* or *neither . . . nor,* the verb usually agrees with the nearer subject part:

Charles or Fred *is* the man to see.
Neither criticism nor ridicule *disturbs* him.
Either the twins or George *is going* to take charge.
Either George or the twins *are going* to take charge.

But if the subject is plural in idea, a plural verb is often used in informal English, especially in questions and in negative sentences:

Have Jim or Tom *arrived?*　[Formal: *Has* Jim or Tom *arrived?*]
Neither the president nor the vice-president *have signed* yet.　[Formal: *has signed.*]

When the subjects are of different persons, in formal usage the verb agrees with the nearer part:

He or you *are* to drive.　　　　　You or he *is* to drive.

People often avoid the necessity of such a choice of verb form by rewording the sentences:

You will drive, or he will.　　　　He will drive, or you will.

In sentences like the following, the verb agrees with the affirmative part, not the negative:

You, not I, *are invited.*　　　　　I, not you, *am invited.*

People often avoid the problem by rewording the sentences:

You are invited, not I.　　　　　I am invited, not you.

d) A collective noun (one that names a group of persons or things) may take either a singular or a plural verb. The verb is singular if the group is thought of as a unit, plural if the members of the group are acting as individuals:

The band *is going* to the Rose Bowl this year.
The band, as usual, *were straggling* into the auditorium in groups of two or three.

(See also **Collective nouns,** section 1.)

e) The meaning determines whether words like *half, all, one third, some, any, none, more, most, lot, part, rest,* and *number* take singular or plural verbs:

Half of the letters *have been mailed.*   [Tells how many.]
Half of this letter *is* illegible.   [Tells how much.]

One third of the students *live* on campus.   [Tells how many.]
Two thirds of the stock *remains* unsold.   [Tells how much.]

(See **number.**)

f) A subject plural in form but singular in meaning takes a singular verb:

Measles *is* an infectious disease.
Three years *is* a long time to wait.
He said five dollars and thirty cents *was* the usual charge.
Seven yards *doesn't seem* enough to me.
"Thirteen Days in the Desert" *sounds* like the best article.
General Motors *is sponsoring* the program.

g) Singular verbs are used with indefinite pronouns and adjectives — *each, every, either, neither, anyone, anybody, one, everyone, everybody, someone, somebody, nobody, no one:*

Each of the delegates *is introduced* in turn.
Everybody in the tents *was awakened* by the crash.
Someone *was shouting* my name.
Every one of the elms and maples *has been sprayed.*
Neither of the clocks *keeps* accurate time.

h) The verb agrees with the subject regardless of the number of the predicate complement:

His greatest delight *was* his children.
His children *were* his greatest delight.

i) Unusual word order does not affect agreement; the verb generally agrees with the subject, whether the subject follows or precedes it:

When *were* **you** in Cleveland?
Last of all *comes* **Amahl** on his crutches.
Are there any **messages** for me?
Wasn't **anyone** willing to help?
The next day there *were* several **notices** and a new cafeteria **schedule** on the bulletin board.   [A compound subject.]

In informal usage the expletive *there* is sometimes followed by a singular verb when the first part of the compound subject is singular:

The next day there *was* a new cafeteria schedule and several notices on the bulletin board.

j) The verb in a relative clause whose subject is *who, which,* or *that* agrees with the antecedent of the relative pronoun:

Tom is the only one of those debaters who *argues* logically.   [Singular verb; the antecedent of *who* is *one.*]
Isn't Judy one of the three girls that *were* told to report?   [Plural verb; the antecedent of *that* is *girls.*]

(See also **one of those who.**)

2 (a) A pronoun generally agrees with its antecedent in person, number, and gender:

Emily checked every answer before *she* handed in *her* paper.   [*She* and *her* agree with the antecedent *Emily* — third person singular, feminine.]
The boy looked back and waved *his* hand just before *he* turned the corner.   [*His* and *he* agree with the antecedent *boy* — third person singular, masculine.]

b) Singular pronouns are generally used to refer to the indefinite pronouns *one, anybody, anyone, each, either, neither, everybody, everyone, somebody, someone, nobody,* and *no one:*

Neither of the men felt that *he* was responsible.
Somebody had caught *her* heel in the escalator.
Before anyone signs the contract, *he* should read the fine print.   [The masculine form *he* is used even if the "anyone" turns out to be female.]

In informal conversation, plural pronouns are often used in such sentences, but the plurals are inappropriate in writing and in formal speech.
Sometimes the indefinite pronouns are so obviously plural in meaning that using singular pronouns to refer to them would sound ridiculous:

When *everybody* had arrived, Mr. Hull told **him** the good news.

In informal English a plural pronoun would be used in sentences like this. In formal English the sentence would be rephrased so as not to violate the grammatical agreement.

INFORMAL: When *everybody* had arrived, Mr. Hull told **them** the good news.
FORMAL: When *all the members* had arrived, Mr. Hull told **them** the good news.

(See also **he or she, his or her.**)

3 A demonstrative adjective agrees with its noun in number:

I prefer *that* kind of shoes.   [*That* is singular, to agree with the singular noun *kind.*]
All *those* kinds of shoes are inferior to the Lastever brand.   [*Those* is plural, to agree with the plural noun *kinds.*]

(See **Demonstratives** and **kind, sort.**)

ain't   Used in nonstandard English as a contraction for *am not, is not, are not, has not, have not.*

Some authorities feel that *ain't* would be a useful addition to informal English, particularly as the contraction for *am I not*, which has none that can be pronounced easily (*amn't I* is hard to say). They defend *ain't I* as an appropriate colloquial expression in questions: "I'm going to ride with you, ain't I?" (For some reason *aren't I*, which is certainly no more "correct" grammatically than *ain't I*, is more readily accepted: "I'm going to ride with you, aren't I?") But because of the strong social and educational pressure against *ain't*, most users of standard English avoid it, even as a contraction for *am I not.*

The problem does not arise in formal English, which avoids contractions.

a la, à la   Originally French; now widely used as an English preposition meaning "in the manner of; in the style of":

This whodunit is masterfully done—suspense a la Hitchcock.

In formal writing and most fashion advertising the accent mark is kept: *à la.* Informal writing usually omits it.

à la mode   This French phrase meaning "according to the fashion" has become part of the English language. It is most frequently used in reference to food: cake à la mode (cake with ice cream), beef à la mode (beef with vegetables cooked in the gravy).

In informal usage it is often written without the accent mark—*a la mode*—or as one word, without the accent mark—*alamode.*

alibi   In formal and legal usage *alibi* means "the plea or the fact that a person accused of a crime was in another place when it was committed":

He had a perfect alibi: he was with Sheriff Fingland at the time of the robbery.

In informal usage the meaning of *alibi* is much broader. It is used to refer to any excuse for any offense, important or unimportant, and also as a verb meaning "to make an excuse":

I wonder what alibi Lynn will have for not showing up.
"I'd like to hear Sam alibi himself out of this," he added.

all and its compounds   1 **All right** is used both as an adjective and as an adverb:

Ben will be all right after a few days of rest.   [Modifies the noun *Ben.*]
Sammy was there all right; he came early and left late.   [Adverb meaning "certainly."]
All right, you can keep it.   [Adverb meaning "very well; yes."]

The spelling *alright* is occasionally found in comic strips, advertisements, and familiar writing, but it is not yet generally accepted in either formal or informal writing. Always write the two words—*all right*.

2 All ready. When in doubt about writing *all ready* or *already*, use this test: If you could use the word *ready* alone, without changing the meaning of the sentence, *all ready* is the one to use:

By six-thirty the house was all ready for company.
I was all ready to resign at the last meeting.

Already is an adverb of time:

Mr. Glanz had already recorded the test grades.

3 All together. The same test applies to choosing between *all together* and *altogether*. If the word *together* could be used alone, without changing the meaning, write *all together*:

The kittens were huddled all together in a corner of the box.

Altogether is a rather formal adverb meaning "completely":

It is altogether impossible to please him.

4 All-around is a compound meaning "having many abilities, talents, or uses":

Jeb was truly an all-around handyman.

In informal English the form *all-round* is often used.

Alliteration   Literary device of repeating the same initial sound several times in rather close succession. Writers of poetry and literary prose often make use of alliteration to gain attention, to bind phrases together, or to create a musical effect:

> Out of the night that covers me,
>   Black as the pit from pole to pole. . . .
>   —W. E. Henley, "Invictus"

Alliteration gives many advertising and political slogans their catchy quality:

Vitamins for Vim and Vigor   Watch Watson Win

Inexperienced writers should be careful in their use of alliteration. Although it can be effective for special purposes, it is usually out of place in everyday factual writing. There it tends to attract attention to the words themselves and away from the ideas.

all of   The preposition *of* is usual with *all* before pronouns:

All of us have season tickets.   Mom packed all of them in one carton.

All of is often used before nouns, also, though the *of* is not necessary and would probably be omitted in formal writing:

GENERAL USAGE: You cannot please all of the customers all of the time.
FORMAL WRITING: You cannot please all the customers all the time.

allow   Used to mean "declare; think; suppose" in some local dialects·

DIALECT: Grandpa allowed it was too early to plow.
STANDARD: Grandpa thought it was too early to plow.

all right   See **all and its compounds,** section 1.

all the farther, all the faster, etc.   Localisms for *as far as, as fast as,* etc.

LOCALISM: This is all the farther the bus will take us.
STANDARD: This is as far as the bus will take us.

allude, refer   Both *allude* and *refer* mean "to speak of something in a way to turn attention to it." But *allude* means "to call attention *indirectly*," in contrast to *refer*, which implies a direct, open, specific mention:

No, Farrell did not actually refer to any of the members by name. But I'm sure I know which ones he was alluding to when he spoke of "opportunists in the club who think only of themselves."

Allusion   A brief reference to a person, place, thing, or event that is familiar to most people. By using an allusion, a writer or speaker can in a few words convey a great deal of meaning. For example, in a short story an author might refer to one of the characters, a Silas Smith, as "the Hitler of Ridgetown." Because almost everyone knows who Adolf Hitler was and what sort of person he was, the author's intended meaning would be immediately clear to readers. They would know the writer was suggesting that Smith was not an admirable man, that he was a dictator, that he was domineering and overbearing. The author might even — depending on the context — be suggesting that Smith controlled the political affairs of Ridgetown. Notice that an allusion like this helps not only to describe Smith but also to indicate the writer's attitude toward him.

History is a rich source of allusions. Literature, the Bible, mythology, and current events also provide many.

Watch for allusions; you will find them used in almost every kind of speech and writing situation — from backyard conversations to cartoons to editorials to commencement addresses. And once you become aware of how an allusion can make meaning vivid and memorable, you will probably want to make greater use of this economical and effective device for getting across ideas and feelings.

allusion   See **illusion, delusion, allusion.**

alma mater   This Latin expression (meaning "bountiful mother") is used to mean "the college, university, or school that a person attended." It is pronounced /al′mə mä′tər/, /äl′mə mä′tər/, or /al′mə mä′tər/.

almost   See **most, almost.**

Alphabetizing   Although business firms and publishers have their own rules to cover special situations, alphabetizing generally follows a few common conventions:

1 Names are listed with the surname first. When the surnames are the same, the order is decided by the first name or first initial. If necessary, the second name or initial is then considered:

Lewis, J. C.
Lewis, James L.
Lewis, James R.
Lewis, Joseph
Lewiss, Cary

Surnames with prefixes are usually alphabetized under the prefix, not under the main part of the name:

De La Rosa, Ernesto
Delcore, James
De Marais, Philip

In some systems, surnames with *Mac* and *Mc* are listed together under *Mac*; in other systems, they are grouped together in a separate section ahead of all other *M*'s. Currently the most common method is to list all such names in strict alphabetical order (Mabry, *MacCarthy*, Maritt, *McCrea*). Surnames with *St.* (St. Aubin, St. Pierre) are sometimes listed with the *Sa*'s (for *Saint*), sometimes with the *St*'s.

2 A title (whether the name of a book, magazine, short story, song, business firm, organization, and so on) is usually listed according to the first word that is not an article:

School for Scandal, The
Science Publications, Inc.
Senior Scholastic
"Sir Patrick Spens"

3 An item in a book index is usually listed according to its important word—the one that users of the index would probably look for first:

Spelling, phonetics applied to, 132

The various phases of a topic are generally listed in alphabetical order after the entry item:

Theater, 293–299, 575–576; Drury Lane, 894, 1084; Elizabethan, 296; in London, 296, 364; in New York, 366–370

already   See **all and its compounds,** section 2.

also   Sometimes used as a connective in spots where *and* would be more appropriate and therefore more effective:

POOR: Uncle Igor had invested his inheritance in Florida real estate, also in blue-chip stocks.
BETTER: Uncle Igor had invested his inheritance in Florida real estate and in blue-chip stocks.

although, though   These two subordinating conjunctions have the same meaning and can be used interchangeably. In modern prose, *though* is much more common than *although*, whether the adverb clause comes at the beginning of a sentence or at the end:

Though (*or* Although) he had heard the joke twice before, he laughed as hard as if it were brand-new.
My report was not very good, though (*or* although) I had spent hours working on it.

The spellings *tho* and *altho* are often used in familiar writing — letters, advertisements, etc. — and are becoming increasingly common in informal writing. But the words should be spelled out in full in formal writing.

altogether   See **all and its compounds,** section 3.

alumnus   *Alumnus* means "a graduate or a former student of a school, college, or university." This borrowed word (meaning "foster son") keeps its original forms in English:

One male graduate:	alumnus	/ə lum'nəs/
Two or more:	alumni	/ə lum'nī/
One female graduate:	alumna	/ə lum'nə/
Two or more:	alumnae	/ə lum'nē/

Alumni is commonly used to refer to both men and women graduates (or former students) of a coeducational school.
To avoid the confusion that may arise in pronouncing the plural ending of these words, many people prefer to use the word *graduates* or, informally, the shortened form *alums* /ə lumz'/.

a.m., p.m.   Abbreviations for the Latin *ante meridiem* ("before noon") and *post meridiem* ("after noon"). These abbreviations are ordinarily used only when the time is given in figures:

The workshop lasted from 10:45 a.m. to 2:30 p.m.   [Not: The workshop lasted from the a.m. to the p.m.]

Since *a.m.* means "before noon" and *p.m.* "after noon," it is redundant to say "The workshop lasted from 10:45 a.m. *in the morning* to 2:30 p.m. *in the afternoon.*" Drop one or the other.

In printed matter, small capital letters are generally used: 8:30 A.M., 9:20 P.M.

M. is the abbreviation for *noon*: *12:00 m.* There is no corresponding abbreviation for *midnight*; *12:00 p.m.* is used.

(See also **Hours.**)

Ambiguity   An ambiguous construction is one that has two or more possible meanings. The most common causes of ambiguity are these:

1 Unclear reference of pronouns.

AMBIGUOUS: Ginny was highly critical of Miss Norton because she is a dyed-in-the-wool perfectionist.

If this sentence appeared in context, the meaning would probably be clear. But to avoid any confusion, the writer should indicate more clearly the specific meaning intended:

CLEAR: Ginny, being a dyed-in-the-wool perfectionist, was highly critical of Miss Norton.

CLEAR: Ginny was highly critical of Miss Norton, who is a dyed-in-the-wool perfectionist.

CLEAR: Ginny, who is a dyed-in-the-wool perfectionist, was highly critical of Miss Norton.

(See **Reference of pronouns.**)

2 Squinting and misplaced modifiers. A squinting modifier is ambiguous because it might refer to either the preceding or the following construction:

AMBIGUOUS: Any waitress who dared to complain frequently was assigned to work at the lunch counter.

CLEAR: Any waitress who frequently dared to complain was assigned to work at the lunch counter.

CLEAR: Any waitress who dared to complain was frequently assigned to work at the lunch counter.

(See **Squinting modifiers.**)

Misplaced modifiers, because of their position in the sentence, do not clearly modify the word they are intended to modify. They are also often a source of humor that the writer does not intend:

MISPLACED: We saw hundreds of acres of beautiful pines flying over northern Wisconsin.

REVISED: Flying over northern Wisconsin, we saw hundreds of acres of beautiful pines.

(See **Misplaced modifiers.**)

3 Incomplete expressions, especially in comparisons:

AMBIGUOUS: The manager distrusted Tim as much as Harold.
CLEAR: The manager distrusted both Tim and Harold.
CLEAR: The manager distrusted Tim as much as Harold did.
CLEAR: The manager distrusted Tim as much as he did Harold.

American   Since no convenient adjective or noun can be formed from the name of our country, the United States, we use *American*, from the name of the continent. This is an obviously inexact term, for citizens of other North American countries and of Central and South America are as "American" as we are. Our use of the term for the people and the products of *our* country is often resented by other Americans. Despite inexactness and complaints, longstanding habit encourages our continuing to use the term. But in situations where the usage might be considered offensive, it would be wise to substitute other words — for example, "a citizen of the United States" instead of "an American"; "a product of the United States" instead of "an American product."

American and British usage   Both Americans and Englishmen speak English, but they do not speak exactly the same kind of English. The most extreme language differences are found, of course, in regional or provincial dialects. You would have a great deal of trouble understanding a Yorkshireman, for instance, or a London cockney. The contrast between the standard language (the language of the majority of educated people) in the two countries is less striking. But there still are differences to be noted.

There are, to begin with, a few variations in spelling. The English prefer the -*re* ending for words like *lustre*, *sabre*, *centimetre*. They still keep the -*our* ending in words like *colour* and *humour*. They use *x* in words like *reflexion* and *genuflexion* (which we spell *reflection* and *genuflection*). And they double more consonants than we do (*medallist*, *marvellous*, *diagrammed*).

There are a number of differences in vocabulary. For example:

AMERICAN	BRITISH
billboard	hoarding
delivery truck	van
dry-goods store	draper's shop
fender	wing
floorwalker	shopwalker
garbage can	dust bin
garters	sock suspenders
hardware dealer	ironmonger
legal holiday	bank holiday
line (of people, cars)	queue
monkey wrench	spanner

newspaper clipping	newspaper cutting
no parking on shoulder	no stopping on verge
patrol wagon	prison van
private school	public school
public school	council school
roller coaster	switchback
scratch pad	scribbling block

Words and phrases belonging peculiarly to the English, we call *Briticisms*; those that belong peculiarly to us (*charley horse, get the hang of it, to have the jitters, minor league, on the fence, sashay, stick-to-it-iveness, gimmick*) the English call *Americanisms*. Such words and phrases are a frequent source of amusement in the two countries—and sometimes also a source of confusion. For instance, by taking words like *wing* and *hoarding* in their usual American sense, you might completely mistake the meaning intended by an English speaker.

You will notice only a few differences in grammar if you compare the standard spoken and written English of the two countries. Collective nouns, for example, are more likely to be plural in British usage: "The government *intend* to correct this"; "The cabinet *are* undecided." And where Americans would say "What *did she have* to do this evening?" Englishmen are likely to say "What *had she got* to do this evening?"

There are enough differences in pronunciation to make an "English accent" and an "American accent" clearly recognizable. The English have different values for the vowels, different stresses, and in general a more rapid speech and a tendency to slur vowels (like the *ar* in *necessary* and the second *or* in *oratory*). American pronunciations are slower and fuller.

But as time goes on, the differences between these two branches of the English language will probably tend to diminish. Modern developments in transportation and communication will bring the two nations closer together through a steady exchange of books, periodicals, movies, teachers, students, tourists, entertainers. As a result, Americans and Englishmen will find it increasingly easier to understand each other.

among, between   See **between, among.**

amount, number   *Amount* is used in referring to "mass nouns"—nouns which name things that can be measured or weighed; *number* is used in referring to "count nouns"—nouns which name things that can be counted:

a small *amount* of dough	a large *number* of doughnuts
a large *amount* of dirt	a small *number* of mud pies

(See also **number.**)

Ampersand   The name for the sign **&**, which means "and." This sign is often used as a space saver in business writing and in charts and tables.

The ampersand is not appropriate as a substitute for the word *and* in general writing.

In addressing or referring to a business firm, you should use the form the firm uses:

Marshall Field & Company   Blaine, Russo and Company

an   See **a, an.**

Analogy   A figure of speech in which a comparison is rather fully developed, suggesting several points of similarity:

. . . Every writer should read and reread what he writes, silently and aloud. His first draft is rather like a road under construction. A reader, like a motorist, would have to go slow and watch for obstructions. A writer, like a builder, must smooth out the bumps and fill in the holes. The final version seems to be effortless because the verbal impediments have been removed and the mental gaps have been bridged. — Sumner Ives, *A New Handbook for Writers*, Alfred A. Knopf, Inc.

and   1 *And* is a coordinating conjunction that connects elements of equal grammatical value:

NOUNS: Mike and Ike; quarters, dimes, and nickels
VERBS: We groaned and moaned.
ADJECTIVES: fat, old, and rich; a dark and stormy night
ADVERBS: slowly and painfully; came closer and closer
PHRASES: in one ear and out the other; arguing stupidly and getting nowhere
SUBORDINATE CLAUSES: You should have asked them who they were and what they wanted.
COORDINATE CLAUSES: I did the work and she got the credit.

2 Inexperienced speakers and writers often use too many *and*'s, with resulting monotony. In some sentences a subordinating conjunction or a *but* or *yet* would express the idea more exactly than *and*:

INEXACT: The fire engines arrived, and a huge crowd had already gathered.
BETTER: When the fire engines arrived, a huge crowd had already gathered.

In other sentences, *and* is used when no connective is needed:

Uncle Harry stood right in the middle of the front row with a phony look of concentration on his face, and secretly wishing he could be a thousand miles away.

The participial phrase *secretly wishing he could be a thousand miles away* is a modifier of the subject *Uncle Harry*. Since it is not a second part of a compound verb, it should not be joined to the rest of the sentence by the conjunction *and*:

Uncle Harry stood right in the middle of the front row with a phony look of concentration on his face, secretly wishing he could be a thousand miles away.

A monotonous succession of *and*'s, as in the following sentences, can generally be avoided by "reducing" some of the details in such a way that all or most of the *and*'s can be dropped:

MONOTONOUS: Mr. Lund was our boss, and he was half owner of the business, and naturally he wanted everyone to work hard every minute and all of us did. And then one day Mick Grady got a job in our department, and he was as lazy as they come.
BETTER: Since Mr. Lund, our boss, was half owner of the business, he naturally wanted everyone to work hard every minute, which all of us did. Then one day Mick Grady, who was as lazy as they come, got a job in our department.

Though the expression *and so* is common (especially in speech), there is no need for using the *and* before the *so*, since it adds nothing to the meaning:

However, Mrs. Vanderpoel had turned down her hearing aid, so she caught only the last two words he said.   [Not: *and so* she caught only the last two words he said.]

3 *And* is sometimes effectively used at the beginning of a sentence, to place special emphasis on the idea that follows:

USUAL: In this letter, Dad said he would never send Uncle Theo another cent, and he meant it.
MORE EMPHATIC: In this letter, Dad said he would never send Uncle Theo another cent. And he meant it.

This device should not be overused, or it loses its effectiveness.

(For punctuation of compound sentences with *and* and of a series with *and*, see **Comma,** sections 1 and 3a.)

and etc.   Since *etc.* is an abbreviation for the Latin *et cetera*, which means "*and* others" or "*and* so forth," the *and* should not be used with *etc.* (See **etc.**)

and/or   A business and legal expression that efficiently indicates three choices — both items mentioned *or* one of the items *or* the other item:

Everyone is asked to contribute toys and/or clothing.

Because many people dislike its business connotation, *and/or* is seldom used in general writing.

and which, and who   *And which* and *and who* are appropriate only when joining a second relative clause to a first one:

We finally replaced our old TV set, which we had bought secondhand and which suffered from every known television ailment.

Using an *and which* or an *and who* (or *but which, but who*) when there is no preceding *which* or *who* clause is a mistake most writers make occasionally. Check your first drafts for sentences like these:

FIRST DRAFT: Dad spent every spare minute looking for a used trailer big enough for all of us, *and which* he could park in a corner of the backyard.
REVISED: Dad spent every spare minute looking for a used trailer big enough for all of us, *which* he could park in a corner of the backyard.

FIRST DRAFT: I myself liked Mrs. Harris, the building manager, a crisp-mannered and crabby-voiced woman, *but who* was concerned about the tenants and did all she could to make life easier for them.
REVISED: I myself liked Mrs. Harris, the building manager, *who* was crisp-mannered and crabby-voiced, *but who* was concerned about the tenants and did all she could to make life easier for them.

angle   A standard American English term for "point of view." Because *angle* has been so overused (especially as a slang term in sentences like "Jake knows all the angles" and "I wonder what his angle is"), it has acquired unfavorable connotations for many people which make it inappropriate for general writing. Use one of its synonyms—*point of view, aspect,* or *standpoint:*

OVERWORKED: Now let's look at the matter from a parent's angle.
SAFER: Now let's look at the matter from a parent's point of view.

Anglicizing   English has borrowed and is still borrowing many words from other languages. We keep the foreign pronunciation and form of some of these words—*coup d'état,* for example, *ciao, soupçon,* and *bravo.* But many borrowed words—especially the ones that prove very useful but are hard for us to pronounce or spell—we *Anglicize.* That is, we bring them into line with English usage by giving them an English pronunciation or form. For instance, the French word *menu* /mə nᵧ'/ is generally given the pronunciation /men'yü/ or /mā'nyü/ in our country. The Spanish *rumba* /rüm'bä/ we usually pronounce /rum'bə/. The German *Gestapo* /gə shtä'pō/ we usually pronounce /gə stä'pō/. And the word *cañon,* borrowed from Spanish, we commonly spell with an *ny* instead of with an *ñ: canyon.* (See **Borrowed words.**)

angry   *Angry at* and *angry about* are used in referring to things:

Hal soon became angry at the waiter's arrogance.
Jeff was sure no one would be angry about the postponement.

In referring to persons, *angry with* is general:

I wasn't angry with him; I was angry with her.

But when the angry feeling is to be stressed, *at* is used:

At this, the boss got so angry at her that he hung up.

(See **mad.**)

annoyed   We are annoyed *at* things and *with* people:

He was annoyed at my interrupting him and said so.
Grandfather will be annoyed with her if she's late again.

By is used when the meaning is "pestered":

Every speaker we've had has been annoyed by hecklers.

Antecedent   The word, phrase, or clause to which a pronoun (or a relative adverb) refers. The pronoun agrees in person, number, and gender with its antecedent, which may precede or follow it:

Uncle Charlie, who has been bald for years, bought himself a toupee for the wedding.   [*Uncle Charlie* is the antecedent of the relative pronoun *who* and the reflexive pronoun *himself*.]
As soon as she saw them, Jane waved to Doug and Larry.   [Here the antecedents follow the pronouns that refer to them: *she—Jane; them—Doug and Larry*.]

anti-   A prefix meaning "against; opposed to; the opposite of; counteracting." It is usually hyphened only before root words beginning with *i* and before proper nouns and adjectives:

antipoverty   anti-intellectual
antirust   anti-Fascist

   Anti- is pronounced /an'ti/ or /an'tī/ or /an'tē/.

Anticipatory subjects   See Expletives.

Anticlimax   In writing, *climax* means the arrangement of two or more items in a rising order—from the least important to the most important, from the least forceful to the most forceful. *Anticlimax* means an abrupt departure from this order. In other words, the writer ends not with the most important item but with a trivial or commonplace one.

   Anticlimax is sometimes used intentionally—and effectively—as a device for humor:

For ours is the age of the four "A's": anxiety, apprehension, agonizing, and aspirin. —James Thurber, *Lanterns and Lances*.

Unintentional anticlimax can make a piece of writing seem ridiculous:

POOR: He was dismissed from the team, expelled from school, disowned by his father, and snubbed by his girl.
BETTER: He was snubbed by his girl, dismissed from the team, expelled from school, and disowned by his father.

Antonym   A word meaning the opposite of another word: *long* and *short* are antonyms, as are *proud* and *humble, cheap* and *expensive, decrease* and *increase, wealth* and *poverty, rough* and *smooth*.

anxious   When *anxious* means "eagerly desirous," it is followed by an infinitive or by *for*:

George was anxious to please the new manager.
Now that he has skis, Hank is anxious for snow.

When *anxious* means "worried," it is followed by *about* or *at*:

You needn't be anxious about Dan; he's an excellent driver.
The director became really anxious at this second postponement.

any and its compounds   1 *Any* is used as an adjective, as a pronoun, and as an adverb:

ADJECTIVE: Do you have any money?
PRONOUN: I haven't had any since the day after payday.
ADVERB: Don't stay any later than ten.

2 As a pronoun, *any* may be either singular or plural (and may take either a singular or a plural verb), depending on the meaning intended:

Wasn't any of the bodyguards paying attention? [Singular; speaker means "Wasn't there even one who was paying attention?"]
I offered to check the list of names and correct any that *were* misspelled. [Plural; speaker expects more than one to be misspelled.]

3 *Anyone* and *anybody* always take singular verbs. They are referred to by singular pronouns in formal English and in most writing:

I can't stand Lola; in fact, I dislike anyone who *acts* as if *she is* always right.
I like anybody who *minds his* own business.
After all, anyone *has* the right to express *his* or *her* opinion.

In colloquial usage, however, plural pronouns are often used. (This is probably because many people feel uncomfortable using *he* and *his* when speaking of both men and women, and because *he or she* and *his or her* seem clumsy.)

I like anybody who minds *their* own business.
After all, anyone has the right to express *their* opinion.

31

4 *Anybody, anyhow, anything*, and *anywhere* are always written as single words. *Anyone* and *anyway* usually are, but when each part has a separate meaning, they are written as two words. (*Any* is then an adjective.) The pronunciation gives a clue to the spelling. If the *any* is stressed, the single-word form should probably be used:

STRESS ON *any*:   Anyone may attend.
STRESS ON *one*:   Any one of these costumes would be better than that.

STRESS ON *any*:   Jim won't go with us anyway.
STRESS ABOUT EQUAL: Any way you look at it, it's the best thing to do.

5 Informal usage sometimes substitutes *anyplace* for *anywhere*. Nonstandard English uses *anywheres* and *anyways*.

Aphorism   See **Epigram.**

Apostrophe (')   **1** The most common use of the apostrophe is in writing the possessive forms of nouns and of some of the indefinite pronouns:

the captain's uniform   the carpenters' tool kits   nobody's business
everyone's opinion   his son-in-law's car   the razor's edge

The apostrophe is not used in the possessive form of the personal pronouns (*hers, its, ours, yours, theirs*) or of *who* (*whose*).
(For further examples, see **Possessive case.**)
2 The apostrophe is used to show the omission of one or more letters in contractions:

don't   I'd   he'll   it's (it is)   they're

It also is used to indicate spots in words in which the speaker does not pronounce certain sounds:

"An' like ever'body else, you're tryin' to talk him out of quittin'," he said.

(See **Conversation.**)
3 For the use of the apostrophe in forming the plural of figures, symbols, letters of the alphabet, and words being discussed as words, see **Plurals of nouns,** section 9.

Apostrophe   A figure of speech in which a speaker or writer addresses an absent person as if he were present, or a thing or idea as if it could understand. For example:

Visit her, gentle Sleep, with wings of healing.—Samuel Taylor Coleridge, "Dejection: An Ode."

Appendix   An addition at the end of a book. It may contain lists of definitions, biographical sketches, maps, charts, or other supplementary material like long tables and documents.

The English plural *appendixes* is much more common now than the Latin plural *appendices* /ə pen′də sēz′/, used mainly in formal writing.

Appositives   **1** *Apposition* means, literally, "a putting beside." An *appositive* is a second noun, or the equivalent of a noun, that is placed beside a first noun to explain it more fully. The appositive often has modifiers.

Mrs. Guevara, *our Spanish teacher*, has a pilot's license.
Little Eddie's favorite form of blackmail, *holding his breath*, always got results.
She discussed her latest theory, *that plants have feelings*.
The word *business* is a common spelling demon.

Introductory expressions (*such as, namely, or, like, that is, for example*) are sometimes used with appositives:

Certain names, such as *Marion* and *Leslie*, are given to both boys and girls.
Some of their furniture—for example, an enormous inflated plastic *armchair*—is downright hideous.

Occasionally an appositive is put before the noun it explains:

A *perfectionist* in everything he did, Mr. Evans did his best to make a perfectionist of his son.

Sometimes the appositive is separated from the noun it explains:

The coral reef lay a few feet under the water—a beautiful, hidden, navigator's *nightmare*.

An appositive is sometimes used to sum up the idea expressed in a preceding group of words:

While driving, Dad often turns around to talk to people in the back seat— a *habit* that makes Mother extremely nervous.

An appositive might sum up a preceding series of nouns:

House, garage, silo, barn—*all* were destroyed by the tornado.

Or a series of appositives may be used to explain a single noun:

The bit parts in our class play—the brattish little *sister*, the gossipy *neighbor*, the inquisitive *mailman*—were far better acting parts than the leads.

2 Appositives agree in case with the words they are in apposition with:

The losers—*Pat* and *I*—had to pay for the hot dogs. [The nominative-case pronoun *I* is used to agree with the subject noun *losers*.]
Mr. Pratt fired us—*Larry*, *Cliff*, and *me*—before the end of the week. [The objective-case pronoun *me* is used to agree with the direct object *us*.]

33

3 For the punctuation of appositives, see **Comma,** section 6, and **Dash,** section 4.

Appropriateness   To be effective, English must be not only clear and lively but also *appropriate*. Language is appropriate when it is suitable to the audience, to the subject, and to the situation. For example, a greeting like "Hiya, Georgie boy" might be quite appropriate for a classmate. But it would be quite inappropriate for an elderly neighbor. For him something like "Hi, Mr. Jones" or "Good evening, Mr. Jones" would be far more suitable. Similarly, the kind of language you would use in a report for the Student Council about a recent (and less than harmonious) committee meeting would be very different from the kind of language you would use in a letter telling your best friend about the meeting. Dignified, objective report language would be appropriate for the first but out of place in the second.

As these examples suggest, there is not just one kind of English, appropriate for every speaking and writing situation; there are different kinds. In general, these different kinds of English can be sorted into three main types: formal, informal, and nonstandard. For a discussion of how these kinds of English differ and how they are used, see **Levels of English usage.**

apt   See **likely, liable, apt.**

Arabic numerals   See **Numbers,** section 5.

Archaic   A term applied to words and expressions once common in the language but no longer in general use. Such expressions are now found only in books of an earlier period or in books that imitate the style of an earlier period: *methinks, certes, howbeit, belike, prithee.*

Argumentum ad hominem   See **Fallacies in reasoning,** section 4.

arise   Situations and difficulties and questions *arise,* but people *rise* (rather formal) or *get up:*

The problems you worry about may never arise.
Be sure to rise (*or* get up) when Mrs. Marsden comes in.

In formal writing and in poetry, *arise* is sometimes used in referring to people.

around, round   In informal English *around* and *round* are used interchangeably. The tendency is to use *round* (or to clip the *a* of *around* so that it sounds like *round*).

They hope to fly round (*or* around) the world some day.
Ted tied a cord round (*or* around) his waist.

Formal English generally uses *around* to mean "here and there" or "in every direction," and *round* to mean "in a circular or a reverse motion":

They walked around a bit and then had dinner.
Magellan's ship was the first to sail round the earth.
Do not turn round now; he is looking this way.

Articles   *A, an,* and *the* are noun determiners generally known as *articles.* *A* and *an* are *indefinite* articles; they point out any one of a group ("*A* boy came"; "I took *an* apple"). *The* is the *definite* article; it points out a certain one of a group ("*The* boy left"; "I ate *the* apple").

Some grammarians regard articles as a class of adjectives. (See **a, an** and **the.**)

as   One of the most versatile words in our language, *as* has several uses:
    1 The conjunction *as* introduces several kinds of adverbial clauses:

In Rome, do *as the Romans do.*   [Shows manner.]
She held her breath as long *as she could.*   [Shows degree.]
The report was as slanted *as a tilted pinball machine (is).*   [Shows comparison.]
As he raised the spear to hurl it at his enemy, a gnat settled on the end of his nose.   [Means "when."]
As it was payday, Neil felt rich enough to order a jumbo hamburger. [Means "since" or "because."]
Mac must have torn his shirt *as he was scrambling over the fence.*   [Means "while."]
Fragile *as she looks,* she is a brown-belt judo expert.   [Means "though."]

The conjunction *as* is a problem in writing. Because of the very variety of its meanings, it is overused. Often a more exact conjunction would make the intended meaning immediately clear:

AMBIGUOUS: As he was busy checking the names and addresses, Kay retyped the first page.
BETTER: Since (*or* Because) he was busy checking the names. . . .
BETTER: While he was busy checking the names. .

    2 As an adverb, *as* shows degree:

Right now he's *as* fat as an outsize elephant.

    3 Used as a relative pronoun, *as* usually follows *the same* or *such*:

The fireplace was *the same* color *as* the walls [were].
You have never seen *such* stupidity *as* I displayed at that moment.

In nonstandard English, *as* is sometimes used for *who* or *that*:

NONSTANDARD: Anyone as has a cold should stay home.
STANDARD: Anyone who has a cold should stay home.

35

4 As a preposition, *as* means "in the role of" or "in the capacity of":

No one in his hometown can imagine him as a great tycoon.
Last summer Ken worked as a busboy at Alfredo's.

(See also **as . . . as** and **like, as.**)

as . . . as   **1** When making a double comparison (like "as much as, if not more than") in speech, we often omit the second *as*:

You are as smart if not smarter than Kay.
Porter's work is as good or better than Clifford's.

In formal writing, this second *as* is generally included:

You are as smart as, if not smarter than, Kay.
Porter's work is as good as or better than Clifford's.

But many people consider these constructions rather clumsy and avoid them by stating the comparison thus:

You are as smart as Kay, if not smarter.
Porter's work is as good as Clifford's or better.

2 Guard against carelessly using *than* for the second *as* in a comparison like this:

Larry paid twice *as* much for his dinner *as* I did.   [Not: twice *as* much for his dinner *than* I did.]

3 In negative comparisons some formal writers use *not so . . . as*, but *not as . . . as* is the more common idiom in all styles:

FORMAL: Mr. Ames is not *so* civic-minded *as* the rest of his family.   [Or: not *as* civic-minded.]
GENERAL: Mr. Ames is not *as* civic-minded *as* the rest of his family.

as, like   For a discussion of the choice between *as* and *like* ("Hold the rod *as* he does"; "Hold the rod *like* he does"), see **like, as.**

as if, as though   In formal English, the subjunctive is generally used after *as if* or *as though*; in informal English, the indicative is often used:

FORMAL: She acted as if (as though) she *were* the supervisor.
INFORMAL: She acted as if (as though) she *was* the supervisor.

(See **Subjunctive.**)

asterisk (*)   The last two letters are *sk*, not *ks*: /as'tər isk/.

as to   A commonly used, but clumsy, substitute for a single preposition — usually *on*, *about*, or *of*:

CLUMSY: Mrs. Kraft had no further comments as to the proposed increase.

BETTER: Mrs. Kraft had no further comments on the proposed increase.

Sometimes *as to* is simply deadwood and should be omitted in writing:

He was not certain [as to] how much the new fares would be.

at   Nonstandard English commonly adds an unnecessary *at* to questions beginning with *where*:

NONSTANDARD: Where are they at?
                Where is he working at?
STANDARD: Where are they?
             Where is he working?

athletics   Pronounced /ath let'iks/ — three syllables, not four. When *athletics* refers to physical sports, games, and exercises, it generally takes a plural verb:

In ancient Rome, athletics *were* popular — especially boxing and wrestling.

When it refers to the principles of athletic training or a system of athletic training, it usually takes a singular verb:

In those days, athletics *was considered* unimportant.

Author card   See **Card catalog.**

Auxiliary verb   A verb used with another verb to help it express the exact meaning intended. An auxiliary verb helps show the tense, person, voice, and mood of the main verb. The most common auxiliaries are the forms of *be*, *have*, and *do* (*is* working, *have been* invited, *did* look). Others frequently used are the "modals": *can, could, may, might, shall, should, will, would, must.* (See **Modals.**)

awful   The original meaning of *awful* is "inspiring with awe" (the *awful* power of God). But informal usage has weakened the meaning of *awful*, making it merely a general word of disapproval (an *awful* movie, an *awful* test, an *awful* game). As a result, the word is rarely used in its original sense; *awe-inspiring* is used instead.

awhile, a while   One word when an adverb; two words when *while* is a noun in a prepositional phrase:

We talked *awhile* and then went back to work.   [Adverb modifying the verb *talked*.]
We worked for *a while* and then left.   [*While* is object of the preposition *for*; the whole phrase modifies the verb *worked*.]

Awkward writing (Awk)   A general term (abbreviated *Awk*) sometimes used in theme correcting to indicate such faults as inappropriate word choice, unnecessary repetition, clumsy phrasing, confusing word order, poor choice of sentence pattern for the intended meaning, or any other weakness in expression that makes reading difficult or obscures meaning.

Many writers have found that reading their first drafts aloud, putting themselves in the reader's place, helps them detect clumsy or unclear phrasing in their work. Once identified, an awkward construction can almost always be improved by rethinking and rewording.

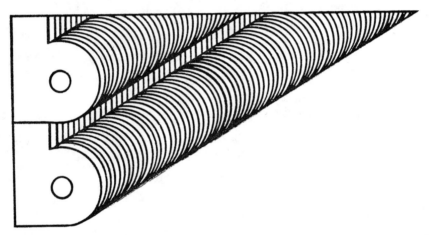

Back formations   Ordinarily a new form of a word is made by adding to an existing base form. For example, adding *-er* to the verb *prowl* and *-ous* to the noun *joy* resulted in two new forms—the noun *prowler* and the adjective *joyous*. But occasionally the opposite is true: A new form is made by dropping a part of an already existing form. For instance, the noun *television* was the original form. Dropping part of it resulted in the new verb form *televise*. Similarly, dropping part of the already existing noun *escalator* resulted in the new verb form *escalate*. Forms made like this are called *back formations*.

The majority of back formations are verbs. Most are formed from nouns—for example, *commentate* from *commentator*, *diagnose* from *diagnosis*, *enthuse* from *enthusiasm*, *reminisce* from *reminiscence*, and *resurrect* from *resurrection*. A few are formed from adjectives: *laze* from *lazy*, *frivol* from *frivolous*.

When a back formation fills a need, as *televise* and *diagnose* do, it usually is quickly accepted and used by all. But not every back formation is welcomed with open arms. For instance, many people frown on *commentate*, a recent back formation, considering it unnecessary and awkward. And *enthuse*, even though it has been around since the 1860's, is still not fully acceptable to some.

back of, in back of   Both of these phrases are now established as standard usages in the United States, though many people consider the preposition *behind* more appropriate in writing, especially formal writing:

STANDARD: No one noticed the man standing back of me.   [Or: in back of me, behind me.]

backward, backwards   Used interchangeably as adverbs:

The wind stung my face, so I walked backward.
The wind stung my face, so I walked backwards.

Only *backward* is used as an adjective:

He took a second backward step and toppled over the edge.

bad, badly   *Bad* is generally used as an adjective, *badly* as an adverb:

Kay had a bad scare.   She was badly frightened.
Al made a bad guess.   He plays chess badly.

In formal English and in informal writing, *bad* — not *badly* — is used as a predicate adjective following a linking verb:

He felt bad about breaking the vase.
Besides, the medicine smelled bad.

In informal speech, *badly* is often used as a predicate adjective, especially after the verb *feel*:

I felt badly about his being fired.   [Written: felt bad.]

But this form is not appropriate in writing.
Informal English uses *badly* to mean "very much":

She needs some new uniforms badly.

Bad and *badly* are both compared irregularly:

bad   worse   worst
badly   worse   worst

Bad grammar   A term of disapproval applied to all sorts of expressions ranging from "He ain't went yet" to "Who does he mean?" (instead of "Whom does he mean?") and "You can go now" (instead of "You may go now"). People who use this term to condemn *all* such expressions believe that there is just one kind of English that is "good," and that any departure from this one kind is "bad." They do not take into account that there are several kinds of English — each one good or appropriate for certain occasions, social groups, or geographical sections.

There is nothing wrong with these expressions in themselves. What makes them wrong is using them in situations where they are not appro-

39

priate. And then the objection to them is not that they are sins against grammar, but that they are sins against usage. For example, in informal speech "*Who* did he want?" and "The reason Sam was chosen was *because* he is tall" are appropriate. In formal English they are not. "*Whom* did he want?" and "The reason Sam was chosen was *that* he is tall" are the appropriate forms there.

Your goal should be to learn enough about the various kinds of English so that you can recognize and use the forms and the sentence structures that are appropriate at different times. (See **Levels of English usage.**)

balance Used in informal English to mean "rest" or "remainder":

Pat kept a few of the flowers and sent the balance to the hospital.

Balanced sentences Sentences in which two or more parts are noticeably similar in length and form. Using balanced sentences is an effective way of emphasizing important ideas, especially ideas expressing comparisons and contrasts:

In science class, Ann's questions were welcomed as thought-provoking; in history class, they were dismissed as impertinent.

Barbarism A term applied to a word or expression that is not in good (standard) use: *their'n* (for *theirs*), *three deers* (for *three deer*), *ain't hardly* (for *is hardly*), *drownded* (for *drowned*), *theirself* (for *themselves*), etc.

barefoot *Barefoot* is used as an adjective or adverb; *barefooted* is used as an adjective:

ADJECTIVE: A barefoot child was sitting on the curb.
ADVERB: I don't like to walk barefoot.
ADJECTIVE: Most of them were barefooted.

be **1 Forms.** *Be* is a highly irregular verb, but since it is used so often, its forms are seldom troublesome:

INFINITIVE: (to) be
PRESENT PARTICIPLE: being
PAST PARTICIPLE: been
PRESENT: I am, you are, he is; we, you, they are
PAST: I was, you were, he was; we, you, they were
SUBJUNCTIVE: be, were

2 As linking verb. *Be* is the most common linking verb, a verb that links a subject with a predicate complement:

Then George is a *fool*. [Predicate noun.]
The real winner is *you*. [Predicate pronoun.]
His explanation was rather *fuzzy*. [Predicate adjective.]

Pronoun complements after the verb *be* are in the nominative case in written English:

I doubt that it was *he* who gave the order.   [Not: *him.*]
The only ones who complained were *she* and *I.*   [Not: *her* and *me.*]

In informal speech and writing "It's me" has practically replaced the formal "It is I." But other objective-case pronouns (It's *him, her, us, them*) are not as yet fully acceptable. (See **It's me.**)

3 As auxiliary verb. Forms of *be* are used with the present participles of other verbs to form the progressive-tense forms:

I am talking.   She will be waiting.
You have been sleeping.   They were grinning.

Forms of *be* are used with the past participles of other verbs to form the passive-verb forms:

I was pushed.   She will be rewarded.
It should have been washed.   We had been seen.

In informal English one form of *be* is often used to serve both as a linking verb and as an auxiliary:

Pedro *was* old and starting to show signs of giving up.

In formal usage the form of *be* is repeated:

Pedro *was* old and *was* starting to show signs of giving up.

beau   The plural is either *beaus* or *beaux* (formal), both pronounced /bōz/.

because   A subordinating conjunction used to introduce a clause that gives the reason for the statement in the main clause:

Because he was the oldest, he thought he could boss us around.

The conjunction *as* is often used instead of *because* in such clauses. But since *because* is more definite and emphatic than *as*, *because* is preferred in written English:

AMBIGUOUS: *As* Dad was busy working out his income tax, I decided it was better not to mention the dented fender right then.   [Seems at first to mean "while."]
DEFINITE: *Because* Dad was busy working out his income tax, I decided it was better not to mention the dented fender right then.

In formal English the coordinating conjunction *for* is often used instead of *because*, especially when the clause is used to give evidence for or to explain the main statement:

INFORMAL: I knew we'd have a fire drill that period, because the fire chief had just pulled into the front parking area.

41

FORMAL: I knew we would have a fire drill that period, for the fire chief had just pulled into the front parking area.

(See **reason is because** and **as**.)

Begging the question   See **Fallacies in reasoning,** section 1.

being as, being that   Certain dialects use *being as* and *being that* in place of the conjunctions *since* and *because*, which are standard:

DIALECT: Being as Leo owned the ball and bat, we had to give in.
STANDARD: Since Leo owned the ball and bat, we had to give in.

DIALECT: Being that he seemed interested, we told him the story.
STANDARD: Because he seemed interested, we told him the story.

beside, besides   *Beside* is most commonly used as a preposition meaning "by the side of":

Tom, of course, wanted to sit beside Becky.

It is also used figuratively in certain rather formal idioms:

Usually what she says is beside the point.
He rushed at Ted, beside himself with rage.

   Besides is used both as an adverb and as a preposition meaning "in addition (to)" or "except":

They gift-wrapped the package for us and delivered it besides.   [Adverb — "in addition."]
Besides criticizing everything we said, he did very little.   [Preposition — "in addition to."]
Nobody besides Emily had skis.   [Preposition — "except."]

Besides is also used as a conjunctive adverb meaning "moreover":

Andy didn't feel like talking to Gloria; besides, he owed her a dollar and had only fifty cents.

between, among   *Among* implies more than two persons, places, or things:

There was a strong feeling of loyalty among the club members.

Between is generally used to refer to only two:

Fitz and Randy had only ninety cents between them.

When used to refer to more than two, *between* suggests that the persons, places, or things are being considered two at a time:

He worked hard to improve the relations between the three countries.
Just what is the difference between nylon, Dacron, and Acrilan?

Between is followed either by a plural (between *acts*, between the *wheels*) or by two expressions joined by *and* — not by *or* or *to*:

ILLOGICAL: He offered the men a choice between paying the fine *or* going to jail.
LOGICAL: He offered the men a choice between paying the fine *and* going to jail.

ILLOGICAL: Between July 1 *to* July 9, we sold two hundred bushels of peaches.
LOGICAL: Between July 1 *and* July 9, we sold two hundred bushels of peaches.

Although expressions like "between each store" and "between every class" are common in speech, it would be more logical to say:

There is a parking lot between each store and the next.
We have a five-minute recess between classes.   [Or: after each class.]

between you and me   In standard English the objective-case pronouns are used as objects of prepositions: *between you and me, between you and her, between you and him, between you and us, between you and them.*

Because so much emphasis is placed on the use of the nominative-case pronouns in sentences like "You and I should help," "Ann and he just left," "It was she," some people mistakenly think that "you and me" and "Ann and him" are always incorrect. So in an effort to be correct, they say "between you and I" and "between Ann and he," not realizing that in these phrases the objective forms, not the nominative, are called for: "between you and me," "between Ann and him."

Bible, bible   *Bible* is capitalized but not italicized or enclosed in quotation marks when it refers to the Holy Scriptures:

Whenever she was worried, Grandma turned to her Bible.

The word is neither capitalized nor italicized when it refers to a book that is regarded as an authority:

John Holt's *How Children Fail* was our teacher's bible.

These are the forms used in referring to parts of the Bible:

the Old Testament   the New Testament
I Thessalonians 3:8–10   [The 8th to 10th verses in the 3rd chapter of First Thessalonians, the first of the Epistles from the Apostle Paul to the Christians of Thessalonica.]
The Sermon on the Mount is in Matthew 5–7 and in Luke 6:20–49.   [The 5th to the 7th chapter of the Gospel of Matthew and the 20th to the 49th verses in the 6th chapter of the Gospel of Luke.]

The adjective *Biblical* is often not capitalized: *biblical.*

Bibliography   Most research papers have at the end a *bibliography*—a list of the books and other published material actually used in writing the paper. (Sources in the "working bibliography" that were consulted but not referred to in the paper are not listed.) The bibliography serves two purposes: First, it shows what research was done for the paper. Second, it indicates to readers who are especially interested in a subject a number of sources that they may find useful.

Although the form of bibliography entries has been pretty well standardized, there are slight differences in the forms used by various writers, as you can see by comparing bibliographies in different books. But these are minor matters; the important thing is to see that the entries contain the necessary information (author, title, facts of publication) and are consistent in form.

In your bibliographies, use the following forms—unless, of course, your teacher prescribes other forms:

1) For a book—one author:

Kahn, Herman, Thinking About the Unthinkable, New York, Horizon
　　Press, 1962

2) For a book—more than one author:

Kennan, Erlend A., and Edmund H. Harvey, Jr., Mission to the Moon, New
　　York, William Morrow & Co., 1969

3) For a book—compiled by an editor:

Lawson, Don, ed., Great Air Battles, New York, Lothrop, Lee & Shepard
　　Co., 1968

4) For a book—only one chapter used:

Cooke, Alistair, "The European's America" in Talk About America, New
　　York, Alfred A. Knopf, 1968, pp. 63–70

5) For a magazine article—author given:

Davidson, Sara, "Open Land: Getting Back to the Communal Garden,"
　　Harper's, vol. 240, June 1970, pp. 91–102

6) For a magazine article—no author given:

"Vanishing Wildlife," Time, vol. 95, June 8, 1970, pp. 52–53

7) For a pamphlet—no author given:

Nuclear Terms: A Brief Glossary, Oak Ridge, Tenn., USAEC Division of
　　Technical Information Extension, 1967

8) For an encyclopedia article—author given:

Pine, L. G., "Genealogy," Collier's Encyclopedia, 1970 edition, vol. 10,
　　pp. 613–617

9) For an encyclopedia article—no author given:

"Mail-Order Business," The World Book Encyclopedia, 1970 edition, vol. 13, p. 60

All the items in the bibliography are to be put in one list, arranged alphabetically by the last name of the author. If no author is given, the first word of the title (not counting *A*, *An*, or *The*) determines the order.

Big words   "Big words" are not necessarily long words. They are words that are too fancy for the subject, too formal for the situation, or too unnatural to the user.

When long or uncommon words are appropriate, you should not hesitate to use them. In a paper on a technical subject for a restricted audience, you may have to use such words as *coleopterous*, *metathesis*, or *ancipital*. Words that are more familiar but less exact would be the wrong words to use. In formal writing, strongly suggestive or rhythmical words, like *ubiquitous*, *ephemeral*, *quintessence*, *debacle*, are often the right words to use. There are no short, everyday words that can match their connotations and rhythm.

But words like *elucidate* (for *explain*), *multitudinous* (for *many*), *habitation* (for *house* or *home*), *salubrious* (for *healthful*), *hyperbolic* (for *exaggerated*), *sobriquet* (for *nickname*), *inculpate* (for *blame*) are generally out of place in ordinary writing. To most readers they sound pompous and showy. Even more important, big words tend to obscure meaning by drawing attention away from what is being said to how it is being said. (See **Gobbledygook.**)

blame   Both *blame . . . for* and *blame . . . on* are standard English. There is only a slight difference in meaning:

Everyone blamed Joel for the accident.   [That is, everyone held him responsible, accused him of being at fault.]
Everyone blamed the accident on Joel.   [That is, everyone claimed that he was responsible, ascribed the responsibility for the accident to him.]

Blend   A coined word made by telescoping two words into one:

ruckus   (from *ruction* and *rumpus*)
dumfound   (from *dumb* and *confound*)
chortle   (from *chuckle* and *snort*)
floatel   (from *float* and *hotel*)
blotch   (from *blot* and *botch*)
medicare   (from *medical* and *care*)
smaze   (from *smoke* and *haze*)

Until a blend has become accepted as part of the general vocabulary, as *motel* (from *motorist* and *hotel*) and *gerrymander* (from *Gerry* and *salamander*) have, it is more appropriate in informal writing than in formal.

45

blond, blonde   As a noun, *blond* is a man; *blonde*, a woman:

The two youngest boys are blonds.   My sister is a blonde now.

Although the adjective is spelled with or without the final *e*, *blond* is the more common spelling:

She has blond hair and brown eyes.

Boners   A slang term used to refer to blunders that result from confusing two similar words or from combining ideas that do not belong together. Boners are generally quite funny — though not in a way intended by the person who makes the mistakes. Here are some examples from student papers:

In case of asphyxiation, apply artificial respiration until the patient is dead.
American citizens have the inalienable right to partition Congress without being put in jail.
The crossing was so rough that even the seasoned sailors were glad to set foot on terra cotta again.
A plenipotentiary is a prison where diplomatic agents from foreign countries are kept.

Watch for amusing boners in the books and magazines you read, and share the fun with your friends. But unless you do not mind a laugh at your expense, check your own writing carefully to catch any boners before they are found by others. (See also **Malapropism.**)

bore   Followed by *with* when it means "make (someone) weary":

He bored us with a blow-by-blow account of his argument with the boss.

born, borne   **1** The past participle of *bear* in most of its meanings is *borne*:

Few men could have borne life at the camp without cracking up.   ["Endured."]
The glider was borne along by the wind.   ["Carried."]
She had borne five children.   ["Given birth to."]

But *born* is the usual spelling in such sentences as:

Hakim was born in India.
Corby was a born leader.
The author, born to wealth, shows great compassion for the poor.

2 Students asked to write their autobiographies often become coy and self-conscious or else try to be humorous in giving the facts of their birth: "I first put in an appearance in this vale of tears on May 14, 1959" or "Early one lovely morning in August — August 21, 1959, to be exact — I entered this confused and confusing world." A simple and natural statement like "I was born May 14, 1959" is usually much better.

borrow   Usually followed by *from*, rarely by *of*:

Len borrowed an alarm clock from the neighbors upstairs.
Ken's father had borrowed the money of the bank.

Borrow . . . off and *borrow . . . off of* are nonstandard:

NONSTANDARD: Then he borrowed a dollar off of Jake.
STANDARD: Then he borrowed a dollar from Jake.

In certain regional dialects *borrow* is used to mean "lend":

DIALECT: Ask her if she can borrow us a cup of flour.
STANDARD: Ask her if she can lend us a cup of flour.

Borrowed words   In the course of its history, English has borrowed words from many other languages. Some of these borrowings have been deliberate: scientists and scholars have often gone to foreign languages for names for new discoveries, ideas, or situations. Others have been brought in by groups of immigrants, introduced through commerce or trade, or picked up by large groups of our citizens (soldiers, for example, or tourists) who have visited foreign lands. Some of these borrowed words retain their original forms and pronunciations (*ersatz, blasé, adagio, joie de vivre*). But many of them—generally the most useful ones—are gradually Anglicized to bring their pronunciation (and sometimes their spelling) in line with English usage. (See **Anglicizing**.)

1 Use. The reason for the common use of many borrowed words is that they supply a real need in our language. Many times they say in a word or two what it would take many English words to say—for example, *nouveau riche*, "one who has recently become rich, especially one who makes a vulgar display of his wealth." Many times they are the only names we have for certain objects or ideas: *zwieback, beau geste, Anschluss, deus ex machina*. In other instances, they carry with them strong connotations that are extremely important in certain contexts: *bon vivant, mot juste, magnifico, persona non grata*. Borrowed words for which there are adequate English equivalents are not so likely to become common or Anglicized, retaining always a foreign flavor: *savoir-vivre, beau monde, bon mot, soupçon* For these we can say *good breeding* or *good manners, fashionable society, witty remark, very slight amount*.

Borrowed words have greatly enriched our language; in fact, it would be practically impossible to communicate without them. This sample list merely hints at the extent of our borrowings:

alligator (Spanish)   bamboo (Malay)
apropos (French)   berserk (Old Norse)
arpeggio (Italian)   blitz (German)

boomerang (Australian)
borsch (Russian)
boss (Dutch)
bungalow (Hindustani)
catastrophe (Greek)
dodo (Portuguese)
factory (Latin)

gape (Scandinavian)
kowtow (Chinese)
polka (Czech)
shawl (Persian)
slalom (Norwegian)
sputnik (Russian)
violin (Italian)

2 Italics. Borrowed words so commonly used that they have become part of the general vocabulary are written without italics. Those that have not been Anglicized and are still thought of as foreign words are usually italicized in print (underlined in writing):

en avant   fait accompli   mañana   paparazzo   sans pareil

When in doubt about whether to italicize a particular word or phrase, consult a dictionary. In recent dictionaries, borrowed words that are not part of the general English vocabulary are indicated by a double dagger (‡), by two parallel bars (‖), by a label (*Italian*, *French*, *German*, etc.) preceding the definitions, or by being set in italics.

both   *Both* is used to emphasize twoness:

His foster parents were both notified.
The Panthers and the Tigers both belong to the Valley League.

In speech *both* is sometimes used in sentences like these:

The novel and the movie were both alike.
Both Florence and Venice are equally fascinating.

But since *alike* in the first example and *equally* in the second express the intended meaning clearly, the word *both* is unnecessary. In writing, it should be omitted as a bit of deadwood.

In some regional dialects *both* is used in place of *two*:

DIALECT: The both girls went into nursing.
STANDARD: The two girls went into nursing.

both . . . and   Used as correlative conjunctions (conjunctions that work in pairs):

He was both ready and willing to help out.

(See **Correlative conjunctions.**)

boughten   Used in some regional dialects to distinguish articles bought at a store from those that are homemade:

DIALECT: None of the women would have served boughten bread.
STANDARD: None of the women would have served bread that was not homemade.   [Or: that was bought at a store.]

Brackets [ ]   Used mainly to enclose an explanation, comment, or correction that is inserted into quoted material:

"The greatest lexicological effort in England in the nineteenth century—perhaps the greatest of any century anywhere—was the *Oxford English Dictionary* [also called the *New English Dictionary* or the *NED*]."

breath, breathe   *Breath,* pronounced /breth/, is a noun; *breathe,* pronounced /brēᴛʜ/, is a verb:

NOUN: You might as well save your breath.
VERB: It was hard to breathe at that altitude.

bring, take   The choice between *bring* and *take* depends on the direction of the action. If the motion is toward the speaker, a form of *bring* is used:

If you come, be sure to bring a warm coat.
He brought the pictures with him when he came over.

If the motion is away from the speaker, *take* is used:

If you go, be sure to take a warm coat.
Didn't he take the pictures with him when he went home?

British usage   See **American and British usage.**

Broad reference   A pronoun that refers to a preceding idea (expressed in a group of words) rather than to a specific, one-word antecedent is said to have "broad reference":

The next month the cost of living went up another 2 percent, *which* caused a serious problem for retired people with a small fixed income. [The *which* refers to the whole idea stated in the main clause.]

(For further examples, see **Reference of pronouns,** section 2.)

Bromide   A figurative term for a commonplace idea or a trite remark:

You can't teach an old dog new tricks.
Haste makes waste.
Well-begun is half-done.

Since the literal meaning of *bromide* is "a medicine used to calm nervousness and cause sleep," the term is an effective—though harsh—name for such expressions. (See **Cliché.**)

brunet, brunette   As a noun, *brunet* is a man; *brunette,* a woman:

My brother is a brunet.   Rebecca was a beautiful brunette.

As an adjective, either *brunet* or *brunette* is used.

bunch   In formal English, *bunch* is used only to refer to things that grow together or can be fastened together

a bunch of grapes   a bunch of violets   a bunch of tags

In informal English, *bunch* is used to refer to a small group of anything —
including people:

He was standing at the back with a bunch of students.

burned, burnt   The past tense and the past participle of *burn* are either *burned* or *burnt*:

The acid burned (*or* burnt) holes in the rug.
He had burned (*or* burnt) both copies of the contract.

Burned is the more common form, except when the participle is used as an adjective before a noun:

A burnt child dreads the fire.

burst   The principal parts are *burst, burst, burst*:

At this point, the door bursts open and he walks in.
She fell against the fence, and the balloon burst.
Before I could answer, they had burst into the room.

(See **bust.**)

bus   The plural is either *buses* or *busses*; the first is more common.

Business letters   See **Letters,** sections 1 to 4.

business world   A pretentious term for *business* or *businessmen*:

PRETENTIOUS: Mr. Halleck hoped that his son-in-law would give up painting and enter the business world.
BETTER: Mr. Halleck hoped that his son-in-law would give up painting and become a businessman.

bust   Used in nonstandard English for *burst* or *break*:

NONSTANDARD: If the water freezes, the pipes might bust.
STANDARD: If the water freezes, the pipes might burst.

NONSTANDARD: He dropped the teapot and busted the lid.
STANDARD: He dropped the teapot and broke the lid.

The expressions *bust a bronco, bust a trust, bust an officer* (reduce in rank) are labeled *Slang* in most dictionaries. But they are so generally used in informal English that they may be considered standard.

but   **1** *But* is a coordinating conjunction used to connect two contrasting expressions. The words, phrases, or clauses joined by *but* should be of the same grammatical form:

ADJECTIVES: Bobby was bright but lazy.
ADVERBS: He advanced slowly but steadily.
PHRASES: She spoke with frankness but without malice.
SUBORDINATE CLAUSES: Dick was one of those students who would always do the assignments but who would never let anyone copy his work.
MAIN CLAUSES: She had written down her address, but I couldn't read her writing.

The parts joined by *but* should actually be contrasting or opposite in thought. If they are not, *but* should not be used to join them:

CONTRASTING IDEAS: Yes, their commercials are amusing, but they don't make me want to buy the products.
NOT CONTRASTING: The message was written in Russian, *and* nobody there could translate it.   [Not: *but* nobody there could translate it.]

But should not be doubled by a word like *however*, which adds nothing to its meaning:

He knew he was wrong, but he wouldn't admit it.   [Not: but *however* he wouldn't admit it.]

(For the punctuation of compound sentences with *but*, see **Comma**, section 1.)

2 *But* is sometimes used at the beginning of a sentence to emphasize the contrast between ideas:

Ian Ray was one of the most ambitious students in the School of Music. He was enthusiastic, hardworking, and intelligent. But he had no talent.

Used too often, however, this introductory *But* loses its effectiveness.

3 *But* is also used as a preposition meaning "except" and as a rather formal adverb meaning "only" or "no more than":

PREPOSITION: Everyone got the point but Elmer.
ADVERB: If I had but known, I would have warned him.
ADVERB: There were but five Democrats in the whole town.

Using *not* with *but* (in the sense of "no more than") makes a double negative:

There weren't but five Democrats in the whole town.

Though this double negative with *but* is found in informal speech, it is not appropriate in writing. There the *not* should be dropped. If the sentence then seems too formal in tone, the *but* can be changed to *only*:

There were only five Democrats in the whole town.

51

but that, but what   In informal written English, *but that* is the usual con-junction in sentences like these:

There is no doubt but that Dale wrote the letter.
She doesn't doubt but that he will get the promotion.

In informal speech, *but what* (or *but* alone) is common:

There is no doubt but what Dale wrote the letter.
She doesn't doubt but what he will get the promotion.

In formal English, *that* alone is preferred:

There is no doubt that Dale wrote the letter.
She does not doubt that he will get the promotion.

but which, but who   See **and which, and who.**

buy   Used with *from*, not with *off* or *off of*:

NONSTANDARD: Buy it off of Mr. Porter; he'll get a commission.
STANDARD: Buy it from Mr. Porter; he'll get a commission.

Buy off is an idiomatic phrase meaning "bribe":

Everyone suspected that Fawcett had bought off the witness.

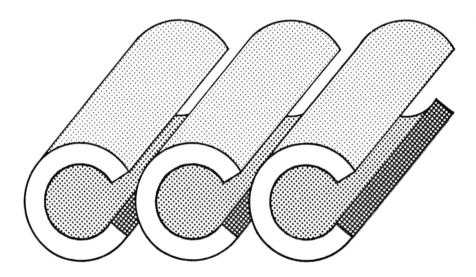

can, may   1 In informal English (both spoken and written) *can* is used to express permission as well as ability:

PERMISSION: Can I have another chance?
              Why can't he go to the movies with us?

ABILITY: Bonnie can type seventy words a minute.
            I can't get this lid off.

May is rarely used except to express possibility:

It may melt.
The butter may turn rancid.

2 In formal English *can* is generally used only to express ability:

I can dive from the high tower.
Can you understand Russian?

To express permission, *may* is generally used:

May we invite him to dinner?
You may take the car on Friday, but not on Saturday.

cannot, can not   Both are used, but *cannot* is more common.

can't help but   A colloquial expression, common in everyday speech and in informal writing:

We can't help but like the rascal.

In formal English, the expression *cannot help* followed by a gerund is more likely:

We cannot help liking the rascal.

Capital letters   **1 Sentence capitals.** (a) The first word of a sentence is always capitalized.
    b) In quotations, the first word of a quoted sentence is capitalized; but if the quoted sentence is interrupted by explanatory words (*he said, she answered, I explained,* etc.), the first word of its second part is not capitalized:

Uncle Bill said, "Eating out is too expensive."
"It wouldn't be," Aunt Hattie reminded him, "if you didn't always order porterhouse steak. Why don't you stick to hamburger?"
"I'd rather just stay home then," he replied. "At least I'd get enough food to fill me up."

    c) A sentence enclosed in parentheses is capitalized when it stands *between* other sentences:

The Firemen's Ball, produced in Czechoslovakia, was the most unusual of the series of foreign films presented by the college. (The program notes suggested that the movie be viewed mainly as political satire.) What made the picture so unusual was the fact that none of the characters seemed to be actors; they were just people that candid cameras kept focusing on.

53

But when a sentence enclosed in parentheses comes *within* another sentence, it is not usually capitalized:

While Herzog was undergoing the worst tortures on the way back from the Himalayas (his hopelessly frozen fingers and toes were being amputated, and he was receiving painful injections that might or might not restore life to his arms and legs), he had only one fear — that he would never be able to go mountain climbing again.

2 Proper nouns and abbreviations of proper nouns are capitalized:

PEOPLE: Jesse Jackson, General Dwight D. Eisenhower

PLACES: Puerto Rico, Isle of Man, Mount Olympus, N.Y.

RACES, LANGUAGES: Indian, Portuguese

POLITICAL PARTIES AND THEIR MEMBERS: the Liberal Party, Republicans

CHURCHES AND THEIR MEMBERS: St. Patrick's Cathedral, Baptists, a Lutheran

BUSINESS FIRMS: Scott, Foresman and Company, General Electric, Sears

DAYS, MONTHS, HOLIDAYS, HOLY DAYS: Wednesday, April, Flag Day, Ascension Day, Yom Kippur

ORGANIZATIONS: the Camp Fire Girls of America, the Daughters of Isabella

INSTITUTIONS: Carthage College, Massachusetts Institute of Technology, Smithsonian Institution

SHIPS, TRAINS, PLANES: U.S.S. *Nautilus*, the *Santa Maria*, the *Rocket*, *Lucky Lady II*

HISTORICAL EVENTS, PERIODS, DOCUMENTS: the Boxer Rebellion, the Space Age, the Charter of the United Nations

BUILDINGS: the Pentagon, the Empire State Building, Rockefeller Center, the Jefferson Memorial

TRADE NAMES: Duz, Royal Crown, Green Giant

SACRED FIGURES, BIBLE, PARTS OF THE BIBLE: God, the Holy Spirit, Lamentations, the Old Testament (See **Bible, bible.**)

3 Adjectives formed from proper nouns are generally capitalized, but the words they modify are not, unless they themselves are proper nouns:

the Welsh countryside   Moorish architecture
Arabian customs   Shakespearean England
a Pyrrhic victory   American Indian

4 The name of the planet earth is generally not capitalized except when used without a preceding *the*:

The earth has one satellite, the moon.
The third planet from the sun is Earth.
Peace to men on Earth.

The names of all other planets (Jupiter, Venus, Saturn, etc.), which are derived from proper names, are always capitalized.

5 The names of the seasons are not capitalized:

In the *spring* we again postponed our trip — to early *autumn*.

6 The points of the compass (south, north, southwest, etc.) are not capitalized when they indicate direction:

The library is *east* of the tracks; the museum is *west*.

They are generally capitalized, however, when used as the names of geographical regions:

He went to college in the *East*, but he hopes to live in•the *West*.

7 School subjects are not capitalized unless they are names of languages or of specific numbered courses:

I signed up for *French, typing,* and *biology*.
We both are taking *Psychology 101*.

8 Words like *street, avenue, river, island, park, building, hospital, hotel, theater, bank, high school, junior,* and *senior* are not capitalized unless they are used as part of a proper noun:

His father owns the *bank* on that *street;* his uncle owns the *theater*.
You can get a good view of the *river* from the *hotel*.
The *juniors* and the *seniors* would like to run our *high school*.

But:	Brown National Bank	Nile River	Tremper High School
	Twenty-first Street	Drake Hotel	Passavant Hospital
	Olympic Theater	Junior Prom	Luder's Island

Note: Many newspapers and magazines do not capitalize words like *street, avenue, park, island,* and *river* when they follow a proper noun: *Lyman avenue, Laurel park, Passmore island, the Missouri river*. But in your school writing you will probably be expected to follow the more conservative practice of capitalizing the words.

9 Personal titles. Nouns showing office, rank, or profession (*senator, captain, archbishop, judge, coach,* etc.) are always capitalized when used with the name of a person and are usually capitalized when used alone as a substitute for a person's name (unless it is preceded by a word like *the, a, an, our,* etc.):

The rulings were approved by *Mayor Higgins*.
"Have you any statement for the press, *Mayor?*" he asked.
When did the *mayor* sign the bill?
Chemistry 2 will be taught by *Professor Blake*. The *professor* I had last year isn't here any more.

The title of our country's highest executive — *President* — is generally capitalized:

The President will report to the nation on Tuesday evening.

10 Nouns showing family relationships. Capitalize words like *uncle*, *aunt*, *cousin*, *grandfather*, *mother*, *father*, etc., only when they are used with a person's name, or as a substitute for a person's name (unless it is preceded by a word like *my*, *their*, *the*, *a*, *an*, etc.):

My *father* and *mother* didn't approve of baby sitters — except for *Uncle Dan* and *Aunt Mary.*
"While you visit *Grandmother Sprague, Mother,* I'll be the cook."

11 Titles of articles, books, etc. The usual practice is to capitalize the first and last words of the title, all important words (nouns, pronouns, verbs, adverbs, adjectives), and all prepositions of more than four letters:

"Devils with Clean Faces"   *Odyssey of a Friend*
"A Prison Without Walls"   *The World We Live In*

12 Lines of poetry. In most poetry each line begins with a capital letter. But in much modern poetry this is not true. Remember that poetry must be copied exactly as it originally appeared — with or without capitals, however the poet wrote it.

13 O and oh. The formal (and rare) interjection *O*, used in direct address, is always capitalized. The interjection *oh* is not capitalized unless it begins a sentence:

Grant us this favor, *O* King.
He fell asleep immediately, and *oh*, how he snored.
Oh, what a scoundrel he is!

Card catalog   An alphabetical list of all the books in a particular library, arranged on cards in a series of drawers. In the catalog you can find (1) whether the library has a book of a certain title, (2) what books it has by a certain author, (3) what books it has on a given subject, and (4) where you will find a book on the library shelves.

The catalog usually contains at least three cards for every book: an *author* card, a *title* card, and a *subject* card. When you know the author of a book, you generally look for the author card. This is filed alphabetically by the author's last name, which appears at the top of the card. When you know the title of a book but not the author, you look for the title card. It is filed alphabetically according to the first important word of the title.

Sometimes you may want to find books on a certain subject, but you have no particular authors or titles in mind. Then you look in the catalog for subject cards, filed alphabetically according to the subject. Under every subject heading there are cards for the books in the library dealing with that subject. Moreover, a book may be listed under several different subject headings. (A study of Eskimo tribes in Alaska, for example, might be listed under ESKIMOS, ALASKA, and ANTHROPOLOGY.) If you do not find the first subject heading you look for, try related subjects. (MAN-MADE MOONS may not be listed, but you may find books treating the subject under SATELLITES, SPACE, SPACE EXPLORATION, or ROCKETS AND MISSILES.)

Here are three catalog cards for Howard G. Smith's *Hunting Big Game in the City Parks*:

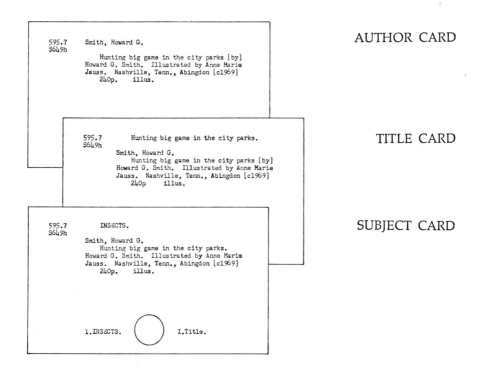

The top lines differ, but otherwise the cards are exactly the same. The *call number* in the upper left corner of each tells where you will find the book in the library. The top line, **595.7**, is the Dewey classification number. (See **Dewey Decimal System.**) The second line, **S649h**, is the author's initial and number followed by the first letter of the first important word of the title. Since this call number is also printed on the spine of the book, it makes it easy for you to find the book on the shelves.

Catalog cards tell you other things that you may want to know about a book: the place and date it was published; the name of the publisher; the number of pages; whether it has illustrations, maps, appendixes; and all the subject headings it is listed under.

Cardinal numbers   See **Numbers,** section 6.

Caret (ʌ)   A mark put in a line of manuscript to show that something should be inserted at that point:

        had
Al said that he ʌ already signed the petition.

57

You will rarely need to use carets in your papers if you take time to revise your first drafts carefully before making final copies. But in general (on exam papers, official forms, committee reports, etc.) there is no objection to your using carets to make corrections, if you do it neatly and not too often.

Case 1 Pronouns change in form depending on how they are used in a sentence (*He* expected Mother to mail *his* to *him*). In grammar, this change of form to match a change in the function of a word is called a change in the "case" of the pronoun.

Personal pronouns (except *you* and *it*) and the pronoun *who* have three different case forms:

NOMINATIVE CASE: I, you, he, she, it, we, you, they; who
OBJECTIVE CASE: me, you, him, her, it, us, you, them; whom
POSSESSIVE CASE: mine, yours, his, hers, its, ours, yours, theirs; whose [The adjective forms are *my, your, his, her, its, our, your, their; whose.*]

a) The *nominative* forms are used as subjects:

Ellen and *she* figured out the answer.   [Not: Ellen and *her.*]
We boys won every game.   [Not: *Us* boys.]
Who do you think ate the pie?   [Not: *Whom. Who* is the subject of the verb *ate.*]
The two older girls — Judy and *she* — offered to baby-sit.   [Not: *her.* The pronoun is in apposition with the subject *girls.*]
Is anyone else as bewildered as *I*?   [*I* is the subject of the elliptical clause *as I am.*]
Aren't you shorter than *he*?   [*He* is the subject of the elliptical clause *than he is.*]
"Who broke the typewriter?"   "Not *I.*"

In casual conversation the objective form of the pronoun is commonly used in sentences like the last two — probably because the pronoun comes at the end of the sentence, where the objective-case form usually comes:

Aren't you shorter than him?
"Who broke the typewriter?"   "Not me."

But in more careful speech, as well as in writing, the nominative-case forms are used.

Usage is divided when a pronoun is used as a predicate complement after the verb *be*. The nominative form is considered preferable in writing and careful speech:

Someone gave me those statistics — I am sure it was *he.*

But in casual conversation you will often hear the objective form:

Someone gave me those statistics — I'm sure it was *him.*

Some people feel that in many situations *he* is too formal to be appropriate, and that *him* is too informal. Then they avoid the problem by expressing the idea in another way:

Someone gave me those statistics, and I'm sure he was the one.

(See also **It's me.**)

b) The *objective* forms are used as objects of verbs and of prepositions:

They wanted *him* and Nan to sit with them.   [Not: *he.*]
She never pays any attention to *us* boys.   [Not: *we* boys.]
"Did they call anyone?" "Yes, Ron and *me.*"   [Not: *I.* The meaning is "They called Ron and me."]
You can come with Ruth and *me.*   [Not: *I.*]
I know both girls, Sue and *her.*   [Not: *she.* The pronoun is in apposition with the object *girls.*]
I like Anita more than *him.*   [*Him* is the object of the elliptical clause *than I like him.*]

c) The *possessive* forms are used to show ownership:

Mine writes better than *yours.*   *Whose* won?

(See also **Gerund,** section 2.)

2 Nouns have only two case forms—a possessive and an ordinary form that is used for all other functions: *sister's, sister; Robert's, Robert.*

(See also **Nominative case; Objective case; Possessive case;** and **who, whom, whose.**)

case   Expressions with *case* are often merely deadwood that could easily be pruned away in revision:

In [the case of] classes for the teaching of English as a second language, a different approach must be used, of course.
He has resorted to this same sort of name-calling before, in [the case of] his guest appearances on various TV shows.
[In] many [cases] students feel that their student council is an ineffectual, do-nothing group.

catalog, catalogue   Though formal English tends to keep the *ue* spelling, the shorter form is becoming more common.

center around (or about)   The phrases *center around* and *center about* are informal idioms:

The story centers around the kidnaping of a pampered poodle.

In formal English *center on* or *center in* is used:

The supreme authority was centered in one person.
All his hopes centered on his winning the contest.

Centuries   A simple rule for naming a century correctly is to add one to the number of its hundred. This present century, the nineteen hundreds, is called the twentieth century. The eighteen hundreds are called the nineteenth century, and so on.

Dates before Christ are figured in the same way as those after: The first century B.C. runs back from the birth of Christ through the year 100; the second century, from 101 through 200; the third, from 201 through 300, etc.

cf.   An abbreviation for the Latin *confer*. It is used in footnotes when the writer wants the reader to "compare" or "see" a given reference for further information.

Chinese   Because the words *Chinaman* and *Chinamen* have acquired belittling connotations, *Chinese* is preferable:

The most articulate of the panel was a Chinese.
Hundreds of Chinese lined the streets along the parade route.

Circumlocution   The use of a larger number of words than are necessary to express an idea clearly and effectively: "in a state of confusion" = "confused"; "filled with embarrassment" = "embarrassed"; "she was made a recipient of" = "she received." "He finally arrived at the decision to compensate us for the time we had worked beyond our regular hours of employment" = "He finally decided to pay us overtime." (For further examples, see **Wordiness**, section 1.)

Cities   In expository writing, the name of the country or state need not be given with the names of well-known cities: *Berlin, Cairo, Dallas, Glasgow, Geneva, New York, Rome, Vienna, Venice*. But cities or towns that are not well known or have the same names as other cities should be fully identified if there is a possibility that readers may be puzzled or misled: *Berlin, Wisconsin; Cairo, Georgia; Warsaw, Indiana; Venice, Florida*.

Clause   A group of words that has a subject and a verb and is used as *part* of a sentence. (A simple sentence like "Ed ordered a hamburger" has a subject and verb, but we do not call it a clause, because it is a whole sentence, not part of a sentence.) There are two classes of clauses: *main* and *subordinate*.

1 Main clause (also called *independent* or *principal* clause). A main clause is one that, though part of a sentence, is grammatically independent; that is, it could stand alone as a sentence. The main clauses are italicized in these examples:

Ed ordered a hamburger, but *Neil got a steak*.
The man that won the car *had just bought a new car*.
As soon as she had left, *I remembered the address*.
Nora wondered what the boss would say.

2 Subordinate clause (also called *dependent* clause). A subordinate clause cannot stand alone as a sentence; it depends on the rest of the sentence to complete its meaning:

The man *that won the car* had just bought a new car.   [Adjective clause.]
As soon as she had left, I remembered the address.   [Adverb clause.]
Nora wondered *what the boss would say*.   [Noun clause used as object of the verb.]

Subordinate clauses, as the examples show, are used in sentences as single words might be used — as adjectives, as adverbs, as nouns.

(For further examples and discussion, see **Adjective clause, Adverb clause, Noun clause, Compound sentence, Complex sentence.**)

Cliché   An expression that has been used so often that it has become commonplace and stale: *clean as a whistle, selling like hot cakes, knee-high to a grasshopper, gone but not forgotten, few and far between.* (See **Bromide.**)

Climax   Climax is the arrangement of a series of words, phrases, clauses, or sentences in an ascending order — that is, each item in the series is longer, more striking, more forceful, or more important in some way than the preceding item:

The prisoners spoke guardedly of home, of the possibility of escape, and of the ceaseless struggle to stay alive.   [Order based on the length of the phrases.]
All that week at the lake it rained: Sometimes it was big, slow, single drops, making countless pockmarks on the surface of the water. Sometimes it was driving sheets of rain, raking across the beach in graceful waves. Sometimes it was a straight-down Niagara torrent so thick it blotted out everything but itself.   [Order based on the amount and intensity of the rain.]
Napoleon's life is a study in adventure, in calm mastery of the situation, in short-lived glory, in heartless indifference to the desires of millions of people, and in monstrous greed for total power over the world.   [Order based on importance of ideas and amount of emotion they will arouse.]

Climax is the natural order for arranging the items of a series unless there is some special reason for another order. Failure to use climactic order usually results in a weak passage or, if the last member of the series is conspicuously less important than the preceding ones, in anticlimax. (For a discussion of this point, see **Anticlimax.**)

Clipped words   Words made by dropping a syllable or more from another word are called *clipped words* or sometimes *clips*. They are used in informal speech and writing: *pro, mums, flu, franks, photo, quad, rhino*. Some clips are shoptalk or slang: *electro, schizo, con, hood*. Since clipped words are not abbreviations, they are not followed by periods.

Coherence   When we say that a piece of writing has coherence (or is coherent), we mean that the ideas move in a smooth, straight, uninterrupted line from beginning to end. Coherence is achieved primarily through order, through presenting the details in an orderly sequence that the reader can easily follow and will find sensible. But order alone is not enough to guarantee coherence. The sentences giving the details must be linked together in such a way that the reader can move smoothly from one to another without being puzzled about the relationship between them. The linking may be done directly, through the use of transitional expressions (e.g., *next, last, afterwards, in the first place, as a result, for this reason, on the other hand, years ago . . . but now*). Or the linking may be done indirectly — by repeating the subject from sentence to sentence, for example, by using synonyms that "echo" key words, or by using pronouns or "summary" expressions (like *all these, that last suggestion of his, this remedy*) to refer back to details mentioned earlier. The effective use of these indirect links will keep the writing from sounding stiff or unnaturally formal, as it might if only direct transitions were used.

Coining words   Making up a new word for a particular occasion (like *frugomania, microspender,* a *wear-you-outster*) or for general use (*me-tooism, serendipity, sloganeer*) is called *coining*. The made-up word is called a *coinage* or, if it is never used again, a *nonce word*.

Collective nouns   A *collective noun* is one that though singular in form names a group of people or things:

audience	club	faculty	group	orchestra
cast	crew	flock	jury	panel

1 Agreement. When the writer intends the collective noun to mean the group taken as a whole, he uses a singular verb and pronoun:

The faculty *has* already *given its* approval.

When the writer intends the collective noun to mean the individual members of the group, he uses a plural verb and pronoun:

The faculty *are* still *debating* the issue among *themselves.*

2 Consistency. In speech we often use a collective noun with a singular verb and then inconsistently shift to a plural pronoun. But in writing, a collective noun should be treated consistently as either singular or plural:

The faculty *is meeting* at ten o'clock and will let us know *its* decision at noon.   [Not: *their* decision.]

Sometimes you will find that the meaning of a collective actually changes from singular to plural within a sentence. Then, rather than be inconsistent, substitute a regular plural noun for the collective:

INCONSISTENT: The panel *has chosen* a subject but *haven't* yet *prepared their* talks.

CONSISTENT: The panelists (*or* The members of the panel) *have chosen* a subject but *haven't* yet *prepared their* talks.

Colloquial   *Colloquial* means "characteristic of conversation." When words and constructions are labeled *colloquial* in this book, it means that they are found chiefly in informal speech but are also generally considered appropriate in informal writing. (There are some colloquialisms that are not considered appropriate in writing; that point is made clear when such expressions are discussed in this book.)

The editors of some dictionaries of usage also use *Colloquial* to label words and phrases like *hot spot, kick him out, monkey around, nit-picking, old-timers, roughneck, skedaddle,* and *tag after,* which are used more often in speech than in writing. Remember when you see this label that, contrary to what many people think, the editors are not frowning on the use of the labeled word. They are simply indicating that the word is inappropriate in formal situations, though acceptable in most informal writing and completely appropriate in informal speech.

Colon (:)   The colon is a rather formal and emphatic mark that directs attention to what follows. As a "go ahead" sign it has three main uses:

1 A colon is used to introduce a list of appositives (at the end of a sentence) that the writer wants to emphasize:

There were three movies that we saw three times, though we really couldn't afford it: *A Man for All Seasons, Becket,* and *The Lion in Winter.* [The three names are in apposition with *movies.*]
At the end of the week two questions still nagged at Elsa: why Frazer had been fired and where he had hidden the photographs.   [The two clauses are in apposition with *questions.*]

Note: The colon is not used before a list unless the items are appositives. When they are simply predicate complements or objects, no mark of punctuation should be used before them:

The three movies we enjoyed most were [ ] *A Man for All Seasons, Becket,* and *The Lion in Winter.*   [The three names are predicate complements.]
At the end of the week Elsa was still wondering [ ] why Frazer had been fired and where he had hidden the photographs.   [The two clauses are direct objects.]

2 A colon is used to introduce a long or formal quotation in factual writing:

In his essay "Speaking of Translation," Maurice Valency says: "To translate word by word and phrase by phrase is virtually to court failure. The gifted translation depends more on magic than on labor."

3 A colon may be used between the clauses of a compound sentence when the second clause explains or illustrates the first:

Ian was dissatisfied with the pictures he had taken: all but two of them were out of focus.
Friday was even worse: the bakery delivery was four hours late, and the dairy truck didn't get to the store at all.

4 The colon has several conventional uses:
a) After the salutation in a business letter:

Dear Mr. Higgins: Dear Miss Bachman: Gentlemen:

b) Between hours and minutes expressed in figures:

6:05 a.m.   7:45 p.m.   at 8:30 this evening

c) Between volume and page numbers of a magazine:

Holiday, 47:41–43

d) Between Biblical chapter and verse:

Luke 6:20   II Kings 17:19–23

Comma   The purpose of the comma is to help make what you write clear. You will find it useful to think of the comma as making a slight separation—just enough to keep words or phrases distinct. It represents the slight pause that we use automatically in speech to help get across our meaning.

Today the tendency in writing is to use as few commas as possible and still make the meaning clear. Narrative writing generally uses fewer commas than expository writing; formal writing generally uses more than informal.

The following sections point out places where commas are likely to be needed, to make reading easier or to prevent misreading.

1 In a compound sentence. A comma is generally used before the coordinating conjunction (*and, but, for, or, nor, yet, so*) that joins the two independent clauses of a compound sentence:

By eleven-thirty all the pews were filled, and people were standing in the side aisles and in the vestibule.
The hijackers permitted the women and children to leave the plane, but the men they kept on board.

When the clauses are short and easily distinguishable, the comma is often omitted. This is especially true in informal narrative:

Jackie saw the wasp fly in and she ran for the Raid.
But: Jackie saw the wasp fly in, and out the back door she went. [Without the comma the clauses are not easily distinguishable. The sentence might first be read "Jackie saw the wasp fly in and out. . ."]

He had to give up his painting or he would be unable to support his family.

But: He had to give up his painting, or his children would starve. [Without the comma the sentence might first be read "He had to give up his painting or his children. . . ."]

(For punctuating compound sentences when the clauses themselves contain commas, see **Semicolon,** section 2.)

2 To set off interrupting elements. Parenthetical expressions like *of course, after all, to be sure, I suppose, as you know;* nouns of address; words like *yes, no, oh, well;* and tags like *isn't it, do they, won't you* added to statements to ask questions are all set off by commas:

Dan is, of course, the world's laziest man.
You, I hope, will have more sense.
Neil is a pro, after all.
Don't forget, Elsie, that we are leaving early.   [Noun of address.]
Keep moving, you slowpoke!   [Noun of address.]
No, he won't eat spinach.
Well, there's no fool like a young fool.
You don't think there's life on Mars, do you?

Remember that expressions like *after all, I hope,* and *of course* are set off only when they are used parenthetically. When they are closely connected in meaning with other words in a sentence, they are not set off: "He will get here *after all* the work is done." "*I hope* that you will have more sense."

Conjunctive adverbs (e.g., *moreover, however, nevertheless, consequently*) coming in the middle of a sentence or clause are considered parenthetical and are set off by commas:

The trip, however, was well worth the cost.

Many writers also set off conjunctive adverbs at the beginning of a sentence or clause, as parenthetical expressions or for emphasis:

He had absolutely no scruples in either his business or his social life; consequently, he had no friends and few admirers.

3 Between items in a series. (a) Words, phrases, and clauses in a series are separated by commas:

My aunt, my uncle, and my cousin were right there to commiserate with me.
We had cookies cooling on the table, on the chairs, on the sink, and even on the windowsill.
The sweaters come in brown and beige, black and gray, pink and green, but not red and white.
No one thought to ask where Dave was, why he had left, or when he would be back.

Commas are generally not used when all the items in the series are joined by conjunctions:

We had to get a plumber and a plasterer and a painter.

The comma before the last item of a series is often omitted, especially in newspaper and in business writing, which tend to use an "open" style of punctuation (in contrast to the "close" style of much formal writing):

OPEN: Ed had a quarter, two dimes and four pennies.
CLOSE: Ed had a quarter, two dimes, and four pennies.

Choose whichever style you prefer. But remember always to use the comma before the last item if there is any possibility of confusion, as in this sentence:

The proclamation was drafted by the two delegates from Taft High, Elizabeth Griffith, and Jim Peterson.

Without the comma before *and* it might seem that *Elizabeth Griffith* and *Jim Peterson* were appositives identifying the two delegates. But the meaning intended in the sentence is that four people — not two — drafted the proclamation.

(For punctuating a series of items that contain commas themselves, see **Semicolon,** section 3.)

b) Commas are used between two or more adjectives in a series:

His talk was a sad collection of inaccurate, incoherent, insignificant remarks.

Since the three adjectives in this sentence are equal modifiers of *remarks*, each should have equal emphasis. Separating the three with commas shows that they are equal modifiers. At each comma the reader pauses slightly and then gives the next adjective as much emphasis as the one before.

When the last adjective in a series is thought of as part of the noun, no comma is used before it:

His son-in-law was a fine young man.
Alan was a polite, generous, articulate young man.

In these sentences the adjective *young* is so closely connected in meaning with *man* that the writer considers the two words together as one noun (like *grand jury*, *small talk*, *hard coal*, *first aid*). The other adjectives in the sentences modify the word group *young man* — not *man* alone.

4 After introductory clauses and verbal phrases. (a) An adverb clause that precedes the main clause is generally followed by a comma:

Whenever I waited on him, I got a fifty-cent tip.

When the adverb clause is short and closely related to the main clause, and the two clauses are distinguishable, the comma may be omitted:

If he enters he will win.
But: If he enters, the contest will attract an enormous crowd.   [Without
the comma the clauses are not easily distinguishable. The sentence might
first be read "If he enters the contest. . . ."]

Before Kay left she told us the latest gossip.
But: Before Kay left, Mrs. Danvig let her read Bob's latest letter from
camp.   [Without the comma the sentence might first be read "Before Kay
left Mrs. Danvig. . . ."]

   b) A modifying verbal phrase at the beginning of a sentence is usually
followed by a comma:

Inspired by his words, Ken and I vowed to become doctors.   [Participial
phrase.]
To keep up with José, Pat had to study twice as hard as before.
[Infinitive phrase.]
By lining up jobs early in spring, we had enough yard work to keep us
busy all summer.   [Gerund phrase.]

   5 To set off nonrestrictive modifiers. *Restrictive modifiers* — those that
are needed to identify which particular one or ones are meant — are not
set off by commas:

The ushers refused to seat anyone who arrived late.   [The adjective clause
who arrived late is essential if the reader is to understand which particular
people the ushers refused to seat.]

   Nonrestrictive modifiers are not essential in getting across the basic
meaning of the sentence. They add details, helping to explain or illustrate
or describe, but the basic meaning would emerge without them. They are
always set off:

My brother Jerry, *who arrived late*, had to wait in the lobby until the end
of the first number.   [Basic meaning: Jerry had to wait in the lobby. The
adjective clause *who arrived late* adds an interesting and important bit of
background information, but it is not essential in identifying who had to
wait.]
She nodded her head in agreement, *although she really didn't understand
what the woman was saying.*   [Nonrestrictive adverb clause.]
Uncle Oscar, *fatter than ever*, met us at the bus station.   [Nonrestrictive
adjective phrase.]
Finally Mr. Pierson, *swallowing his pride*, apologized.   [Nonrestrictive
participial phrase.]
Nora was sitting in the back, *her head bent over a puzzle with movable
squares.*   [Absolute participial phrase; this construction is always nonrestrictive.]
Both our fathers were working the midnight shift, *from midnight to eight.*
[Nonrestrictive prepositional phrase.]

Remember that a modifier may be either restrictive or nonrestrictive, depending on the meaning intended by the writer. In both of the following examples, the italicized modifiers are punctuated appropriately, each one for a different meaning:

A month later we checked the three boxes again. The cereal *packed in heavy foil* was still crisp; the others were quite limp.   [The context makes it clear that there were several boxes of cereal; therefore the phrase *packed in heavy foil* is necessary to identify which particular cereal had stayed fresh.]

We searched the cupboards but found nothing except a box of cereal and a can of powdered milk. The cereal, *packed in heavy foil*, turned out to be quite fresh.   [The context makes it clear that there was only one box; therefore *packed in heavy foil* is not being used to identify which particular cereal was meant. To show that the modifier is included simply as an explanatory detail, the writer sets it off.]

6 To set off appositives. Appositives are set off by commas when they are nonrestrictive — that is, when they are added to give additional information about the preceding noun:

The ambassador's favorite was lox, a delicious smoked salmon.
Mr. Hale, the librarian at the college, was quite cooperative.

When the appositive is used to specify the particular person or thing, it is restrictive and is not set off:

his son Emil [He has more than one.]   Ethelred the Unready
the adjective *unique*   his play *Crisis*

7 For emphasis and contrast. (a) Since a comma tends to make the reader pause, it is sometimes used before a construction that the writer wants to emphasize:

Maurie was immensely popular with the girls because of his light-hearted charm, and the sleek Corvette he drove.   [Ordinarily a comma would not be put between the parts of a compound object of a preposition; here it is used to call attention to the second part.]

b) This use of the comma is especially common before contrasting expressions introduced by *not* or *but*:

We discovered that the real genius was Mrs. Lloyd, not Mr. Lloyd.
It was not a migraine, but a football game, that kept him home.

c) With certain idioms like *the more . . . the greater, the fewer . . . the better* formal writing uses a comma for emphasis; informal writing does not:

FORMAL: The louder he barked, the less we listened.
INFORMAL: The less we see of him the better we like it.

8 For clearness. Often a comma is used to prevent reading together two parts of a sentence that do not belong together:

After that, dinner was served promptly at 5:30. [To prevent: After that dinner. . . .]
To her, parents were love and security. [To prevent: To her parents. . . .]
We advised him to pay the full amount now, and then ask for a rebate at the end of the month. [To prevent: We advised him to pay the full amount now and then. . . .]
The ones who came, came because they were really interested in helping. [To prevent the reader from tripping over the repeated word.]

9 Routine uses of the comma. (a) To set off the second and all following items in addresses and dates:

Honolulu, Hawaii   Elmhurst, DuPage County, Illinois
Kenosha, Wisconsin   Port-au-Prince, Haiti
Please send all manuscripts to Miss Jan Kohler, 1921 Orrington Avenue, Evanston, Illinois 60201, before the May deadline.

January 14, 1973 [When the day of the month is not given, usage is divided — either *January, 1973* or *January 1973*.]
On June 23, 1974, the watercolor classes will begin.

b) After the salutation in personal letters and the closing in all letters:

Dear Ozzie,   Dear Miss Jens,   Sincerely,   Cordially yours,

c) In figures, to separate thousands, millions, etc.:

$6,170,166   32,000 students

d) To set off degrees and titles:

Arthur G. Flatley, D.D.S.   Robert MacNamara, Jr.
Leslie Bixby, LL.D., will give the keynote speech.
The newest board member is Atwood P. Wilson, Sr., a lawyer.

e) To show omission of a word required to fill out a grammatical construction if confusion would result without the comma; if the meaning is clear, the comma may be omitted:

The British prefer tea for breakfast; the French, chocolate. [Sentence would be hard to understand without the comma.]
Jack took the pie and she the last brownie. [Meaning is clear without the comma.]

10 Unnecessary commas. A comma should not be used:
a) Between the parts of a compound subject:

Out of the limousine stepped a tall young woman with flaming red hair [ ] and a handsome six-year-old in a cowboy suit.

b) Between a subject and its verb:

Who will get the nomination [ ] is anybody's guess.

c) Between a verb and its object or complement:

The next morning she realized [ ] why he hadn't been in class.
The big question in everyone's mind was [ ] who would take Mr. Benedict's place.

d) Between the parts of a compound predicate — unless the comma is needed for clearness or is wanted for emphasis (as in section 7):

He struggled with the report for an hour or so [ ] and then gave up.
Sue resented his taking credit for her work [ ] and resolved to tell him so.

e) At the end of a series of words, phrases, or clauses unless the series is part of a construction that requires a comma:

Ted's fondness for potatoes, rolls, butter, and desserts [ ] had added fifty ugly pounds.
But: If you would cut down on potatoes, rolls, butter, and desserts, you'd soon get back into shape.   [The comma after *desserts* is there to set off the introductory adverb clause.]

f) Between an adjective and the noun (or word group) it modifies:

At the end of the bumpy, winding [ ] road was a flagpole.
It was the most pretentious, bombastic, cliché-ridden [ ] campaign speech of the year.

g) Between a coordinating conjunction and the words that follow it — unless it is followed by an interrupting expression:

Clarence was short, blond, and [ ] homely.
Mr. Fritz tried to help, but [ ] he knew nothing about the new math.
But: Mr. Fritz knew nothing about the new math, but, as you might expect, he did his best to help us.

h) Before an indirect question or an indirect quotation:

The waitress asked [ ] who had ordered oyster stew.
She told him [ ] that they were fresh out of oysters.

i) Before directly quoted words and phrases that are built right into the construction of a sentence:

It took him a year to get [ ] "He don't" out of his speech.
His answer to all of these questions is [ ] "Perhaps."

j) Before a title, unless it is used as a nonrestrictive appositive:

The author said [ ] "Glory Be" was his best short story.
At times like these he liked to quote the poem [ ] "Ozymandias."
But: The first story he wrote, "Instant Failure," was made into a movie.

70

k) Before *that* in a *so . . . that* construction:

Dorothy was so nervous about taking her driving test [ ] that she couldn't remember her name when the examiner asked for it.

Comma fault   When you put two independent statements into one sentence, you ordinarily join them with a conjunction and a comma, or separate them with a semicolon. If you use a comma alone between the clauses, you have a comma fault—or, as it is called in this book, a *run-together sentence*: Dad refused to eat the mushrooms, he was afraid they were poisonous. (Correctly punctuated: Dad refused to eat the mushrooms; he was afraid they were poisonous. Or: Dad refused to eat the mushrooms. He was afraid they were poisonous.) For further discussion of this writing fault and how to avoid it, see **Run-together sentence.**

Commands and requests   1 Direct commands are expressed by the simple form of the verb (the infinitive form). The subject is not usually expressed unless special emphasis is wanted:

Look!	Turn on the lights, someone.
Get out.	Steve, you hang on to that side.

The helping verb *do* is used in negative commands:

Don't worry about a thing.	Do not ask Bill for a loan, Ed.

Commands are usually punctuated with periods, unless the writer wants to suggest strong feeling by using an exclamation mark.

2 Softened commands or polite requests may be expressed in several different ways:

Please return the stapler to Don Abramson.
Do visit us again.
Let's just forget about the thirteen cents.
Suppose you take your complaints to the manager.
Try to be more quiet, please.
You will be home by midnight, of course.

Often polite requests have the word order of questions—but these are generally punctuated with periods:

Will you please bring your passbook with you.
Would you kindly let us know how many copies you will need.

committee   See **Collective nouns.**

common, mutual   See **mutual, common.**

Common noun   A noun used as the name of any one of a class or group of persons, places, or things: *woman, actor, kitten, village, mountain, taxi,*

junior college, comet, plant, book, typewriter, carton.
(See **Proper noun.**)

compare   Differs from *contrast*, which always points out differences. *Compare* has two meanings: (1) Used with *to*, it means "point out similarities between":

He was at his most entertaining when he compared his classroom to a zoo.   [He showed various ways in which the two were alike.]
Grandma, who had been a movie buff in her day, had fun comparing our camping experiences to *The Perils of Pauline*.   [She described the ways in which our experiences resembled Pauline's.]

2) Used with *with*, it means "point out similarities and differences between":

You will find it interesting to compare the novel with the movie.
Our assignment was to compare the *Tribune*'s account of the meeting with the write-up in the *Daily News*.

Comparison of adjectives and adverbs   **1** To show a greater degree of the quality or characteristic named by an adjective or adverb, *-er* or *-est* is added to the word or *more* or *most* is put before it:

ADJECTIVE—
POSITIVE: Our dog is noisy.
COMPARATIVE: The Reeds' dog is even noisier.
SUPERLATIVE: He is the noisiest dog on the block.

POSITIVE: Ted is an eccentric fellow.
COMPARATIVE: I don't know anyone more eccentric than he.
SUPERLATIVE: He is probably the most eccentric man in town.

ADVERB—
POSITIVE: Elaine can work fast.
COMPARATIVE: You can't possibly work faster than she.
SUPERLATIVE: She works the fastest of all of us.

POSITIVE: The man next door speaks Spanish fluently.
COMPARATIVE: Of course I speak Spanish more fluently than he.
SUPERLATIVE: Of the three of us, I speak it most fluently.

The *-er* and *-est* endings are usual for words of one syllable and for many of two syllables. *More* and *most* are generally used with longer adjectives and adverbs, and with all adverbs ending in *-ly*. But for many words both forms are possible. Then the choice depends partly on the sound and partly on the emphasis wanted in a particular sentence:

Mother was *stricter* than Dad.   [Emphasis is on the strictness.]
Dad was far *more strict* than Herbie's father.   [Emphasis is on the degree of strictness.]

72

But both forms should not be used together, as in *more stricter* and *most strictest*. This "double comparison" was usual in Shakespeare's time but is nonstandard today.

Some adjectives and adverbs have irregular comparisons:

	POSITIVE	COMPARATIVE	SUPERLATIVE
ADJECTIVES:	bad	worse	worst
	far	farther, further	farthest, furthest
	good, well	better	best
	little	less, lesser	least
	much, many	more	most
ADVERBS:	well	better	best
	little	less	least
	much	more	most

The *comparative* forms are ordinarily used in comparing two things or people, and the *superlative* forms in comparing more than two:

Carol's idea was *better* than mine.
Isn't Tom *more conservative* than his brother?

Harry is the *fastest* runner in the league.
Of the three stories, Sue's was the *most suspenseful*.

But in informal speech, the superlative is frequently used for comparing two:

Both coats were attractive, but I liked the blue one *best*.
What we have to decide is which of the two plans is *most likely* to succeed.

2 In formal English, adjectives and adverbs like *perfect, perfectly, unique, fatal, round, dead, impossible* are generally used only in their exact, original meanings—that is, to name qualities that do not vary in degree. A thing is either perfect or not perfect, unique or not unique, dead or not dead. If it is perfect or unique or dead, something else cannot logically be *more* perfect, *more* unique, or *more* dead; it can only be *more nearly* perfect, *more nearly* unique, *more nearly* dead.

But in informal English these words are not always used in their exact, original sense. *Dead*, for instance, is used to mean not only "without life" but also "dull; quiet." *Unique* is used to mean not only "the only one of its kind" but also "rare; unusual; remarkable." *Impossible* is used to mean not only "not possible" but also "not easily possible." When the words are used in these broader meanings, they are often compared:

The carnival this year is even deader than last year's.
She is the most unique person I have ever met.

(See also **Faulty comparisons.**)

Complement of a verb   See **Predicate complement.**

73

Complex sentence   A sentence made up of one independent clause and one or more subordinate clauses (italicized in these examples):

Mrs. Higby has a parrot *that speaks German.*
When the reporters arrived, Mrs. Higby explained *that the parrot never spoke before strangers.*

(See **Clause.**)

complexioned, complected   In such phrases as "a light-complected man," *complected* is colloquial or dialectal for "a light-*complexioned* man."

Compound-complex sentence   A sentence that contains two or more main clauses and one or more subordinate clauses:

Coach Palmer invited us in and listened sympathetically as we presented our arguments, but he did not change his decision.

The two main clauses *Coach Palmer invited us in and listened sympathetically* and *he did not change his decision* make the sentence compound. The subordinate clause *as we presented our arguments* makes it compound-complex.

Compound predicate   A predicate consisting of two or more verbs (with or without complements and/or modifiers) that have the same subject:

Yes, we *live* and *learn.*
Keith *pulled* a pen from the drawer, *drew* a mustache on the photograph, and *put* it back in the frame.

Compound sentence   A sentence made up of two or more independent clauses (each could stand alone as a sentence). The clauses are joined either by a comma and a coordinating conjunction or by a semicolon:

The screw worked itself loose, and the handle fell off.
There was great gloom in Mudville; their great Casey had struck out.

(See **Clause.**)

Compound subject   Two or more nouns (or noun equivalents) used as the subject of one verb:

Jim and *I* hated each other.
The *waitress*, the *busboy*, and the *cashier* were questioned a second time.

(For the agreement of verbs with compound subjects, see **Agreement,** sections 1b, 1c, and 1i.)

Compound words   Combinations of two or more words, some of which are written as one word (*blueprint, carefree, easygoing, heavyweight,* *ingroup, letterman, roughneck*); some as hyphened words (*blue-green, chain-smoke, flip-flop, ill-gotten, know-it-all, mischief-maker, wheeler-dealer*); and some as separate words (*blue chip, cake flour, egg roll, grade school, jump shot, old maid, totem pole*). Regardless of how it is written, a compound word is thought of as a single word.

If you are not sure how to write a given compound, look it up in a dictionary. (See also **Hyphen** and **Plurals of nouns,** section 8.)

conclude   Used with *by* before a gerund:

Uncle Hal concluded his lecture by patting Willie on the shoulder.

Used with *with* before a noun:

She concluded her letter with her usual best wishes to all.

Used with *from* when it means "infer":

Dad concluded from her flustered look that she had spent the money.

Concrete words   Concrete words name persons, places, and things that can be seen and touched: *infant, park, mesa, elevator, sugar, rose, silo.* They contrast with abstract words, which name ideas, qualities, states: *goodness, evil, humility, ethics, terror, democracy, success.*

Conditions   In simple, straightforward conditions—those that state a condition that is likely or possible—indicative verb forms are used:

If Lou *is* on the four-thirty bus, Sam will give him a lift.
If you *will proofread* those for me, we can beat the deadline.
If he *has* the money, he'll be glad to lend you a dollar or two.

When a condition is less likely or possible, the helping verb *should* or *would* or the past tense is used:

If he *should get* the job, we would move to Chicago.
If he *got* the job, we would move to Chicago.

In conditions that are contrary to fact—those that cannot be met—the subjunctive is often used in formal English, but rarely in informal:

If I *were* that rich, I would buy a helicopter.   [Informal: If I *was* that rich.]
If she *were* the supervisor, I would resign.   [Informal: If she *was* the supervisor.]

Had with the past participle (not *would have*) is used if the condition refers to past time:

If I *had known* the answer, I would have told him.   [Not: If I *would have known* the answer.]
Had he *moved* one inch more, he would have gone off the edge.   [Informal: If he *had moved* one inch more.]

Conjugation   A verb has various forms to show person, number, voice, mood, and tense. An orderly arrangement of the forms of a particular verb is called a *conjugation*. For a typical conjugation, see **Tenses of verbs.**

Conjunctions   Connecting words used to join words, phrases, clauses, and sentences. For discussion of specific conjunctions, see the following entries: **Coordinating conjunctions** (*and, but, for, yet, or, nor, so*); **Conjunctive adverbs** (*therefore, thus, moreover, consequently,* etc.); **Correlative conjunctions** (*both . . . and, either . . . or, neither . . . nor, not only . . . but also*); **Subordinating conjunctions** (*after, because, so that, while,* etc.).

Conjunctive adverbs   **1** Adverbs used as connectives to join two independent clauses (or sentences) by showing the relationship in meaning between them are called *conjunctive adverbs* (or *transitional adverbs* or *sentence connectors*):

By the end of the second day Reilly had lost his ten-point lead and seemingly had no chance to win; *nevertheless*, he would not give up.   [*Nevertheless* points up the contrast between the clauses.]
Next week their production schedule will be cut from three shifts to two; *consequently*, a thousand more men will be out of work.   [*Consequently* shows that the second clause is the result of the first.]

   2 The most common conjunctive adverbs are:

accordingly	indeed	nonetheless
besides	in fact	now
consequently	later	otherwise
finally	moreover	still
furthermore	nevertheless	then
however	next	therefore

   Some of these—*accordingly, consequently, furthermore, however, moreover, nevertheless, nonetheless, therefore*—are "heavy" connectives, rather stiff and formal. Simpler conjunctions are generally more appropriate in informal writing, especially narrative writing:

HEAVY: Frank, who is nearsighted, wanted us to get seats on the main floor. However, I had only two dollars left. Therefore I persuaded him to sit in the balcony with me.
IMPROVED: Frank, who is nearsighted, wanted us to get seats on the main floor. But I had only two dollars left, so I persuaded him to sit in the balcony with me.

   3 When the clauses of a compound sentence are linked by a conjunctive adverb, a semicolon (not a comma) is used between them—whether the adverb begins the second clause or comes within it:

Being a bellboy, I told myself, would be fun; besides, I did need the money.
I felt a yank on the line; then I saw the marlin.

76

Mr. Blair was skeptical; he decided, however, to let us present the proposal at the next assembly.

When the adverb comes within the clause, as in the third example, it is generally set off by commas. When it comes first in the clause, as in the first and second examples, it may or may not be followed by a comma. If the writer intends it to be parenthetical, he uses a comma, otherwise not.

connected with, in connection with   Wordy phrases that often can be effectively replaced by a simple *in, for, with*, or *about*:

WORDY: First she explained the regulations connected with using the library.
BETTER: First she explained the regulations for using the library.

WORDY: Did Mr. Metz say anything in connection with the bus strike?
BETTER: Did Mr. Metz say anything about the bus strike?

Connotation   Besides its recognized dictionary meaning (its denotation), a word may have an additional shade—or shades—of meaning (its connotation). *Statesman* and *politician*, for instance, both have the denotation "a person actively engaged in the business of government," but their connotations are different. *Statesman* suggests or connotes approval (a statesman is able, wise, high-principled); *politician* connotes disapproval (many politicians are scheming and opportunistic).
   (See **Loaded words**.)

considerable   Although in speech a clear distinction is not always made between the adverb *considerably* and the adjective *considerable*, in both formal English and informal writing it is:

He influenced us considerably during that year.   [Adverb modifying the verb *influenced*.]
He had considerable influence on the students.   [Adjective modifying the noun *influence*.]

   In nonstandard English *considerable* is used as an intensifier, but not in standard English:

NONSTANDARD: She was considerable upset by it all.
STANDARD: She was extremely upset by it all.   [Or: *very* upset.]

   In informal speech *considerable* is sometimes used as a noun:

SPOKEN: I'd say Al has already done considerable for his family.
WRITTEN: I'd say Al has already done a great deal for his family.

Context   Used to mean (1) "the parts that come before or after a word or sentence," (2) "the whole passage, speech, or situation in which a word or sentence occurs." The context always determines the intended meaning of

77

a particular word or sentence; therefore, to understand words and ideas exactly and completely, you must see them or hear them in context.

Contractions   Contractions are shortened forms of words, made by "telescoping" syllables when speaking the words; in writing, the letter or letters representing the omitted sounds are indicated by an apostrophe:

I have — I've	he is — he's	should have — should've
we are — we're	he has — he's	they are — they're
do not — don't	we had — we'd	has not — hasn't
she will — she'll	they had — they'd	did not — didn't
you are — you're	it is — it's	could not — couldn't

Contractions are ordinarily out of place in formal writing. But because they are typical of spoken English, they are often necessary in informal writing — especially, of course, in the dialogue in stories and plays.

Conversation   A great deal of writing — exposition as well as narration — can be made more interesting and vivid by the use of direct quotation and conversation. Notice how quotation enlivens this passage from a biography:

Then came the Boer War. Bruce and Mrs. Bruce found themselves besieged in Ladysmith with nine thousand other Englishmen. There were thirty medical officers in the garrison — but not one surgeon. With each whine and burst of the shells from the Boers' "Long Tom" the rows of the wounded grew — there were moanings, and a horrid stench from legs that should be amputated. . . . "Think of it! Not one of those medicos could handle a knife! Myself, I was only a laboratory man," said Bruce, "but I had cut up plenty of dogs and guinea pigs and monkeys — so why not soldiers? There was one chap with a bashed-up knee . . . well, they chloroformed him, and while they were at that, I sat in the next room reading Treve's *Surgery* on how to take out a knee-joint. Then I went in and did it — we saved his leg." So Bruce became Chief Surgeon, and fought and starved, nearly to death, with the rest. — Paul de Kruif, "Bruce: Trail of the Tsetse," *Microbe Hunters*, Harcourt Brace Jovanovich, Inc.

Quoted speech is effective, of course, only if it sounds real. If you are interested in learning to write good conversation, start by observing carefully how you talk and how people around you talk. You will find that contractions, clipped expressions, and informal words and idioms are typical of everyday speech, and that the use of them will help make your written conversation sound natural. But don't overdo them. Though written conversation is based on real speech, it should not be a word-for-word reproduction. If you wrote down conversations as they were actually spoken, you would often end with a hodgepodge of apostrophes, distorted spellings (*shootin', kin, gotta, hyar, wuz, sich, fust, ya, 'em, aincha, keerful*), and coarse expressions. This would be confusing, distracting, and possibly offensive to your readers. In reproducing speech on paper, it is better to use just enough such spellings and expressions to *suggest* the way speech is supposed to sound. For example:

He began again. "It's a funny story," he said. "Get ready to laugh. Get ready to bust your sides, for it is sure a funny story. It's about a hick. It's about a red-neck, like you all, if you please. Yeah, like you. He grew up like any other mother's son on the dirt roads and gully washes of a north-state farm. He knew all about being a hick. . . . "—Robert Penn Warren, *All the King's Men*, Harcourt Brace Jovanovich, Inc.

It is quite likely that the speaker would actually say *git* for *get, t'* for *to, an'* for *and, bein'* for *being*, and so on. But these distorted spellings are not needed; for the use of expressions and words like *bust your sides, hick, red-neck*, and *Yeah* and the general rhythm and tone of the sentences strongly suggest the man's speech pattern, personality, and background.

A few words about the speaker, coming before or after his quoted words, sometimes help tell the story:

"All right, all right. I'm coming; I'm coming," she yelled, her irritation doubling with each step she took.

Jerome scooped up another handful of the slushy snow, packed it around the snowball Phil had handed him, and muttered maliciously, "When this hits old man Crawford, he'll know he's been hit."

But this kind of description or explanation should not be overdone. For instance, it isn't always necessary when labeling speeches to use a picturesque synonym for *said* (*grunted, murmured, squealed, thundered, stuttered, whimpered*). In fact, unless there is a good reason for using one of these more specific words, *said* is preferable because it is less conspicuous.

And you need not even indicate who is speaking if the conversation leaves no question in the reader's mind:

Ozzie stuck the envelope back in his pocket and opened the door. A sleepy-looking fellow slouched at a table watched him as he peered around the dark room. The fellow stood up. "Looking for someone, kid?"
"Yes. Is George Leasa here?"
"No. Georgie's lying low for a couple days."
"Can you tell me where he lives?"
"Why do you want to know?"
"I've got a pawn ticket to give him."
"Oh, you're the guy, huh? Well, hand it over, kid. I'm Georgie-boy."

Some of the conventions of paragraphing and punctuating conversation are illustrated in the examples you have just read. More details can be found in **Quotation marks.**

Coordinating conjunctions   **1** The coordinating conjunctions—*and, but, for, or, nor, yet, so*—are used to connect words, phrases, subordinate clauses, independent clauses, and sentences (parts of equal grammatical value):

WORDS: nuts and bolts; Tom, Dick, or Harry; fat but pretty; today or tomorrow
PHRASES: by the people and for the people; watching the practice and finding fault with every play
SUBORDINATE CLAUSES: They were looking for someone who could run the office but who would work for peanuts.
INDEPENDENT CLAUSES: According to the polls Eaton didn't have a chance, yet he won by a landslide.
SENTENCES: The old man promised Mr. Brenner that some day he would repay the loan. And he did.

2 The conjunction *and* is badly overworked. Sometimes it is used when there is no need for it; sometimes it is used where another conjunction would express more exactly the relationship between two parts. For a discussion of this point, see **and**, section 2.

3 There is a special group of coordinating conjunctions that are used in pairs—*both . . . and, either . . . or, neither . . . nor, whether . . . or, not only . . . but also*. For a discussion of their use, see **Correlative conjunctions.**

Correction marks In correcting your papers, your teacher may indicate some of the revisions that are needed by using certain abbreviations or symbols. The following list gives some of the most common correction marks. Each one is followed by a reference to an article where you will find help in making the appropriate revisions.

Ab	Abbreviations	Frag	Sentence fragment
Agr	Agreement	Local	Localism, Dialect
Amb	Ambiguity	Mis	Misplaced modifiers
Apos	Apostrophe	Prep	Preposition
Awk	Awkward writing	Pn	Punctuation mark misused.
Big W	Big words		See article on appropri-
Cap	Capital letters		ate mark.
CF	Comma fault	Ref	Reference of pronouns
Comp	Faulty comparisons	Shift	Shifted constructions
Dang	Dangling modifiers	Sp	Spelling
Dead	Deadwood	Tense	Tenses of verbs
Div	Division of words	Wordy	Wordiness

¶ This symbol means a new paragraph is needed.

Correlative conjunctions Coordinating conjunctions used in pairs:

not only . . . but also	either . . . or
not only . . . but	neither . . . nor
both . . . and	whether . . . or

The main purpose of these connecting words is to emphasize the fact that two items are involved. Therefore the two items that are connected should be "parallel"—or similar—in form. If the first conjunction is followed by a prepositional phrase, the second should be followed by a prepositional phrase; if the first is followed by a verb, the second should be followed by a verb; and so on.

NOT PARALLEL: Uncle Theodore calmly predicted that we would find Maxie either *working* on his motorcycle or *he would be reading* some hot-rodder magazines at the library.

PARALLEL: Uncle Theodore calmly predicted that we would find Maxie either *working* on his motorcycle or *reading* some hot-rodder magazines at the library.

NOT PARALLEL: Aunt Helen couldn't decide whether *to go* to Europe with two of the other teachers or *if she should take* some graduate courses at the college.

PARALLEL: Aunt Helen couldn't decide whether *to go* to Europe with two of the other teachers or *(to) take* some graduate courses at the college.

PARALLEL: Aunt Helen couldn't decide whether *she should go* to Europe with two of the other teachers or *(should) take* some graduate courses at the college.

NOT PARALLEL: Jay spent the whole two weeks either *arguing* with me or *with Sam*.

PARALLEL: Jay spent the whole two weeks arguing either *with me* or *with Sam*.

PARALLEL: Jay spent the whole two weeks either *arguing* with me or *writing* letters to the newspaper.

Counter words   Vague, general adjectives (like *nice, wonderful, cute, super, darling, awful, terrible, punk, frightful, ghastly*) that are used not for their exact meanings but only for expressing approval or disapproval. Counter words are common—and useful—in conversation, but they are seldom appropriate in writing. There it is important to use words that express exact meanings, words that help give the reader a specific picture.

Count nouns   See **Mass nouns, count nouns.**

couple   Strictly, the noun *couple* means "two persons or things that are associated in some way":

The Petersons were a handsome couple who lived next door to us.

In informal speech and writing, *couple of* is used to mean "two or three; a few; several":

Fred won't be gone more than a couple of weeks.
Don't wait for me; I have a couple of letters to type.

In informal speech the *of* is often omitted:

Pete ate a couple doughnuts and left.

But this usage is not considered appropriate in expository writing.

credible, credulous   *Credible* means "believable"; *credulous* means "too ready to believe":

It hardly seems credible that he earns that much in a week.
Only a child—a credulous child—would believe those ads.

creek   Pronounced /krēk/ or /krik/.

criterion   A rule, standard, or test on which a decision or judgment is based. The plural is *criteria* or *criterions*.
  Though *criteria* is sometimes used colloquially with a singular meaning, this use is avoided by careful writers and speakers:

His only criterion of success is how much money a man makes. [Not: His only criteria of success is. . . .]

curriculum   The plural is *curricula* or *curriculums*.

Dangling modifiers   A modifier that has no word in the sentence which it can sensibly modify is said to be *dangling*:

DANGLING: *Having spent three summer vacations in Chicago*, the Shedd Aquarium was quite familiar to Jerry. [Who had spent three vacations in Chicago? The sentence seems to say that the Shedd Aquarium had.]
REVISED: Having spent three summer vacations in Chicago, *Jerry* was quite familiar with the Shedd Aquarium. [Now there is a sensible word—*Jerry*—for the modifier to relate to.]

The most usual way of correcting a dangling phrase is to provide a word — a subject — that it can sensibly modify:

DANGLING: *After taking a shower,* the bathroom floor usually has to be mopped up by Clint.
REVISED: After taking a shower, *Clint* usually has to mop up the bathroom floor.

DANGLING: *To be eligible for a student-government office,* your grades must be above average.
REVISED: To be eligible for a student-government office, *you* must have above-average grades.

But sometimes rewording the modifier is the best solution, especially when the dangler is a prepositional phrase or an elliptical clause:

DANGLING: *At the age of six,* Judy's father sold his advertising agency and bought a farm.
REVISED: *When Judy was six,* her father sold his advertising agency and bought a farm.

DANGLING: *While in the drugstore getting a prescription filled,* a meter maid ticketed his car.
REVISED: *While he was in the drugstore getting a prescription filled,* a meter maid ticketed his car.

Dash   Since dashes are conspicuous and emphatic marks of punctuation, they should be used sparingly — only when they serve a specific purpose, when no other marks will carry the intended meaning as well. They should not be used as substitutes for all other marks, as some writers use them.

1 A common use of the dash is to mark an abrupt change in the thought of a sentence:

Just then Mr. Fiedler called and — no, that was later, about nine-thirty.
"Where did I — oh, here it is in my pocket."

2 Dashes are used to set off parenthetical expressions — explanatory comments or side remarks — that make an abrupt interruption in the thought or structure of a sentence:

At the start of the twelfth inning — it was getting pretty dark by then — Rube Heller decided he had had enough.
They bought that house for five thousand dollars — does it seem possible? — and last week they sold it for twenty-eight.
Laura believed his hard-luck story — how naive she is! — and let him borrow their car.

Notice that the first word of the interrupting expression begins with a small letter, even though the interrupter is a sentence. A period is not used after an interrupter, but a question mark or an exclamation mark is—right before the second dash.

Parentheses, which are more formal than dashes, are sometimes used to set off interrupting expressions. Parentheses tend to lessen the emphasis, to make the interrupter seem less conspicuous. Dashes make the interrupters stand out more than parentheses would. In informal writing—unless it is serious expository writing—dashes are more common than parentheses, though both should be used sparingly.

3 Nonrestrictive modifiers are usually set off by commas. But when special emphasis is wanted, dashes are used. And dashes are usual if the modifiers themselves have commas.

Mrs. Pedderlin was an extremely patient, sympathetic teacher—when the supervisor was in the room.
Yes, you will love the hotel—if you can afford forty dollars a day for a room.
Ordinary pork—which Hindus relish, but Moslems detest—was one cause of friction in nineteenth-century India.

4 Nonrestrictive appositives are usually set off by commas; but when the writer wants to call special attention to an appositive or when the appositive phrase itself has commas, dashes are better:

As a reporter for the school paper he got a chance to interview one of my childhood crushes—the glamorous Lena Horne.
Some of these euphemisms—*to pass away*, for example, and *the dear departed*—are justifiable because they help to soften misfortunes.
Ambassador Wilson was a good choice for the post in India, for he knew three Indian languages—Hindustani, Bengali, and Tamil.

If a comma were used instead of a dash in the third example sentence, a reader might think that Ambassador Wilson knew six languages. The dash shows clearly that the three names are appositives identifying the Indian languages.

5 A dash is used before a word or phrase (like *these* or *all these*) that sums up a preceding list of items, to clearly mark the division between the list and the statement that follows:

Pettiness, envy, selfishness, vindictiveness—these neatly summarized her opinion of him.
Julie, Tricia, Pat, Martha—all were in agreement.

6 A double-length dash is used at the end of a sentence to show that it is left unfinished or that a speaker is interrupted. No period is used after the dash:

Uncle Ben insists it is the principle, not the money, but — —

"Well, I for one don't think — —"
"No one cares what you think," she cut in sharply.

7 In handwriting, distinguish between a dash and a hyphen by making the dash twice as long. On the typewriter, you will have to use two hyphens (not spaced away from the words before and after), since the standard keyboard has no dash.

data   Pronounced /dā'tə/, /dat'ə/, or /dä'tə/. *Data* (from Latin) is the plural of the singular *datum*, which is rarely used. Since to most people its meaning is singular—"a group of facts" or "a mass of information"—*data* is generally used with a singular verb in informal English:

His data *is* accurate, all right, but *it is* not complete.
This data *seems* to contradict that.

In formal English *data* is usually regarded as plural:

The data he collected *have* to be carefully analyzed.

Dates   The usual form for writing dates is:

July 14, 1789   June 6, 1968

The form *6 June 1968* (with no comma) is used by the armed services.
     In personal letters and in business memos and forms, figures only are often used:

1/27/72   12/29/72

The month is put first, then the day of the month, then the year.
     The *st, nd, rd, th* are now generally omitted from the day of the month when the day is given as a figure:

November 1   Not: November 1st
February 12   Not: February 12th

     In very formal style the day of the month is often written out in full when the year is not given:

September fourteenth   April first

But the year is not written out in words except in formal social announcements or invitations, which are usually engraved or printed.
     If it is necessary to save space (in business memos, for example), the names of months may be abbreviated. Here are some of the abbreviations in use:

Jan., Ja.   Feb.   Mar.   Apr., Apl., Ap.   Jun., Ju., Je.
Jul., Jl., Jy.   Aug., Ag.   Sept., Sep.   Oct.   Nov.   Dec.

(See also **Centuries**.)

Dative case   Nouns or pronouns used as indirect objects of verbs are sometimes said to be in the *dative case*. Actually English (unlike Latin or

85

German) has no distinctive form for the dative case. A noun used as an indirect object is in the ordinary case form and a pronoun is in the objective case form:

Jane bought *Larry* a hideous hand-painted tie.
Dad gave *me* a pat on the back

Deadwood   A term used to describe words or phrases that add nothing to the meaning of a sentence:

[It was] on one of our daily walks [that we used to take every day that] Carl noticed an abandoned shack [that no one was living in at the time].
[The way in which] my brother usually managed to make the hamburgers palatable [to the taste was] by smothering them with mustard, ketchup, and piccalilli.

Omitting the deadwood in sentences like these makes for clearer, crisper writing.

deaf   Pronounced /def/. At one time the pronunciation /dēf/ was standard, but it is now used only in some nonstandard dialects.

decided, decisive   Good English makes a distinction between *decided*, meaning "definite" or "unmistakable," and *decisive*, meaning "having or giving a clear result; settling something beyond question":

By the end of that semester there was a decided improvement in his work.
The sixth round proved decisive; Morgan himself knew the match was lost at that point.

Declarative sentences   Sentences that make statements:

The fight started in the chemistry lab.
Mr. Hill asked who had started the fight.
Mr. Hill turned to Ted and asked, "What happened to your eye?"
"It got in the way of Rob's fist!" exclaimed Gordon.

Declension   The change in the form of nouns, pronouns, and adjectives to show *number* (book—books, mouse—mice, child—children); *case* (girl—girl's, I—me—mine); or *gender* (his—hers—its). In a highly inflected language like Latin or German, declension plays an important part in grammar. But in English, where so few words change in form to show case or gender, declension plays a relatively small part.

Deductive reasoning   See **Inductive and deductive reasoning,** section 2.

Defining words   Many times in your writing you use words or phrases whose meaning your readers may not know. To make your meaning clear, you should find some way to explain what the words mean. If the word is abstract (like *liberty, conservatism, success, glamour*), the best way to explain is to give concrete examples of what it means to you. If the word is concrete, you can often make its meaning clear by tucking in a synonym that your readers are likely to know. For example:

Uncle Pat enjoyed telling us stories of his days on the Burlington line as a gandy dancer—or section hand, to use a more familiar term.

By adding the synonym *section hand*, you make clear what the job was and still keep the term *gandy dancer* with its picturesque connotation that helps readers get a vivid picture of the uncle.

There are two other common ways of clarifying the meaning of words for your readers—one direct and rather formal, the other indirect and informal:

My first assignment was to collate the new books—a job far less impressive than it sounds. *To collate* is a librarian's term meaning to examine a book page by page to see that none are missing.
My first assignment was to check each new book page by page to make sure none were missing—a rather boring job which the librarian dignified by the high-sounding term "collate."

In the first example *collate* is defined directly; in the second its meaning is made clear indirectly. This indirect way of explaining is preferable in narrative writing, since it does not interrupt the story with a formal definition.

In expository writing a formal definition is often best—especially to define a term for which there is no well-known synonym that will explain its meaning fully. In defining a word, give (1) its general class and (2) the characteristics that make it different from other things in that class:

Fiberglass [the word being defined] is a material [the class it belongs to] consisting of filaments of glass that are extremely fine and so flexible they can be made into yarn to be woven into fabrics or can be used in woolly masses as an insulator [characteristics that distinguish fiberglass from other materials].
A *gambrel* is a roof that has two slopes on each side, the lower slope of which is generally steeper than the upper.

The number of distinguishing details you should use depends on how much information you think your readers need to understand fully your intended meaning.

In your written work, avoid using *when* and *where* in defining words. Definitions like "A claque is when someone hires some people to go to a play or a concert and to applaud enthusiastically in order to promote the success of the performance or the performers" and "An epithet is where you call someone by a word that names or describes one of his main qualities, like *the Terrible* in *Ivan the Terrible*" make the meaning clear enough, but they sound amateurish. They are better stated in a more sophisticated way—by giving the general class first and then the distinguishing characteristics: "A claque is a group of people hired. . . ." "An epithet is a word or phrase naming or describing. . . ."

Definite article   The adjective *the* (called a *noun marker* or a *noun determiner* by some grammarians). (See **the** and **a, an.**)

Degree (of adjectives and adverbs)   One of three stages in the comparison of adjectives and adverbs:

POSITIVE DEGREE:	tall	bravely
COMPARATIVE DEGREE:	taller	more bravely
SUPERLATIVE DEGREE:	tallest	most bravely

(See also **Comparison of adjectives and adverbs.**)

Degrees   Academic degrees (titles granted by a college or university to show the completion of a required course of study or as an honor) are not ordinarily given with a person's name except in college publications or in reference works. When used, they are set off by commas:

Albert R. Dawe, B.A., M.A., Ph.D., and Harold Weaver, B.S., M.S., Ph.D., served as consultants.

delusion   See **illusion, delusion, allusion.**

Demonstratives   *This, that, these, those*—used to specify or point out—are called demonstrative adjectives or demonstrative pronouns, depending on how they are used in a sentence:

ADJECTIVES: This jacket costs more than that suit.
　　　　　　　These papers are heavier than those tiles.
PRONOUNS: Why is this more expensive than that?
　　　　　　Aren't those heavier than these?

(See **kind, sort.**)

Denotation   The *denotation* of a word is its exact, literal meaning as contrasted with its *connotation*, the added meaning the word suggests or implies. The adjectives *assertive* and *pushy* have the same denotation ("conspicuously or obtrusively energetic or active"), but their connotations differ. *Assertive* suggests desirable characteristics like determination and self-confidence; *pushy* implies such undesirable qualities as officiousness, rudeness, and offensive forwardness.

Dependent clause   See **Clause,** section 2.

Derivational endings   See **Endings (of words).**

Dewey Decimal System   To make it easy to find available material on a particular subject, most libraries classify and arrange their books according to the Dewey Decimal System, devised by a New York librarian, Melvil Dewey, in 1876. In this system, all subject matter is divided into ten main classes and assigned certain numbers:

000–099   Generalities (encyclopedias, periodicals, etc.)
100–199   Philosophy & related disciplines (psychology, ethics, etc.)
200–299   Religion (Bible, churches, church history, etc.)
300–399   The social sciences (economics, law, education, etc.)
400–499   Language (grammar, derivations, etc., of various languages)
500–599   Pure sciences (mathematics, chemistry, astronomy, etc.)
600–699   Technology (agriculture, medicine, business, etc.)
700–799   The arts (sculpture, music, sports, theater, etc.)
800–899   Literature & rhetoric (novels, plays, essays, poetry, etc.)
900–999   General geography, general history, etc. (including collective biography)

Each of these ten classes is subdivided into ten more specific groups. For example:

700	The arts	750	Painting and paintings
710	Civic and landscape art	760	Graphic arts
720	Architecture	770	Photography and photographs
730	Sculpture and the plastic arts	780	Music
740	Drawing and decorative arts	790	Recreation

Each of the ten groups is in turn divided into ten smaller fields:

790	Recreation	795	Games of chance
791	Public entertainment	796	Athletics; sports and games
792	Theater	797	Aquatic and air sports
793	Indoor games and amusements	798	Equestrian sports; racing
794	Indoor games of skill	799	Fishing; hunting; shooting

Still smaller subdivisions are made by using decimals. For example, books dealing with the Olympic games are classified under the number 796.48; those dealing with mountain climbing, under 796.522.

In most small libraries, books of fiction are not given a classification number. Instead, they are marked with an **F** and are arranged on the shelves alphabetically by the last name of the author.

Individual biographies are marked **B** in some libraries; in others they are given number **92** or **920**. The biographies are arranged alphabetically by the last name of the person the book is about.

The Dewey classification number, which is part of the *call number*, is placed on the spine of the book. The call number is put in the upper left corner of the author, subject, and title cards in the card catalog. Once you know the call number of a certain book, you can easily find it on the shelves. (See also **Card catalog.**)

Diacritical marks   Marks like ‾, ˆ, ¨, and · used to show how letters of words are pronounced. Diacritical marks are used most often in the *phonetic spelling*—the pronunciation respelling—of a word in a dictionary entry: **find** /fīnd/, **scorn** /skôrn/, **rule** /rül/, **germ** /jėrm/.

For the most part, dictionaries use the same marks. But there are some slight variations. In the front of every dictionary there is a complete key explaining the pronunciation symbols it uses. There is also usually an abbreviated one at the bottom or top of alternate pages. For a key to the pronunciation symbols used in the phonetic spellings in this book, see **Pronunciation.**

Dialect   The speech of people in one section of a country that has characteristics making it different from the speech of people in other parts of the same country. Dialects differ in vocabulary; in one region, for example, *doughnut* is common; in others, *fossnock*, *ring*, or *fried cake*. (Do people in your locality say *faucet*, *hydrant*, or *spigot*? *quilt*, *puff*, *comforter*, or *comfortable*? *kerosene* or *coal oil*? *sweet corn*, *green corn*, or *roasting ears*?) They differ in idioms (*he resembles*, *he features*, or *he favors; they played hookey*, *they hooked Jack*, or *they bagged school*), and particularly in pronunciations. In some New England regions, for example, a broad *a* is used in words like *mask*, *glass*, *wrath*—which people of other regions pronounce with a short *a*. Easterners and Southerners slight the *r* in words like *farm*, *curl*, *hard*, yet in certain instances sound an *r* where there is none in the spelling (as in "the lawr of the land" and "the hyenar in that cage"). Westerners sound their *r*'s more strongly than other people, and use an "ah" sound for the *o* in words like *block* and *spot*.

Dialects exist because groups of speakers are now—or once were—separated from each other. They are not limited to users of nonstandard English, as many people mistakenly think. Educated, as well as uneducated, people of the South speak somewhat differently from educated Westerners or New Englanders. The prestigious speech of Boston is just as much a dialect as is Brooklynese or the speech of the Scandinavian sections in the Midwest. All of us speak a dialect (or several dialects), though we may not realize that we do, since our neighbors for miles around speak the same way we do. Only when we visit other sections of the country or listen to the speech of a visitor from far away do we realize that there are regional differences in our language. A dialect is, after all, speech that does not attract attention to itself among the people of a region.

Linguistic scholars now believe that there are three major dialect regions in our country: the *Northern*, the *Midland*, and the *Southern*. Within these three main areas there are minor dialects, as in the Ozarks, in New York City, in New Orleans, in Milwaukee.

The differences between the dialects of our country are fewer than those between the dialects of other countries—England, for example, or France or Italy. This is due in part to travel, but even more to movies, radio, and television, and to the nationwide circulation of books and magazines. Because of these factors, people in all parts of the country become familiar with and tend to use the same language forms.

Dialectal words, phrases, and pronunciations are sometimes called *localisms* or *provincialisms*. In dictionaries they are usually labeled *Dial.* (for *Dialect* or *Dialectal*). In speaking to or with people of your region it is entirely appropriate for you to use localisms, avoiding of course those not in good standing among the educated people of your community. In speaking with others or to a general audience, it is best to avoid words, phrases, or pronunciations that might seem overly conspicuous or might be confusing or distracting.

In informal writing, localisms are often appropriate — in stories or personal narratives especially, where they help make the setting seem real and the conversation of people seem natural. In formal writing, localisms are generally avoided; the rare ones used for special effect are usually put in quotation marks.

(See also **Idiolect.**)

Dialogue   For the use and punctuation of dialogue in writing, see **Conversation** and **Quotation marks.**

die   Generally used with *of* — not *from* or *with* — before the name of an illness: He died *of* cancer. But we say *died from a wound, died by violence, died through neglect, died from lack of care.*

differ   Followed by *from* when the meaning is "be unlike or dissimilar":

The Italian spoken in Venice differs from that spoken in Rome.

When the meaning is "disagree; have or express a different opinion," *differ* is followed by *with* or *from*:

On the third point, however, Frank differed with (*or* from) me.

different   In formal English and in informal writing, *different* is generally followed by *from*:

Dad's attitude was different from Mom's.
His design turned out to be quite different from what we had been led to expect.

Colloquial usage is divided; occasionally *from* is used, sometimes *to* (very common in England), and most often *than*:

You will find his latest novel different than nis others.

In both speech and writing, *different than* is becoming more common before a clause:

His design turned out to be quite different than we had been led to expect.
The old town was completely different than I remembered it.

Direct address   The name or descriptive term by which persons (or animals) are addressed:

Ladies and gentlemen, let's consider both sides of this question.
What are you doing here, *young man*?
Stop talking, *Polly*, and eat your cracker.

Words in direct address are set off by commas—one comma if they come at the beginning or the end of a sentence, and two commas if they come in the middle of a sentence.

Direct object   A noun or pronoun (or phrase or clause used as a noun) that tells who or what receives the action expressed by the verb is called a *direct object*. The direct object usually follows the verb, and it answers such questions as "What was it that Gene tore?" or "Who was it that the coach suspected?"

Gene tore the *photograph* into tiny pieces.
The coach suspected *Harold* from the start.
I hate *walking barefoot on cement*.   [Gerund phrase.]
Marileta wondered *who he was*.   [Noun clause.]

Occasionally, for emphasis, the object is put first in a sentence, before both the subject and the verb:

      O   S   V
The *letters* from Bob she kept in a secret drawer.

Direct quotation   The actual words used by a speaker; in contrast with *indirect quotation*, in which the sense rather than the actual words is given:

DIRECT: "How much money do you have left?" asked Rita.
INDIRECT: Rita asked me how much money I had left.

(For punctuation, see **Quotation marks.**)

discover, invent   These verbs are not interchangeable. *To discover* is "to see or learn of for the first time something already existing"; *to invent* is "to make or work out something that did not exist before":

Roald Amundsen, a Norwegian, discovered the South Pole.
Someone should invent a dictionary that always opens to the right page.

disinterested, uninterested   A distinction is generally made between these two words. *Disinterested* is used to mean "having no selfish interest or personal feelings in a matter and therefore no reason or desire to be anything but strictly impartial"; *uninterested*, to mean "not interested":

Yes, but can Craig be trusted to write a disinterested review of a book by an author he despises?
She was quite uninterested in hearing my side of the argument.

In colloquial usage, *disinterested* is sometimes used as a synonym for *uninterested.*

Ditto marks (")   Ditto marks are used in accounts, lists, and tables to avoid repeating words that appear directly above:

derelict, derived from Latin
diplomat,   "   "   French

Ditto marks are not appropriate in most of your written work (themes, tests, reports, letters) nor in footnotes or bibliographies.

dived, dove   Both forms are used as the past tense of *dive; dived* is more common, especially in writing.

Divided usage   The spellings, pronunciations, and constructions used by speakers and writers of the same education often differ. Whenever there are—in the same level of language—two or more forms that are equally acceptable, usage is said to be *divided.* There are many more of these divided usages than most people realize. Here are just a few:

IN SPELLING: bazaar *or* bazar   dryly *or* drily
                beaus *or* beaux   employee *or* employe
                coconut *or* cocoanut   inquire *or* enquire
                cookie *or* cooky   pinochle *or* pinocle
                clue *or* clew   poky *or* pokey
                dialogue *or* dialog   rhyme *or* rime

IN PRONUNCIATION: abdomen: /ab'də mən/ *or* /ab dō'mən/
                     blithe: /blīᵺ/ *or* /blīth/
                     bovine: /bō'vīn/ *or* /bō'vēn/
                     harass: /har'əs/ *or* /hə ras'/
                     kiln: /kil/ *or* /kiln/
                     Nazi: /nät'sē/ *or* /nat'sē/

IN VERB FORMS: Past tense: dived *or* dove, sank *or* sunk
                  Past participle: woven *or* wove, swelled *or* swollen

Remember that in all such instances of divided usage either of the forms is acceptable. Use whichever seems to you the most appropriate in a particular situation. You may choose the one that you think is preferred by the audience you want to reach or, better still, the one that comes most naturally to your own speech.

Division of words   Though the right-hand margin of your papers does not have to be absolutely even (as the margin at the left should be), your papers will look better if you keep a fairly straight right margin. To do so, you may occasionally have to divide words at the end of lines. Whenever it is necessary to divide a word, break it between syllables. The following rules will help you determine in general where the divisions should be made. If you are in doubt about a particular word, consult a dictionary.

1 Both parts of a divided word should be pronounceable; words of one syllable—like *league, breadth, reigned, through, groaned, smudged, you've, they'll*—should not be divided.

2 Words should not be divided so that a single letter stands by itself For example, do not divide a word like *aboard* (which would leave a lone *a* at the end of a line) or *catchy* (which would put a lone *y* at the beginning of a line).

3 As a rule, divide a word after a prefix or before a suffix:

non-porous	depend-able
over-charge	legal-ize
re-phrase	thought-ful

4 As a rule, divide between double consonants:

cor-rect	rac-coon
quit-ter	sum-mer
hop-ping	siz-zling

But if the double consonants come at the end of the root word, they are not split; the division is made after the double consonants, before such endings as *-ing*, *-er*, and *-able*:

fall-ing	refill-able
putt-er	buzz-er

5 Two consonants that come between two vowels may be divided if the consonants are pronounced separately:

tar-get	res-cued
sul-fur	dig-nity

6 Two vowels may be divided if they are pronounced separately:

li-onize	cre-ative
ole-ander	mani-ac
ge-ology	circu-itous

7 If two consonants or two vowels are pronounced as one sound, do not divide them:

fash-ion	bea-ver
hock-ey	crou-ton
periph-ery	nau-tical

8 As a rule, divide between parts of a compound word:

journey-man	motor-cycle
down-trodden	pillow-case
fault-finder	law-breaker

If the compound word itself is actually spelled with a hyphen, divide at the hyphen to avoid the awkwardness of two hyphens in one word:

feeble-minded   jet-propelled
helter-skelter   shilly-shally

9 If a single consonant comes between two sounded vowels, the consonant generally is put at the beginning of a syllable with the second of the vowels:

se-dan   To-le-do
no-ve-na   de-fer

But if the preceding vowel is *short* and *accented*, the consonant is kept with that vowel:

sed'-entary   tol'-erance
nov'-el   def'-erent

10 Try to avoid dividing words in a way that will at first glance cause readers to be confused about the meaning or pronunciation:

Not: hide-ous   But: hid-eous
      Gene-va   Ge-neva
      miser-able   mis-erable

do   **1** Besides its use as a predicate verb meaning "perform; make; accomplish; bring about; etc.," *do* has five uses (as a helping verb) where it has no definite meaning of its own:

a) For emphasis, especially in answer to a question or in a statement contradicting a preceding statement:

Yes, we *do* have season tickets.
But Perry *did* leave early; I left with him.

b) In asking questions:

Does he really think he's going to win?
Did she marry that fellow she met at the zoo?

c) With negative verbs:

Don't just stand there; get a brush.
He didn't say *yes*, and he didn't say *no*.

d) As a substitute for a verb that has just been used, to avoid repetition:

His wife knows more about the business than he does.
Tina dared him to jump off, so he did.

e) In inverted sentences, after such adverbs as *rarely*, *little*, *hardly*:

Only rarely did he get a chance to play.
Little did we suspect what Dave was planning.

2 *Do* has many meanings and is part of many idiomatic phrases: you may *do* your hair or *do* the dishes; your sister may *do up* the week's wash or *do up* a package; you may have a generous neighbor who *does well* by his relatives; after one has *done time* for *doing a partner out of* large sums of money, he could *do without* the suspicious glances he gets and could *do with* a bit of kindness.

doff, don   Rather formal words for *take off* and *put on*, which most people prefer because *doff* and *don* sound affected or old-fashioned in everyday speech and writing. (See **Big words.**)

don't, doesn't   These contractions are universally used in informal writing, especially in sentences where *do not* or *does not* would seem too emphatic or where the rhythm seems smoother with the contraction.

In nonstandard English *don't* is used with a third-person singular subject ("He don't like coffee"; "It don't cost much"). Educated speakers and writers avoid this usage, using *doesn't* with a third-person singular subject and *don't* only with a plural:

He doesn't like coffee.   They don't like tea.
It doesn't cost much.   They don't earn much.
His money doesn't impress her.   Her parents don't approve of him.

Double comparison   See **Comparison of adjectives and adverbs,** section 1.

Double negative   In formal and in informal English two negative words are not used together to express one negative meaning. In nonstandard English this "double negative" construction is often used, especially when the negative meaning is to be emphasized:

NONSTANDARD: I didn't tell him nothing.
STANDARD: I didn't tell him anything.
STANDARD: I told him nothing.

NONSTANDARD: We won't never win with him on the team.
STANDARD: We won't ever win with him on the team.
STANDARD: We will never win with him on the team.

The objection to the double negative is not, as many people like to explain, that "two negatives make an affirmative." No one (unless he is being stubbornly contrary) ever mistakes the intended meaning of "He won't never pay you back"—the double negative makes it only too clear. The real objection is that double negatives are just not used by educated people, except in a joking mood. Centuries ago double negatives were common in all levels of English; you have probably seen examples in Chaucer and in Shakespeare. But they are out of fashion now in the standard language.

Obvious double negatives like those in the examples above are easy to spot. Somewhat more tricky are those made with the adverbs *hardly*, *scarcely*, and *barely*, which have a negative meaning and should therefore not be combined with other negative words:

NONSTANDARD: The box was so heavy that Fred couldn't hardly lift it.
STANDARD: The box was so heavy that Fred could hardly lift it.

NONSTANDARD: There wasn't hardly nobody at the game.
STANDARD: There was hardly anybody at the game.

Double prepositions   In colloquial usage double prepositions like *off of* (for *off*), *inside of* (for *inside*), *outside of* (for *outside*) are common. In informal writing all of these but *off of* are acceptable, though the *of* is unnecessary and could neatly be dropped, since it adds nothing to the meaning. In formal English these double prepositions are avoided.

Doubling final consonants   See **Spelling**, section 1a.

doubt   In negative statements (where there is no real doubt) *doubt that* is used in formal English, *doubt but that* in informal writing, and *doubt but what* or *doubt but* in informal speech:

FORMAL: I do not doubt that he knows his subject.
INFORMAL WRITING: I don't doubt but that he knows his subject.
INFORMAL SPEECH: I don't doubt but what he knows his subject.

In positive statements (where doubt really exists) *doubt whether* is used in formal English and *doubt if* in informal English:

FORMAL: I doubt whether he can help us.
INFORMAL: I doubt if he can help us.

When unbelief rather than doubt is intended, *doubt that* is used:

I doubt that he can help us.

draft, draught   The two are pronounced the same: /draft/ or /dräft/. Since the simpler spelling clearly indicates the pronunciation, it is more common than the spelling *draught*. *Draft* is always the spelling for a *bank draft*, the *military draft*, a *football draft*, a *draft of a composition*, the *draft of a fireplace*, a *draft of air*. *Draught* is more common for a *draught of fish*, a *draught of ale*, *beer on draught*, a *ship's draught*—though there is a growing tendency to use the simpler form for these.

Usage is divided on the word meaning "a person who makes plans or sketches"; either *draftsman* or *draughtsman* is used. The first is more common.

drought, drouth   Both forms are in good use; *drought* /drout/ is perhaps more common in formal English and *drouth* /drouth/ in informal.

drowned   In standard English, pronounced as one syllable /dround/ — not two /droun'did/.

drunk   Since one meaning of *drunk* is "intoxicated," some people shy away from using it as the past participle of *drink*, saying "Sam had drank all the lemonade" to avoid saying *drunk*. But *drunk* is the form to use: "Sam had drunk all the lemonade."

The past-tense form is *drank*: "Sam drank all the lemonade."

due to   Originally *due* was used only as an adjective, and in formal English it is still restricted to this use:

The delay was due to a three-day strike at the Chicago plant.   [*Due* modifies *delay*; *due to* means "caused by" or "attributable to."]

In informal English *due to* is commonly used as a preposition meaning "because of":

Due to the star's jealousy, Lori's scene was cut from the movie.
Dad missed his plane due to the flat tire.

Since in spite of its commonness there is some prejudice against using *due to* as a preposition, it would be wise to avoid this use when writing for readers who you know are rather formal in language. You can easily substitute *because of* or *owing to*:

Dad missed his plane because of the flat tire.

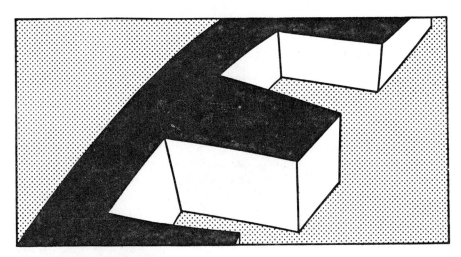

each   **1** *Each*, used as an adjective or pronoun, is singular; it takes a singular verb and is referred to by singular pronouns:

Each candidate *is* to submit a report of *his* expenses.
Each of the candidates *has submitted* a report of *his* expenses.

Each of the waitresses kept *her* thoughts to *herself.*
Each of the waiters kept *his* thoughts to *himself.*

In colloquial usage, the pronoun *each* is sometimes regarded as a plural and is referred to by a plural pronoun:

If *each* of the men had done *their* best, we would have won.

But in formal writing, either singular or plural forms should be used together:

If *each* of the men had done *his* best, we would have won.
If *all* of the men had done *their* best, we would have won.

2 *Each* is sometimes used as a pronoun in apposition with a plural subject:

Tom, Dick, and Harry *each* expect a share.
They *each* are to pay for their own board and room.

Notice that in these sentences the pronoun *each* does not affect the number of the verb. Since the subjects are plural, the verbs (and the pronoun referring to the subject of the second sentence) are plural. (See also **Agreement,** section 2b.)

each other, one another   In formal English a distinction is often made between these pronouns: *each other* is used in reference to two; *one another,* to more than two:

Our boxer and their dachshund eyed each other warily.
Unfortunately, the three women on the staff distrusted one another.

Informal English does not make this distinction, using *each other* and *one another* interchangeably, to refer either to two or to more than two:

Our boxer and their dachshund eyed one another warily.
Unfortunately, the three women on the staff distrusted each other.

economic, economical   *Economic* is generally used to mean "having to do with business or economics — the production, distribution, and consumption of wealth"; *economical,* to mean "avoiding waste; thrifty":

The company's decision to move its plant to another state proved to be an economic disaster for our town.
Uncle Alfred, who had been brought up in an economical household, was stunned by Aunt Flossie's wild extravagance.

Editorial   An article in a newpaper or magazine written by the editor or under his direction, stating opinions and attitudes (of the editor, the publisher, or the owner) on a subject of current interest. Editorials are generally printed on a special page, called the "editorial page," to set them apart from other material. The problems or events discussed in newspaper editorials are usually covered in news stories in the same issue. The news stories are supposed to give just the facts, which the editorials interpret according to the political or social theories that the paper represents. Although most editorials are intended to influence opinion, they are sometimes written to inform or merely to entertain.

Editorial we   See **we**, section 2.

effect, affect   See **affect, effect.**

e.g.   Abbreviation of Latin *exempli gratia*, which means "for the sake of example." Usually not italicized, *e.g.* is a formal abbreviation appropriate in documents, legal statements, and academic writing:

Some of these transitional adverbs, e.g., *however* and *nevertheless*, are relatively heavy connectives and are thus likely to seem stilted in informal narratives.

In informal writing, the expressions *for example* and *for instance* are more appropriate than *e.g.*

ei, ie   For the spelling of words with *ei* and *ie*, see **Spelling**, section 1f.

either, neither   **1** The usual meaning of *either* is "one or the other of two":

ADJECTIVE: We had many relatives in Rome and in Florence, but I had never visited *either* city.
PRONOUN: Polly could not find *either* of the twins.

With reference to more than two, *any* or *any one* is generally preferable:

Each person who opened a savings account could choose a desk set, a key case, or a silver vase as a gift. I didn't like *any one* of them.   [Not: *either* of them.]

The same distinction applies to the negative *neither*. *None* is used for more than two:

Mr. Lerner suggested Ralph or Gordon for the lead, but *neither* is tall enough.
Tom or Keith or Maury would be tall enough, but *none* of them can act. [Not: *neither* of them.]

2 *Either* and *neither* are usually regarded as singular, although informal English sometimes uses plural verbs with them, especially in questions:

Is either of you strong enough to lift a sledge hammer? [Informal: *Are* either of you strong enough?]
Neither *was* willing to try.

3 *Either* meaning "each" is considered formal English and is seldom used now:

RARE: Tanya always wore a heavy gold bracelet on either arm.
USUAL: Tanya always wore a heavy gold bracelet on each arm.

4 In all but a few sections of the United States, the pronunciations /ē′ᴛʜər/ and /nē′ᴛʜər/ are generally heard; /ī′ᴛʜər/ and /nī′ᴛʜər/ are regarded as affectations except in some New England communities or among families or groups in which they are naturally used.

either . . . or, neither . . . nor   Used as correlative conjunctions (linking words that work in pairs):

The hamburgers at Kelly's are either underdone or overdone.
Neither Frank nor Paul ever admitted being there.

(See **Correlative conjunctions.**)

Ellipsis   A punctuation mark of three spaced dots (. . .) used to show an omission in writing or printing. (Plural: *ellipses*.)
   1 An ellipsis is used chiefly to show where one or more words not essential to the meaning have been omitted from a quoted sentence:

Children want . . . to make sense of the world, of themselves, of others.

When an ellipsis comes at the end of a quoted sentence, a fourth mark is needed for the period:

Often, words are used to gain attention and status. . . . Time and again, the desire to appear intellectual leads a person to use words like *multitudinous* and *pourboire* instead of plain *many* and *tip.*

   2 An ellipsis is sometimes used in narrative writing to show that a statement is left unfinished:

The mothballs looked like candy and Billy was hungry, so . . .

(See also **Dash,** section 6.)

Elliptical clauses   Clauses in which a word or words necessary for grammatical completeness but not for meaning are not used. The meaning of elliptical clauses is clear from words borrowed from the rest of the sentence or from the context:

Well, I do think I'm as smart *as he* [is].
We worried about Eddie more *than* [we worried about] *them.*
We worried about Eddie more *than they* [worried about him].
When in Rome, do as the Romans do.   [The meaning is obviously "When you are in Rome."]

(See also **Dangling modifiers.**)

else　**1** Since *else* follows the word it modifies, the sign of the possessive is added to *else* rather than to the modified word:

Is anyone else's car parked in the alley?　[Not: anyone's else.]
By mistake I was given someone else's pay check.

　2 In everyday speech, *else* is sometimes used for emphasis in sentences where it actually adds nothing to the meaning. This use is not appropriate in writing. You can check the use of *else* in this way: if it is followed by *but*, *except*, or *besides* and an object, *else* is deadwood and should be omitted:

There was nobody but Laura in the kitchen.　[Not: nobody *else* but Laura.]
Do you know of anyone besides Hank who has a typewriter?　[Not: anyone *else* besides Hank.]
But:　Hank is out of town; do you know *anyone else* who has a typewriter?

eminent, imminent　These words are sometimes confused, probably because of the similarity of their pronunciations. But their meanings are quite different. *Eminent* means "distinguished; outstanding; noteworthy":

In drawing up the new revenue act, the legislators sought the advice of several leading jurists, including Judge Harold B. Watkins, an eminent authority on constitutional law.

Imminent means "likely to happen without delay; threatening to occur soon":

At ten o'clock the commanding officer of the garrison received a report that a rebel attack was imminent.

employee, employe　Both spellings are standard. *Employee* is more common.

empty out　*Out* is not necessary since it adds nothing to the meaning:

My first job was to empty [out] the flour bin and wash it.

Endings (of words)　Two kinds of endings are added to words in English:
　1 A **derivational** ending is a syllable like *-ize*, *-ment*, *-ly*, and so on, that is added to a word or a word part to form a new word, generally of a different class. For example, adding the ending *-ize* to the noun *idol* results in the verb *idolize*; adding *-ment* to the verb *improve* makes the noun *improvement*; and adding *-ly* to the adjective *smooth* produces the adverb *smoothly*. (See also **Suffix**.)
　2 An **inflectional** ending is a letter or syllable added to a word to indicate number (dog—dogs), gender (alumnus—alumna), possessive case (girl—girl's—girls'), tense (rock—rocked), or degree (tall—taller—tallest).

End-stop A mark of punctuation—usually a period, a question mark, or an exclamation mark—used at the end of a sentence. (See **Period, Question mark, Exclamation mark, Ellipsis,** and **Dash,** section 6.)

ensure, insure *Ensure* is preferred when the meaning is "make sure or certain": "The letter Mr. Potter wrote *ensured* Bert's getting the job." *Insure* is used to mean "arrange for money payment in case of loss, accident, or death." Remember *insure* in connection with *insurance*: "They were advised to *insure* their luggage against theft."

enthuse A verb formed from the noun *enthusiasm*. Although *enthuse* has gained wide acceptance as the colloquial expression for the more formal *be enthusiastic about* or *be enthusiastic over*, many people object to it and would avoid it in writing.

COLLOQUIAL: Aunt Martha enthused over the new styles.
WRITTEN: Aunt Martha was enthusiastic about the new styles.

Epigram A short, pointed, often witty statement of fact or opinion, either in verse or prose. Such statements are useful for focusing attention on a particular idea, making it easy to remember and to quote:

Nothing so needs reforming as other people's habits. — Mark Twain.
Be nice to people on your way up because you'll meet 'em on your way down. — Wilson Mizner.

Aphorisms are similar to epigrams, but are more likely to be abstract and not necessarily witty:

Injustice anywhere is a threat to justice everywhere. — Martin Luther King, Jr.

Proverbs are short, wise sayings, generally about character or conduct, that have been used for a long time by many people. Most proverbs have no known author. The terms *adage* and *maxim* are also used.

He that riseth late must trot all day.
Wealth is not his who has it, but his who enjoys it.
He who swells in prosperity will shrink in adversity.

A special type of epigram is the *paradox*, which presents an idea in seemingly contradictory terms:

To be not as eloquent would be more eloquent. — Christoph Wieland

epithet An adjective or noun used to express a descriptive detail about a person or thing: William *the Conqueror*, Ethelred *the Unready*, Elaine *the Fair*, America *the Beautiful*.

In recent years the word *epithet* has acquired for many people an unfavorable connotation as a result of its being used so often to refer to a word or phrase expressing abuse, contempt, or hostility: *dirty liar, fink, goon, double-crosser*. Notice the contrast between these epithets and the historical and literary ones above.

err   Generally pronounced /ėr/, as in *her;* but the pronunciation /er/ is becoming more common, probably because of the similarity between *err* and *error* /er'ər/.

Esq. (Esquire)   A formal title of respect written after a man's name in the inside and outside addresses of a letter. *Esq.* is frequently used in England, where it signifies a definite social position. Its use in the United States — chiefly with names of professional men — has become rare, though it is still used occasionally, particularly with lawyers' names.

Preceding titles (Mr., Dr., Hon.) are not used when *Esq.* follows a name: Ronald A. Baumann, Esq.

et al.   An abbreviation of the Latin *et alii*, meaning "and others." It may be used in a footnote to indicate that a book has several authors, only the first of whom is named: Stephen Ellis et al. But the English *and others* is becoming more common: Stephen Ellis and others.

etc.   **1** *Etc.*, the abbreviation for the Latin *et cetera* (literally "and others"), is usually read *and so forth* or *et cetera* /et set'ər ə/. It is appropriate in reference and business usage:

Included in the woodwind group are the bassoons, clarinets, flutes, etc.
The *conifers* — pines, firs, spruces, larches, etc. — are cone-bearing trees.

As you can see from the examples given, only one period is necessary when *etc.* comes at the end of a sentence, but other punctuation marks are used after *etc.* according to the needs of the sentence. When *etc.* comes inside a sentence, it is set off by commas:

Pine, spruce, hemlock, etc., are softwoods.

2 *Etc.* is out of place in both formal and informal writing, which avoid abbreviations in general. If you want to write out the term, the English *and so forth* is less conspicuous — and better — than *et cetera*. But the best advice is to avoid all such terms. An *and so forth* weakens your writing by giving the impression that either you are too lazy to complete a list or you are bluffing — indicating that you know more than you actually do. One solution is to rephrase the sentence, using *such as* or some other expression to show that the list is not intended to be complete:

WEAK: To qualify as a detective-novel buff, you have to know the classic writers — Dorothy Sayers, Dashiell Hammett, etc.
BETTER: To qualify as a detective-novel buff, you have to know such classic writers as Dorothy Sayers, Ngaio Marsh, Dashiell Hammett, Raymond Chandler, and Rex Stout.

And etc. should never be used, since the *et* of *et cetera* means "and." Remember *et* also to fix the correct spelling of the abbreviation in your mind: *etc.* — not *ect.*

Etymology   The branch of linguistics that deals with the origin and historical development of words. The term *etymology* is also used in referring to the brief history, or derivation, of a word given in brackets in a dictionary entry. (See **Word formation.**)

Euphemism   A mild, indirect word or phrase used instead of one that is more direct or harsh or that may have unpleasant connotations for some people: *memorial park* for *cemetery, passed on* for *died, people in the low-income bracket* for *the poor, guest house* for *boarding house, dentures* for *false teeth*, and so on.

ever   In colloquial usage, *ever* is sometimes added after the interrogatives — *who, where, what, why, how, when* — for emphasis: "Who ever would have suspected him?" "Where ever did she park the car this time?" "What ever gave you that idea?" "How ever can they afford such a trip?"

In writing you will sometimes see the two words joined (*whoever, wherever, whatever* . . .).

every and its compounds   1 The adjective *every* and the pronouns *everybody* and *everyone* are grammatically singular; they take singular verbs and are usually referred to by singular pronouns:

Every man on the team *has* to pay *his* own expenses.
Why *does* everybody *park his* car in front of our house?
Everyone *has* a right to express *her* own opinion.

In colloquial usage, plural pronouns are sometimes used to refer to *everybody* and *everyone*, especially when they are thought of as plural in meaning:

Everybody in our neighborhood insisted on having *their* say.
Everyone on the staff had done a poor job, but *they* wouldn't admit it.   [Not: *he* wouldn't admit it. A plural meaning is clearly intended.]

In formal usage, singular pronouns would be used or — if the meaning is clearly plural — the sentence would be rephrased:

Everybody in our neighborhood insists on having *his* say.
All the staff members had done a poor job, but *they* wouldn't admit it.
Everyone on the staff had done a poor job, but *nobody* would admit it.

(For further examples, see **Agreement,** section 2b.)

2 *Everybody, everything,* and *everywhere* are written as one word. *Everyone* may be written as one word or two, depending on the meaning intended. The pronunciation can help you decide which form to use. If

105

every is stressed, use the one-word form. If *one* receives an equal amount of emphasis or more, use two words:

Everyone misspells a word now and then.
Every one of us had misspelled at least three words.

When used as an adjective, *everyday* is one word; when *day* is a noun modified by *every*, two words are used:

These raucous arguments were an everyday occurrence.
Every day he grew more obstinate.

3 Informal usage sometimes substitutes *everyplace* for *everywhere*. There are several other useful informal idioms formed with *every* but, like *everyplace*, they should be avoided in formal speech and writing:

INFORMAL: There was a thick coat of dust everyplace.
FORMAL: There was a thick coat of dust everywhere.

INFORMAL: The leaves he had just raked were blowing every which way.
FORMAL: The leaves he had just raked were blowing in every direction.

INFORMAL: Every so often his grandson would visit him.
FORMAL: Occasionally his grandson would visit him.

ex-   A hyphen is used when *ex-*, meaning "former; formerly," is prefixed to words indicating position, rank, occupation, status, profession:

ex-king   ex-mayor   ex-prodigy   ex-child actor

Exaggeration   See **Hyperbole.**

except, accept   See **accept, except.**

Exclamation mark (!)   A mark used after a word, phrase, or sentence that the writer intends to be very emphatic. Such a word, phrase, or sentence is called an *exclamation*:

Hey!   Help!   Get me out of here!
Bosh! He's nothing but a phony!   What an outrageous price!

Exclamation marks are used more frequently in narrative writing than in other types. They should always be used thoughtfully and sparingly (and only one at a time!) because too many exclamation points weaken the emphasis they are intended to provide:

OVERDONE: There was that clicking noise again! It wasn't the wind! It couldn't be the wind! Someone must have broken in!! Those muffled sounds coming closer were footsteps!!!
BETTER: There was that clicking noise again. It wasn't the wind. It couldn't be the wind. Someone must have broken in. Those muffled sounds coming closer were footsteps!

excuse, pardon   Minor faults are *excused*; more serious faults and crimes are *pardoned*:

Excuse me; I didn't mean to block your view.
Such treachery cannot be pardoned.

But in some circles "Pardon me" is considered more elegant than "Excuse me" and would be used in a sentence like the first.
   Excuse is also used to mean "ask or give permission to leave":

Excuse me please; I have to see if the baby is all right.

"I beg your pardon" is often used to mean "I didn't hear what you said."

Expletives   *It* and *there* are called *expletives* when they begin sentences in which the real subject follows the verb:

It is useless *to complain to Mr. Plunkett.*
It seems to me unbelievable *that anyone really likes caviar.*
There was a battered old *Ford* parked in the alley.

Since the only function of *it* and *there* in sentences like these is to point ahead to (or "anticipate") the subjects, they are sometimes called "anticipatory subjects."

Expository writing   See **Story.**

extracurricular   Written as one word, without a hyphen. *Extracurricular* means "outside the regular course of study":

A student with a job has little time for extracurricular activities.

fact (the fact that)   Often used as a roundabout expression for *that*, which would express the same meaning more concisely:

Ted seemed completely unaware [of the fact] that Bob was angry.

fall, falls   Both *fall* and *falls* are used in referring to a waterfall. Although plural in form, *falls* takes a singular verb when preceded by the noun marker *a*, and usually when a particular falls is named:

There is a falls in the photograph that won first prize.
Minnehaha Falls dries up at this time of year.

When preceded by *the*, *falls* usually takes a plural verb:

Actually, the falls are not as lovely as the guidebook reports.

Fallacies in reasoning   As a writer or speaker who wants others to accept his point of view on some matter, you have the obligation to provide well-reasoned, convincing evidence to support your conclusions. And as a reader or listener who is a straight thinker, you want to make very sure, before accepting any conclusion as valid, that it is based on sound evidence and reasoning. Here are examples of four common **fallacies** — errors in thinking — to watch for, not only in the reasoning of others but also in your own:

   1 Begging the question. A speaker or writer who offers as evidence an assumption that needs to be proved is *begging the question*. For example, consider this statement made at an employee meeting: "Anyone who truly believes in the principles of democracy will surely vote against continuing the undemocratic system of giving merit raises to only a select few."

   In this statement the speaker offers no evidence to prove that the merit-raise system is "undemocratic." Even though it is just an assumption, he evidently expects his listeners to accept it as true. But his merely saying that the system is undemocratic (whatever he means by that) does not make it so. No clear-thinking listener, no matter how devoted he is to democratic principles, would vote against a merit-raise system on the basis of an unproved contention that the system is undemocratic.

   2 Post hoc. The error of thinking that Happening A must be the cause of Happening B merely because Happening A came first is called the *post hoc* fallacy. (The name comes from the Latin phrase *post hoc, ergo propter hoc*, which means "after this, therefore because of it.") Notice the post-hoc thinking in this argument: "Unfortunately too many people, blinded by partisan loyalties, refuse to admit how disastrous the policies of the Demopublicans are. Yet history itself makes this only too clear. Every time a Demopublican administration has taken over, this state has suffered a severe recession."

   The mere fact that the Demopublicans came into office *before* the recessions does not, by itself, justify the conclusion that Demopublican policies were the *cause* of the recessions. A severe recession is unlikely to have a single cause. Demopublican policies might have been one cause of the recessions. But if so, the speaker has not proved it.

   3 Ignoring the question. Consider this argument: "I think the judges made a bad mistake; I think Roy Fernandez should have won the state piano competition, and I can prove it. Roy is the best pianist in town; he has won every local piano competition for the last three years. I know for a fact that he practiced a minimum of eight hours a day before the contest. Besides, it's high time someone from our school won; almost every year the winner has come from Tansley Conservatory. Anyone who can afford to go to Tansley doesn't need a scholarship, while someone like Roy—without a father to help him through school—needs it badly."

Notice that not one of the speaker's statements, true though they may be, has anything to do with proving the question at issue: whether or not Roy Fernandez should have won the state piano competition. Not one of the statements tells anything about how the contest was judged, for example, or how Roy played. All the statements are beside the point. Or, to put it another way, the speaker has *ignored the question*.

4 Argumentum ad hominem. Here is an example of *argumentum ad hominem* ("an argument directed to the man"): In a TV news interview Mr. Zee, an automobile company executive, is asked to reply to a magazine article in which the author, a Dr. Redan, charges that automobiles are being made of shoddy materials. Mr. Zee makes a brief statement: "Redan's claims are ridiculous. What does a surgeon know about manufacturing cars? He should stay in his operating room."

Notice that instead of sticking to the point (the quality of materials used in making automobiles), Zee launches into an attack on Dr. Redan. Since it is likely that the average surgeon does not know much about car manufacturing (though this may not be true of Dr. Redan), an unwary listener might accept Zee's statement as a valid reply. But it is not. By shifting the attack to Dr. Redan, Zee is sidestepping the real question, the one he should be answering: Are cars being made of shoddy materials?

(See also **Generalizations** and **Inductive and deductive reasoning**.)

Familiar English   Familiar English is a casual sort of English, the kind of language you use in talking to members of the family or intimate friends, and in writing friendly letters, personal notes, diaries, or journals. Familiar English is not necessarily slovenly or slipshod; it is simply more free and easy than the English used in situations requiring greater formality. Since familiar English is based on everyday speech, it shows all the traits common to informal conversation: contractions, abbreviations, clipped words, nicknames, shortened constructions, localisms, shoptalk, and slang. The use of some or all of these is entirely appropriate in any writing intended only for the eyes of close friends. In fact, avoiding these traits will generally result in writing that lacks the warmth and intimacy your friends have a right to expect from you.

famous   *Famous* should not be used to label people who are obviously well known to everyone:

The Agony and the Ecstasy is a novel about [the famous] Michelangelo.

But if you were writing about someone whose fame was limited to a certain period of time or to a certain field that your readers might not be familiar with, *famous* would be appropriate:

Clarence Darrow, a nationally famous jurist, was the lawyer for the defense.
The award is named for a famous English actress of the eighteenth century, Sarah Siddons.

(See also **notorious, famous.**)

farther, further   In formal English some people distinguish between these words, using *farther* to refer to physical distance and *further* to refer to abstract relationships of degree or quantity:

By that time we were too tired to hike any farther.
She would like to go further into his family background.
He promised to investigate the matter further.

In informal English the distinction is not kept and there seems to be a definite tendency for *further* to be used in all these senses. (See also **all the farther.**)

Faulty comparisons   When making comparisons, writers sometimes fail to express their intended meaning accurately. Comparisons should be phrased so that the reader can see at first glance what two things are being compared:

FAULTY: The repairs on the Impala cost more than the Cadillac. [Repairs are being compared with a car.]
IMPROVED: The repairs on the Impala cost more than those on the Cadillac.

FAULTY: The *Tribune*'s gourmet recipes are not as reliable as Julia Child. [Recipes are being compared with a person.]
IMPROVED: The *Tribune*'s gourmet recipes are not as reliable as Julia Child's. [Or: . . . as those of Julia Child.]

In making comparisons between persons or things of the same class, be sure to use phrases like "than any other," "than anyone else," or "than the other" with adjectives or adverbs in the comparative degree:

FAULTY: We agreed that Mike Royko writes more entertainingly than any newspaper columnist.
IMPROVED: We agreed that Mike Royko writes more entertainingly than any *other* newspaper columnist.

FAULTY: She has probably appeared in more hits than anyone in the theater.
IMPROVED: She has probably appeared in more hits than anyone *else* in the theater.

Phrases with "any" and "other" should not be used after adjectives and adverbs in the superlative degree:

FAULTY: Bixby was the least knowledgeable of any other member on the panel.
IMPROVED: Bixby was the least knowledgeable member on the panel. [Or: the least knowledgeable *of the members*; the least knowledgeable *of all the panelists*.]

(See also **Comparison of adjectives and adverbs** and **other**.)

faze   An informal verb meaning "disturb; bother; disconcert." *Faze* is usually used negatively:

Their heckling did not faze the first speaker.
Professor Hale's sarcasm had never fazed me before.

Faze is less commonly spelled *feaze* and *feeze*, both pronounced /fēz/ or /fāz/.
Do not confuse the verb *faze* with the noun *phase*, meaning "aspect" or "stage of development":

His book treats only one phase of linguistics.
Mother explained that Jimmie was going through a show-off phase and we were just to ignore him.

Feature   A *feature* is a special story, article, column, comic strip, or cartoon in a newspaper or magazine. The feature, often prominently displayed, attracts attention because of its subject matter or because of the reputation of the writer.
A *feature story* is an unusual article or story whose appeal lies in some factor other than its news value. It holds attention by dramatizing the human-interest element contained in everyday incidents. Such unimportant but interest-arousing incidents as the birth of a hippopotamus; the finding of her own false teeth by an elderly woman who had lost them in the surf two weeks before; and the display of unusual bravery, courtesy, or discourtesy are the kinds of subjects on which the feature writer of a newspaper thrives.

feel   For the use of *feel* as a linking verb, see **bad, badly**.

fewer, less   See **less, fewer**.

fiancé, fiancée   *Fiancé* refers to the man, *fiancée* (with two *e*'s) to the woman. Both are pronounced the same: /fē'än sā'/ or /fē'än sā/. The plurals are *fiancés* and *fiancées*.

Fiction   Prose writings, particularly novels and short stories, that tell about imaginary people and events.

field (in the field of)   Often used unnecessarily in sentences like these:

The company is looking for an expert in [the field of] finance.
That summer Loren became interested in [the field of] geology.

Figurative and literal use of words   Words can be used in one of two ways, either literally or figuratively. In a literal sense we use them for their ordinary meanings:

The *wall of rough stones* that Grandpa Porter had built was starting to crumble.   [An actual structure.]

Words can also be used figuratively—that is, for meanings that are suggested by their literal meanings:

Dave tried repeatedly, but he could not break through the *wall of suspicion* that had been built up in the past few weeks. [The suspicion (though it existed only in the mind) was so strong and had increased to such a degree that it functioned just as an actual wall would—to cut people off from each other.]

Figures (1, 61, 598 . . .)   See **Numbers** for the use of figures and the choice between figures and words in writing.

Figures of speech   Figures of speech are expressions in which words are used in an unusual sense, out of their literal meaning, or in an unordinary construction—to add beauty, force, or clarity. The most common figures are *simile* (The old mansions along Ninth Street, S.E., [were] like aged dandies in filthy linen.—Sinclair Lewis, *Babbitt*), *metaphor* (The average Ph.D. thesis is nothing but a transference of bones from one graveyard to another.—J. Frank Dobie, *A Texan in England*), and *personification* (I don't understand why . . . some days smile and others have thin slitted eyes and others still are days which worry.—John Steinbeck, *Journal of a Novel*).
    See also the articles on various figures of speech: **Alliteration, Analogy, Apostrophe, Epigram, Hyperbole, Irony, Litotes, Metaphor, Metonymy, Onomatopoeia, Personification, Pun, Simile, Synecdoche.**

fine   In "a fine white thread," "a robe of fine linen," "fine distinctions between the two," "made of fine gold," "covered with fine sand," "a fine-edged sword," the adjective *fine* has a specific, exact meaning and is a useful and effective modifier. But *fine* (like *nice, grand, cute*) is often used as a counter word—a vague modifier that expresses only general approval. As a counter word, it has little value and is usually better omitted:

Leo has turned out to be a [fine,] capable stage manager.

first   See **former, latter; first, last.**

fish   The plural is also *fish*, unless different kinds or species are being discussed:

The men had their picture taken holding the three biggest fish.
Of these unusual fishes, my favorites were the angler and the archer.

fix   In general usage *fix* has several meanings: "fasten tightly" (fix the pole in the ground), "set" (fixed the price at fifteen cents), "direct" (fix your eyes on the center dot), "put definitely" (fixed the blame on Farrell), "repair" (fixing the lawn mower).

In informal English *fix* is used to mean "punish" or "get revenge on" (She'll fix you!) and "an awkward situation" (He's really in a fix). Both *fix* and *fix up* are used informally to mean "put in order" (fixed her hair, fixed up her room). And although *fix* is in general usage to mean "repair," *fix up* used in the same sense is considered informal English.

flaunt, flout   Though these words are frequently confused, careful writers and speakers keep their meanings distinct. *Flaunt* means "to show off; parade; display ostentatiously":

Many of the miners who struck it rich flaunted their newly acquired wealth by building huge, ornate mansions.

Flout means "to treat with contempt; scornfully disregard":

The other players resented the way Nemo flouted every training rule— and got away with it.

folk, folks   The plural of *folk*, meaning "people; persons," is *folk* or *folks*:

He liked the simple mountain folk he met that summer.
"Don't forget that folks will talk," he warned.

In informal usage *folks* is used to mean "parents; relatives":

Her folks did not approve of him at first.

Folk is used as an adjective and in some compounds: *folk dance, folk tale, folk song, folk music, folklore, folkways.*

Footnotes   In papers based on the writings of others, common courtesy demands that you give credit for the ideas and words of theirs which you use in your work. Such acknowledgments, usually made in *footnotes*, tell your reader where you got your facts, so that he can judge for himself the sources your material is based on and can turn directly to them for further information. Footnotes are used in scholarly articles and books. You will need to know how to use them in research papers:

1 Footnotes are used:

a) To give credit for other people's ideas even though you write them in your own words

b) To give the source of a direct quotation

c) To give the source of diagrams, tables, statistics, and figures

d) To give additional information that may be of interest to the reader but is not important enough to be given in the text

2 In a research paper, number the footnotes consecutively (1, 2, 3) throughout the paper. Place the number slightly above the line at the end of the sentence to be footnoted. Type or write the footnotes at the bottom of each page, below a short line to separate text from notes. Be sure to allow room enough for footnotes at the bottom of each page.

The first time that reference is made to a book, give the author's name, the title of the book (underlined to represent italics), and the page or pages:

---

[1]S. I. Hayakawa, Language in Thought and Action, pp. 203–205.

[2]Neil Postman and Charles Weingartner, Linguistics, p. 129.

To refer to a magazine article, give the author's name, the title of the article (in quotation marks), the name of the magazine (underlined to represent italics), the date of issue, and the page or pages:

[3]Norman Cousins, "Are You Making Yourself Clear?" Saturday Review, February 22, 1969, p. 31.

If the author's name is not given, use this form:

[4]"Warning . . . Danger . . . Loaded Words Ahead!" Senior Scholastic, March 11, 1966, p. 6.

If the reference is to an article in an encyclopedia, give the author's name, the title of the article, the name of the encyclopedia (underlined), volume, and page:

[5]Anatol Rapoport, "Semantics," Grolier Universal Encyclopedia, vol. 9, pp. 195–196.

If the author's name is not given, use this form:

[6]"Logic," Compton's Pictured Encyclopedia, vol. 13, p. 334.

For a reference to a newspaper article, use one of these forms, depending on whether the author's name is given or not:

[7]Hilton Kramer, "A Modish Revision of History," New York Times, October 19, 1969, sec. II, pp. 29 and 30.

[8]"Prose and Cons: Succinct Looks at New Books," National Observer, October 13, 1969, p. 23.

If you have a number of references to the same source, use a shortened form for the footnotes after the first. To refer to a source mentioned in the immediately preceding footnote, use *Ibid.* (an abbreviation of the Latin *ibidem*, meaning "in the same place"). If the page number is different from the one given above, place a comma after *Ibid.* and write the new page number:

[9]Leonard F. Dean and Kenneth G. Wilson, eds., Essays on Language and Usage, p. 61.
[10]Ibid.
[11]Ibid., p. 72.

When you refer to a work quoted earlier but not in the immediately preceding footnote, you may write the author's last name alone if no more than one source by this author is used:

[12]Hayakawa, p. 239.

If there is more than one source by the same author, write his last name and one or two key words from the title:

[13]Hayakawa, Language, p. 251.

In print, each footnote is generally indented like a paragraph, but there is no objection to beginning each one flush with the left margin.

for   A comma is usually needed between two coordinate clauses joined by the conjunction *for*, to prevent misreading *for* as a preposition:

He didn't mind working until six, for Mr. Preston had done him many favors.   [To prevent: He didn't mind working until six for Mr. Preston.]

(For the distinction between *for* and *because*, see **because.**)

Foreign words in English   See **Borrowed words** and **Anglicizing.**

for example   The abbreviation used for *for example* is *e.g.* (from the Latin *exempli gratia*, meaning "for the sake of example"). *E.g.*, which rarely appears in informal writing, is particularly appropriate in scholarly papers, definitions, scientific writing, and legal documents. (For punctuation, see **namely and other introductory words.**)

Formal English   Formal English is the English used by educated people on formal occasions. For discussion and examples, see **Levels of English usage,** section 1.

formally, formerly   Although these words are similar in spelling and pronunciation, they are quite different in meaning. *Formally* indicates the manner in which something is done — "in a formal way":

The new library will be formally opened at a special dedication ceremony next Sunday.

Formerly indicates time; it means "in the past; some time ago":

The present dean was formerly a physics teacher at Dooley High.

Form classes   Through the years, various ways have been devised for classifying, or grouping, the words in the English language. One method, introduced by structural grammarians, is to divide the words in the language into two main groups: form-class words (words that primarily carry meaning) and function, or structure, words (words that primarily show relationships). (See **Function words.**)

The majority of English words fall into one of the four form classes, generally called nouns, verbs, adjectives, and adverbs. The classification is based on the forms of the words and their typical position in basic sentence patterns. For example, a word is classified as a noun if it meets one or more of these criteria: (1) if it has a typical noun ending like -*dom*, -*ism*, -*ment*, -*ness*; (2) if it has a singular, a plural, a singular possessive, and a plural possessive form (girl — girls — girl's — girls'); (3) if it is usually preceded by a noun marker like *a, an, the, some, her*; (4) if it will fit in one of the blanks in these sentence patterns: The _____ is good. He saw (the) _____.

Form classes are sometimes referred to as "open" classes, because new words are continually being added to them.

(See also **Words: classes of.**)

former, latter; first, last   *Former* and *latter* refer to two units only:

At eight o'clock a KTIZ reporter will interview Mrs. May Clare and Mr. Hugh Gordon. The former is a spokesman for the union; the latter, the president of the school board.

First and *last* are used with three or more in a series:

Destiny Waits, Three Cousins, and *The Poor Poor* would all make interesting movies, though the first might seem too romantic to today's audiences and the last too starkly realistic.   [Not: though the former . . . and the latter. . . .]

When used with a number, *first* precedes the number:

The first three suspects had unassailable alibis.

Though *first* and *firstly* are both used as adverbs meaning "in the first place," *first* is generally preferred. Say *first, second, third, last*:

First, the bus service is so poor that it might as well be discontinued entirely. Second, the available parking space is hardly enough for the people who work in the downtown stores. Third. . . .

(See **last, latest.**)

Fractions   Fractions are written in figures when they are attached to other figures (23¾), when they are in a series that is being written in figures (6, ¼, 17, ½, 21, 11), and when they are in tables or reference material. Usually in ordinary writing they are written in words.

Fractions used as adjectives or adverbs are hyphened:

A motion to close debate needs a two-thirds majority.
The gas tank was only one-fourth full when we started.

Usage is divided in writing fractions used as nouns:

At least one half (*or* one-half) of the merchandise was damaged.
We sold three fourths (*or* three-fourths) of the books on the first day.

But if the fraction contains a compound number from twenty-one to ninety-nine, the compound number is always hyphened:

Yes, but five twenty-fifths is less than one fourth!

Decimals are increasingly used in place of fractions in expository writing. They are always written in figures:

.333   .8   .75   3.14159

(See **Numbers.**)

Fragmentary sentences   See **Sentence fragment.**

freshman, freshmen   Because they are pronounced alike—/fresh'mən/— these words are sometimes misspelled. (It is *a freshman, several freshmen*.) The adjective is *freshman* (freshman Latin, freshman electives). *Freshmen,* the plural form, should not be used to modify a noun.

You need not capitalize *freshman* (or *sophomore, junior, senior*) unless courtesy or emphasis makes a capital appropriate, as when you refer to the Freshman Class (or the Sophomore Chorus, the Junior Boosters) as a definite organization.

Friendly letters   See **Letters,** sections 5 and 6.

full, -ful   The adjective has two *l*'s: a *full* day, a *full* moon. The suffix has only one *l*: *helpful, tearful, wonderful.*

The standard plural of nouns ending in *-ful* is made by adding *-s*: *cupfuls, bucketfuls, handfuls, shovelfuls, teaspoonfuls.* Colloquially *cupsful, bucketsful,* etc., are sometimes heard.

Functional shift   In all languages, but more easily in English, the function of a word can be shifted—that is, a word can be used as more than one part of speech. For example, in the sentence "He grabbed the hammer" the word *hammer* functions as a noun (as direct object). In the sentence "He hammered the nail into the wood" the word *hammer*—with an *-ed* past ending added—functions as a verb (as predicate). And notice the various ways in which the word *short* functions in these four sentences:

AS ADJECTIVE: You have a short memory.
AS ADVERB: We ran short of milk.

AS NOUN: There was a short in the cable.

AS VERB: The cable shorted out.

Generally, as these examples indicate, no change is made in the word except the addition of inflectional endings (plural, possessive, past, etc.) where needed.

Function words   Some grammarians, especially structural grammarians, classify, or sort, the words of English into two main groups — form-class words and function words. (See **Form classes.**)

Among the various kinds of function words are prepositions (*under, with, at* . . .), coordinating conjunctions (*and, but, or* . . .), subordinating conjunctions (*that, because, while* . . .), auxiliary verbs (*could, may, do* . . .), and noun markers (*a, the, some* . . .). Though function words carry some meaning, their primary job is to show relationships between words in sentences.

There are only about two hundred function words in English, grouped into fifteen or so categories. And since new words are rarely added to these groups, they are sometimes referred to as "closed" classes.

funny   In formal English *funny* means "amusing; comical"; in informal English it also means "strange; odd":

INFORMAL: It's funny Dr. Meyer wasn't consulted.

FORMAL: It is odd that Dr. Meyer was not consulted.

Future tense, future perfect tense   See **shall, will** and **Tenses of verbs.**

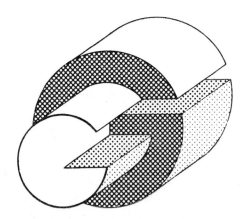

Gender   A classification of words to show whether they are masculine, feminine, or neuter.

1 In many languages nouns and the adjectives modifying them have special endings to show gender. However, in English there are relatively few nouns of this type: *aviator, aviatrix; blond, blonde; equestrian, equestrienne; fiancé, fiancée; hero, heroine; masseur, masseuse; waiter, waitress.*

2 Usually gender in English is indicated simply by the meaning of the word. Words referring to males are masculine (*he, boy, uncle, grandfather, buck*); words referring to females are feminine (*she, girl, aunt, grandmother, doe*); words referring to inanimate things are neuter (*it, desk, calendar, courage, reliability*).

3 Many English nouns can be either masculine or feminine, depending on the person they refer to in a certain situation. Their gender is shown by the pronouns used with them:

We ran up to the singer and asked *him* for *his* autograph.　[The singer here is masculine.]
The speaker declared that *she* was opposed to the whole idea of Medicare.　[The speaker here is feminine.]

4 English often uses compounds to specify gender: *madame chairman, male nurse, woman driver, boyfriend.*

5 Neuter nouns are sometimes given masculine or feminine gender through a type of personification:

Death has left *his* mark on the families of many soldiers.

In informal usage particularly, intimacy or affection are frequently shown by making neuter objects feminine:

Not only is *she* the fastest dune buggy around, *she* is also by far the safest.

(See **he or she, his or her.**)

Generalizations　　General statements, principles, or rules inferred from particular facts or instances. When a generalization is based on enough facts or on enough particular instances, it is valid: "A balanced diet is an aid to good health," "The planets in our solar system revolve around the sun." Generalizations like these, which check with the facts, are sound and valuable; in fact, it would be impossible to reason or think without them.

Although generalizations may often sound impressive, they must be viewed with caution, for many of them are false (or at least partially false) and may be dangerous. Many generalizations are made with only one or two facts or instances to support them. Propagandists, unscrupulous politicians, and many advertisers use generalizations of this type as their chief means of influencing public opinion, of making unthinking people do as they want them to.

A great majority of unsound generalizations are the product of well-meaning, but careless, writers and speakers. In conversation and in some kinds of informal writing, generalizations of this kind are common; often they seem almost unavoidable. And ordinary conversational generalizations, such as "Girls have better table manners than boys" or "French is the most valuable language you can study" or "The Polish and the Irish never get along" normally cause no particular harm; both the speaker and his listeners recognize them as just a "manner of speaking."

But in serious expository writing and speaking, where every statement should be as valid as possible, you must guard against using hasty or unsound generalizations. This is particularly true when these statements are meant to influence others. By saying "Chicago is a dangerous place to live" or "Girls go to college just to find a husband" or "Buying stock when prices are down is a wise idea," you are making statements that are hardly warranted by the facts, yet these statements may be believed by many people.

It would be much more accurate to qualify such statements in some way: "I think that Chicago is a dangerous place to live," "Some girls go to college just to find a husband," "Many experts believe that buying stock when prices are down is a wise idea." Then you must back up the qualified statement with evidence.

While you should guard against making inaccurate generalizations in your own speech and writing, you must be equally careful not to accept as true all of the generalizations that are hurled at you daily in books, in newspapers, over the radio, and on television. Challenge the generalizations you run across. Ask yourself such questions as: Is this statement always true? What evidence is given to prove it is sound? Is it only partially true? Is it just one man's opinion? Why is the statement made? Is it intended to give me important information? Or is it used to persuade me to feel as the writer does so that I will think and do as he wants me to? (See **Inductive and deductive reasoning.**)

General usage   Words, forms, and constructions that are used in all kinds of English—formal, informal, and nonstandard. For a discussion, see **Levels of English usage,** section 4.

Genitive case   See **Possessive case.**

gentleman   See **man, woman.**

Gerund   A verb form ending in -*ing* that is used as a noun.
   1 A gerund can be used wherever a noun can be used. For example:

SUBJECT: *Pole-vaulting* is a great spectator sport.
DIRECT OBJECT: Dad quit *smoking* years ago.
PREDICATE NOUN: Her hobby is *complaining.*
OBJECT OF PREPOSITION: Our faces hurt from all that *smiling.*
APPOSITIVE: The next step, *proofreading,* is most important.

Nouns are often used as modifiers: *flour* sack—"a sack for flour," *soup* bowl—"a bowl for soup." Gerunds, too, may be used as modifiers: *drawing* board—"a board for drawing," *coloring* book—"a book for coloring."

120

2 A pronoun or proper noun immediately preceding a gerund is usually in the possessive form:

Their quarreling upset everyone.   It was caused by *Jane's* meddling.

Usage is divided when a common noun directly precedes a gerund. In formal English the possessive form is usual; in informal English, the ordinary form is often used:

FORMAL: My aunt was unhappy about my *cousin's* enlisting.
INFORMAL: My aunt was unhappy about my *cousin* enlisting.

The ordinary form is generally used for plural nouns:

He doesn't approve of *men* doing housework.

When emphasis is wanted for the noun or pronoun rather than for the gerund that names the action, the ordinary form of the noun and the objective form of the pronoun are used:

Can you imagine *Arthur* enlisting?
Can you imagine *him* enlisting?

3 Do not confuse the gerund with the present participle. Both have the same form. But the gerund is used as a noun; the present participle is used as an adjective:

GERUND: *Stuttering* was Cathy's worst handicap.   [*Stuttering* names an action; it is the subject of the sentence.]
PRESENT PARTICIPLE: *Stuttering* in protest, the prisoner was led from the courtroom.   [*Stuttering* modifies *prisoner*.]

Gerund phrases   **1** Gerunds, being verb forms, can have objects, complements, and adverb modifiers. These words, headed by a gerund, form a *gerund phrase*. The phrase—as a unit—functions as a noun in sentences:

Winning the lottery made them momentarily rich.   [The gerund phrase is subject of the verb *made*; *lottery* is the object of the gerund *Winning*.]
He was very proud of *having been mayor for fifteen years*.   [The gerund phrase is object of the preposition *of*; *mayor* is the complement of the two-word gerund *having been*; and *for fifteen years* is an adverb phrase modifying the gerund.]
Judy's biggest mistake was *talking back to the boss*.   [The gerund phrase is a predicate complement after the linking verb *was*; *back* and *to the boss* are adverb modifiers of the gerund.]

2 A gerund phrase used as the object of a preposition should be related to the subject of the sentence. Otherwise, the phrase will dangle:

DANGLING: After waiting for two hours, my patience ran out.
REVISED: After waiting for two hours, I ran out of patience.

(See **Dangling modifiers.**)

get   **1** The principal parts are *get, got, got* or *gotten*:

Some people get hives from eating oranges.
The twins got a tandem from their grandparents.
By noon I had got (*or* gotten) four subscriptions.

In England the past participle *gotten* — once the usual form — has been re-placed by *got*. But in America both forms are acceptable, although *gotten* is probably more commonly used. The choice between them depends on which form a person is in the habit of saying, on the rhythm of a particular sentence, or, in some cases, on the exact meaning of the sentence.

2 In informal usage *get* is often used as an emphatic helping verb in passive forms:

I don't think he is getting paid enough.   [Less emphatic: he is being paid enough.]
Mr. Lund got hit by a car last night.   [Less emphatic: Mr. Lund was hit.]

3 In colloquial usage *have got* (never *have gotten*) is sometimes used instead of *have* alone as an emphatic way of expressing possession or obligation:

You, Ed, have got to grow up; and you, Al, have got to stop teasing him.
Have you got an extra dime? I haven't got enough for my fare.

In these sentences the *have* alone would carry the meaning, but many speakers feel it is not emphatic enough and so expand the verb to *have got*. This usage, though common in informal speech, is avoided in formal English.

Given names   Given names are usually spelled out in full, although initials may be used. Ordinarily the second and other given names are not written out unless specifically needed (as in legal documents, wills, diplomas) to make identification more certain. Abbreviations like *Chas., Jas.,* and *Wm.* are seldom used now except in the names of long-established business firms and in telephone and other directories, to save space.

Charles K. Schmidt	C. K. Schmidt
Emily R. Butler	Jay F. W. Pearson

Names of well-known people should generally be given in the form that is best known: Martin Luther King, Jr. (*not* M. L. King), J. William Fulbright (*not* James W. Fulbright), H. L. Mencken (*not* Henry Louis Mencken), Billy Graham (*not* William Graham).

go   In colloquial usage *go and* — used when no actual movement is meant — is a common form of emphasis:

You have to get up now, so don't *go and* fall asleep again.
When Dad came in to see what was going on, I didn't say anything, but Steve *went and* told him all our plans.

This usage is appropriate in informal narrative writing, but not in exposition or in formal writing. In these, the *go and* would be omitted: "Don't fall asleep," "Steve told him all our plans."

Going on is a common colloquial idiom in stating ages (The twins are going on thirteen) or time (It is going on eight o'clock). The more formal—and less emphatic—expressions are "nearing thirteen," "almost eight o'clock," "nearly eight."

Gobbledygook   A word (said to have been coined by the late Congressman Maury Maverick) for speech or writing that is hard to understand because technical terms, involved sentences, and "big words" have been used too much. *Gobbledygook*, so called after the sound made by a turkey (a gobble followed by a gook), applies especially to government and business writing that sounds like this:

Extra supplies may be requisitioned in accordance with procedures outlined in the revised operational manual by entering on the appropriate form the source of the extraordinary requisition request, the amount in which said extraordinary request exceeds the annual budgetary allotment designated for that supply category, and a written statement of permission for filing said request from the highest-ranking operational authority available.

(See **Big words.**)

good, well   *Good* is used as an adjective, *well* as either an adjective or an adverb:

ADJECTIVE: I always feel good after a swim.   ["Pleasant."]
ADJECTIVE: Rest now, and you should be well tomorrow.   ["Not ill."]
ADVERB: The radio was working well until you touched it.   ["In a satisfactory or favorable way."]

Nonstandard English almost always uses *good* in place of *well*:

NONSTANDARD: Look that over good before you buy it.
STANDARD: Look that over well before you buy it.

Avoid this nonstandard usage in your own speech and writing.

good and   *Good and* is used colloquially before modifiers as an intensifier meaning "very" ("I'm good and mad at her"; "He had to talk good and fast to get out of that jam"). But this usage is not appropriate in most writing other than dialogue.

Good English   Good English is language that most effectively serves the user's purpose. To be good, language must be clear, lively, and appropriate—to the subject and the situation, to the listener or the reader, to the speaker or the writer. For further discussion, see **Levels of English usage.**

graduate from   *Graduate from* has generally replaced the formal and somewhat archaic idiom *to be graduated from*:

RARE: My sister Barbara was graduated from high school last year.
USUAL: My sister Barbara graduated from high school last year.

Nonstandard English sometimes uses the verb *graduate* alone (My sister Barbara graduated high school last year). This usage should be avoided.

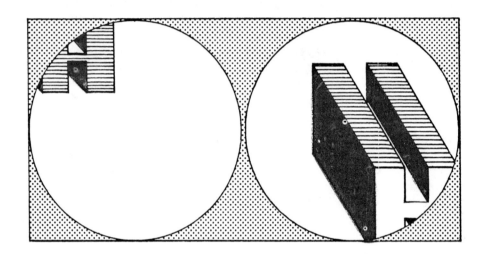

Habitual action   *Would* is commonly used as a helping verb to express habitual action in the past:

He would practice on those drums for hours every evening.

Habitual action is also shown by *used to* or by the past form and an adverb:

He used to practice on those drums for hours every evening.
He constantly practiced on those drums.

had   Used (now rather rarely) in formal writing as the introductory word in a subordinate clause of condition:

RARE: Had we made reservations, we could have seen the play.
USUAL: If we had made reservations, we could have seen the play.

had better, had best   These are the usual idioms for giving advice and making indirect commands:

You had better turn the matter over to a lawyer.
Peter had better prepare his notes for the meeting.
You had best not believe all of his stories.

In informal speech the *had* is sometimes dropped:

You better turn the matter over to a lawyer.

In formal English and in most writing (unless you are reporting directly what a person said) the *had* should be used.

had of   In nonstandard English *had of* (and its contraction *'d of*) is often used for *had* in clauses beginning with *if*:

NONSTANDARD: If he'd of started right away, he'd be done by now.
STANDARD: If he had started right away, he'd be done by now.   [Or: If he'd started right away.]

had ought   *Had ought* and *hadn't ought* are nonstandard forms of the standard *ought* and *ought not*:

NONSTANDARD: They had ought to be here soon.
STANDARD: They ought to be here soon.

NONSTANDARD: You hadn't ought to leave your room in such a mess.
STANDARD: You ought not to leave your room in such a mess.

had rather, would rather   Both expressions are used to show preference; the second is more emphatic and perhaps more common:

He had rather face a hungry lion than apologize to her.
Judy would rather eat fried oysters than filet mignon.
I would rather not answer all the questions on this application.

In speech the *had* or *would* is often slurred or contracted (He'd rather face a hungry lion) so that it is impossible to tell which is being used.

half   The generally used idiom is *half a(n)*; the more formal is *a half*:

GENERAL: It took them half an hour to go half a mile.
FORMAL: It took them a half hour to go a half mile.

Expressions with the article *a* coming both before and after *half*, like *a half a year* and *a half a dollar*, are common in speech. However, such repetition is unnecessary and not often used in writing.

hanged, hung   In formal English the principal parts of *hang* when referring to execution or suicide are *hang, hanged, hanged*; in other senses they are *hang, hung, hung*:

In those days a man could be hanged for stealing a loaf of bread.
We hung the flag of Ireland just below the American flag.

In informal usage there is a tendency to use the forms *hang, hung, hung* in all senses.

hardly   Since *hardly* has a negative meaning ("not easily; not quite"), it should not be combined with another negative word:

NONSTANDARD: He couldn't hardly expect an answer so soon.
STANDARD: He could hardly expect an answer so soon.

NONSTANDARD: There wasn't hardly enough room for our own gear.
STANDARD: There was hardly enough room for our own gear.

(See also **Double negative**.)

have   See **of,** section 3.

have got   See **get,** section 3.

Headword   A word that is modified by another word or other words:

brave *men*   *leaped* quickly to his feet
a long, thin, wrinkled *face*   very nearly *fell* overboard
the *first* of several exacting experiments

healthful, healthy   Formal English distinguishes between these words, using *healthful* to mean "giving health" or "good for the health," and *healthy* to mean "having or showing good health":

He was told to move to a more healthful climate.
How can anyone be healthy if he does not eat healthful food?

In informal English *healthy* is often used to mean "healthful":

This isn't a very healthy place for someone who has bronchitis.

height   In nonstandard English often pronounced /hīth/; in standard English always pronounced /hīt/.

he or she, his or her   Since English has no third person singular pronoun to refer to antecedents that mean either or both men and women, the language has developed three different ways of referring to such words:
    1 Generally *he* and *his* are used, even when some of the persons meant are female:

Every doctor and nurse in the area can be proud of the unstinting help *he* has given during this emergency.
Mr. Pasco and Mrs. Bly spoke first, each giving *his* opinion of the proposed new constitution.

When the majority of the people in the group referred to are women, *she* and *her* are used:

Each committee member is to interview as many parents as *she* can before making *her* report to the chairman.

2 Sometimes the phrase *he or she* (or *his or her*) is used, but it generally is clumsy and sounds pedantic:

A good still-life painter will study *his or her* subject from every angle before *he or she* begins to paint.

The single pronouns *his* and *he* would be less awkward in this sentence, and the meaning would be just as clear.

3 People who avoid *he or she* (and *his or her*) as unnecessarily awkward, and dislike using *he* (and *his*) alone when women as well as men are meant, solve the problem by using a plural pronoun:

Has anyone in your class given *their* report yet?
Ed and Sue were present, but neither expressed *their* views.

The plural pronoun is becoming more and more common and is appropriate in all but formal usage.

here, there Nonstandard English often adds an unnecessary *here* to *this* (and *there* to *that*):

NONSTANDARD: This here book is mine, so that there one must be his.
STANDARD: This book is mine, so that one must be his.

Often in conversation an expression such as *this desk here* or *that one there* is used to clarify or emphasize meaning:

"Which shirt do you want?" "I'll take this one here."
"Where did you ever get such an idea?" "It says so right in that magazine there."

These expressions, in which *here* and *there* function as adverbs rather than adjectives, are standard colloquial usage.

high school Capitalized only when used as part of a proper name:

Across from Lincoln High School is a girls' high school.

When used as an adjective, *high school* is often hyphened:

The high-school speech tournament was held last Saturday.

himself, herself See **Reflexive pronouns.**

Historical present For the sake of vividness or liveliness the present tense is sometimes used in narratives about the past. This usage is called the "historical present":

So Ann stands up very slowly and starts walking toward Tom. Tom looks at her angrily and then turns away. . . .

Although it is quite common to use this method in telling stories aloud, as a rule you will find it easier and more effective to stick to the past tense in written narratives. Used throughout a story, the "historical present" can become quite monotonous. And unless you are careful, you may find yourself shifting without reason from present to past and then back—to the confusion of your reader.

home   Nonstandard English uses *to home* for the generally used *at home* or *home*:

NONSTANDARD: The whole family was to home when Robert called.
STANDARD: The whole family was at home when Robert called.   [Or: was home.]

home, house, residence   At one time a distinction was made between *house* (a building) and *home* (a lived-in house; the center of one's family ties). Although some writers and speakers still make this distinction, in general usage, especially in real-estate usage, the two words have become synonymous.

Residence is used mainly to refer to a large dwelling with considerable surrounding grounds—a mansion or a palace, for example. Using it to refer to an ordinary house, especially one's own, is considered rather formal and pretentious.

homely   In formal English *homely* means "simple, unassuming; suited to home life": *homely ways, homely meals*. But in general usage it is most often used to mean "not good-looking; ugly; plain": Although her face was *homely*, her beautiful hair made her seem almost attractive.

Homographs   Words that have the same spelling but a different origin and meaning: *sole* ("single"), *sole* ("the bottom of the foot or the bottom of a shoe, slipper, etc."), *sole* ("a kind of flatfish").

In most dictionaries homographs are entered separately, and a small superscript number is put before or after each entry word (sole[1], sole[2], sole[3], for example) to indicate that there are other entries (or another entry) which may have the definition a person needs.

Homonyms   Words that have the same pronunciation but different meanings: *brake—break; fair—fare; metal—mettle*.

The meaning of such words is usually made clear by the context, but their spelling is likely to cause trouble. Keeping the words separated in your mind by visualizing them in phrases that give a clue to their meaning will help you spell them correctly:

stepped on the *brake*	a *break* for coffee
the *bridal* party	on the *bridle* path
the predicate *complement*	a sincere *compliment*
a meeting of the *council*	the *counsel* for the defense
going to the *fair*	money for bus *fare*

128

a *grate* for fire	a *great* man
the *heir* to millions	campaigning for clean *air*
a *hoarse* voice	a *horse* of a different color
idle men and *idle* machines	worshiping an *idol*
a *metal* like aluminum	a true test of *mettle*
smoking a *peace* pipe	a *piece* of pie
the art of *plain* talk	*plane* geometry
the *principal* and faculty	based on a moral *principle*
a *stationary* engine	the box of *stationery*
threw the ball to first	tunnel *through* the mountain
Who's there?	*Whose* is it?

Honorable   When used as a title of respect for persons in high political offices (congressmen, judges, governors, mayors), *honorable* is capitalized, is usually preceded by *the*, and is followed by the first name or initials as well as the surname:

The last speaker was the Honorable Osee B. Farmington.

In addresses, when the first name or initials are used, *Honorable* may either be abbreviated or written out in full. Generally, the full spelling is preferable:

Hon. John Pratt	The Hon. John Pratt
Hon. J. E. Pratt	The Honorable John Pratt

hopefully   Originally the adverb *hopefully* meant only "in a hopeful manner":

She waited hopefully for news of his safe return.

But in recent years it has come to be used also in the sense of "it is hoped":

Hopefully, our campaign will be a success.
The bill will be passed, hopefully, on Wednesday.

However, since careful speakers and writers frown on this usage, it would be wise to avoid it when you think it might annoy your audience and take their attention away from what you are saying.

Hours   Generally hours are written in words:

The wedding reception is to begin at half-past six.
The movie will run from eight-thirty until eleven o'clock.
The water-safety class has been rescheduled for seven o'clock.

When the time is to be particularly emphasized, figures are used:

Flight 317 leaves Chicago at 10:11 this evening and arrives in Indianapolis at 11:00.

With the abbreviations *a.m.* and *p.m.*, figures are always used:

The only buses going from Green Bay to Milwaukee today are at 10:35 a.m. and 2:15 p.m.

Notice that a colon is used between hours and minutes written as figures, and that the phrase *o'clock* is not added after *a.m.* and *p.m.*

how come?   A colloquial shortening of the question "How does (did) it come that?": Then *how come* you didn't tell me about the picnic?

however   See **Conjunctive adverbs.**

human, humane   At one time these words were merely spelling variants, meaning the same thing. But today they have different meanings, which are sometimes confused. *Human* is used in referring to any good or bad traits, especially feelings or faults, characteristic of man as distinguished from God or from animals:

Although Gerald rejoiced at his brother's good fortune, he was human enough to be somewhat envious.

Humane is generally used to refer to noble, compassionate feelings and actions of man, especially toward distressed, suffering, or helpless people and animals:

The Geneva Convention provides for the humane treatment of prisoners of war.

Hyperbole   /hī per'bə lē'/ Exaggeration for the sake of effect and not meant to be taken literally:

Big? He weighs just a pound or two less than a whale.
Stop rolling in that snow or you'll turn into a piece of ice.

Hyphen (-)   A connecting mark used between words or parts of words.
    1 With compound modifiers. A compound modifier (two or more words used as a single adjective) preceding a noun is generally hyphened:

first-base umpire	his record-shattering time
formica-covered counter	a grin-and-bear-it attitude
light-blue scarf	stop-and-go traffic

If a compound modifier of this type comes after the noun or if its first part is an adverb ending in *-ly*, no hyphen is used:

The scarf that came with the purple dress was *light blue*.
His time in the relay was certainly not *record shattering*.
The *heavily loaded* flatboats were swept along by the *swiftly moving* current.

Compound proper adjectives or compound proper nouns used as adjectives are not hyphened:

Southeast Asian conflict   Revolutionary War hero
Mother's Day card   Currier and Ives print

2 With numbers and fractions. Hyphens are used in compound numbers from twenty-one to ninety-nine:

seventy-five   two hundred forty-second time
He paid his hotel bill with twenty-five dollar bills. [Compare with "twenty five-dollar bills" ($100) — in which the hyphen is used for a compound modifier.]

Fractions used as modifiers are always hyphened:

By then the arena was three-fourths empty.   [Adverb modifier.]
We were short of a two-thirds majority.   [Adjective modifier.]

But usage is divided in writing fractions used as nouns:

Only one tenth (*or* one-tenth) of the voters turned out.
One half (*or* One-half) of the floats were badly damaged by the rain.

3 With prefixes. A hyphen is used:
a) Between a prefix and a proper noun or adjective:

anti-American   pre-Columbian
ex-President Roosevelt post-Reformation

b) Between a prefix ending in *i* and a root word beginning with *i*:

anti-intellectual   semi-independent

c) After the prefixes *self-* and *ex-* (when *ex-* means "former" or "formerly"):

self-employed   ex-friend
self-made   ex-governor

d) To avoid confusion with another word that has the same spelling but a different pronunciation and meaning:

We will *re-collect* the raffle books next Monday.   /rē'kə lekt'/
I cannot *recollect* reading any such article.   /rek'ə lekt'/
Miss Lewis told me to *re-solve* the equation.   /rē solv'/
Fran should *resolve* to eat less and exercise more.   /ri zolv'/

4 With compound nouns. There is no simple rule for hyphenating ordinary compound nouns, since usage varies so widely. For example, although the compounds *close-up* and *half-truth* are hyphened, *close call* and *half nelson* are written as two words. And related compounds — *closeout* and *halfback* — are written as one word. Sometimes even the same word is spelled differently. In three different magazine articles you may find *prize-fighter*, *prize fighter*, and *prizefighter*.

Many compound words go through three steps before they are written as one word. Not too long ago, for instance, the name of the great Spanish pastime was written as two words: *bull fight*. For a time, the word was spelled with a hyphen: *bull-fight*. Now it is almost always written as one word: *bullfight*.

Since there is no simple rule to guide you in spelling compounds, the safest practice is to consult a dictionary for words you are in doubt about. If the dictionary does not list the compound you are looking for (either as one word or with a hyphen), write it as two words, without a hyphen.

5 For dividing words. A hyphen is used to mark the division of words at the end of a line of writing. The problem here is to divide the word between syllables. For a list of rules to guide you, see **Division of words.**

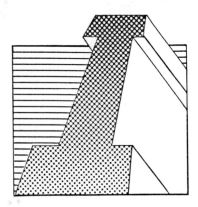

I   *I* is written as a capital simply because in the old handwritten manuscripts a small *i* was likely to be lost or joined to a neighboring word. Contrary to a widespread belief, using *I* as the first word in a letter (or the first word in a series of sentences in a paragraph) is not a sign of conceit. *I* can be used wherever it is needed to express ideas simply and clearly. People who use roundabout expressions to avoid using *I* usually turn out awkward, unnatural sentences that are far less effective than sentences with *I*:

AWKWARD: It seems plausible that a good grade will be given to me on that paper.
BETTER: I think that I will get a good grade on that paper.

If every sentence in a paragraph you have written begins with *I*, you may feel that the pronoun is too conspicuous, that too many *I*'s will be annoying to your reader. By shifting a modifying phrase or clause to the beginning of two or three of the sentences, you can take the emphasis away from the *I*:

After trailing my opponent for three laps, I won the race.   [Instead of: I won the race, after trailing my opponent for three laps.]

Ibid.   An abbreviation of the Latin *ibidem*, meaning "in the same place." It is used in a footnote to refer to the work mentioned in the immediately preceding footnote. (For punctuation and examples, see **Footnotes.**)

Idiolect   An *idiolect* is a person's own particular set of speech habits. For example, one person may be in the habit of saying "the words *on* the list"; another, "the words *in* the list." One person may generally pronounce the word *coupon* /kü'pon/; another, /kyü'pon/. People with similar idiolects speak the same dialect. (See **Dialect.**)

Idiom   An idiom is a combination of words that seems perfectly natural to the native speakers of a language but seems odd or peculiar to other people (usually because it has a meaning different from the literal meaning of the words):

be on pins and needles	run across an old friend
catch a cold	strike a bargain
make the fur fly	walk on air

(For a discussion of idiomatic prepositions, see **Preposition,** section 3.)

ie, ei   For the spelling of words with *ie* and *ei*, see **Spelling,** section 1f.

i.e.   An abbreviation of the Latin *id est*, meaning "that is." It is now seldom used except in reference works; *that is* is used instead. (For punctuation, see **namely and other introductory words.**)

if, whether   **1** *If* is used to introduce a clause of condition; *whether* (with *or*) is used to introduce alternatives:

If she means what she says, we'll have to pay the full amount.
What should we do if he refuses to leave?
Whether she means it or not, I can't tell.
They can't decide whether they should buy a house or rent one.

2 In formal usage *whether* (usually with *or*) is used to introduce indirect questions and expressions of doubt:

INDIRECT QUESTION: They asked whether she had finished the book.
INDIRECT QUESTION: He asked me whether I was arriving or leaving.
DOUBT: Everyone wondered whether she would believe the story.
DOUBT: I am not sure whether his drawing is an original or a copy.

In informal usage *if* rather than *whether* is generally used in such sentences:

They asked if she had finished the book.
He asked me if I was arriving or leaving.
Everyone wondered if she would believe the story.
I'm not sure if his drawing is an original or a copy.

Ignoring the question   See **Fallacies in reasoning,** section 3.

Illogical comparisons   See **Faulty comparisons.**

illusion, delusion, allusion   An *illusion* is "a false impression" or "a deceptive appearance":

Carefully used make-up can often create an illusion of beauty.
The puddle you think you see on the road is an optical illusion.

A *delusion* is "a false belief or opinion":

For years Mark had the delusion that his teachers picked on him.
That poor woman has the delusion that she is a famous actress.

An *allusion* is "an indirect reference to something or someone generally familiar":

Mr. Dmitri's poetry contains many allusions to mythology.
Everyone in the class smiled knowingly when the speaker made an allusion to *Macbeth.*

Imagery   Imagery in writing is the use of words that appeal to the senses: sight, hearing, touch, smell, taste, and the muscular tension known as the kinesthetic sense. Although many words may appeal to more than one sense (*mink* to sight and touch; *fried chicken* to sight, smell, and taste), usually one of the sense appeals is dominant, as in the following:

SIGHT: pink and gold sunset, glittering ruby, new-fallen snow
HEARING: bellowing steer, crackling leaves, roaring waterfall
TOUCH: crushed velvet, starched collar, jagged rocks
SMELL: perfumed hair, bayberry candle, boiling sauerkraut
TASTE: sweet and sour beans, salted pistachios, anchovy pizza
KINESTHETIC: squirming puppy, twitching muscle, pinching shoes

Imagery is an important part of writing, and you will see it used in all but the most abstract discussions of ideas. Try to use images in your own writing, but remember they are most likely to be effective when they come directly from your own experience. The things you are interested in — clothes, sports, pets, hobbies, anything — should be the source of many images, images that you can use in writing about a variety of different topics.

Imitative words (Onomatopoeia)   A number of words imitate or suggest the sound associated with a certain thing or action: *katydid, cuckoo, bang, buzz, fizz, plop, clank, clatter, crunch, ding-dong, zip, whir, whiz, thump.*

The use of imitative words to gain a special effect in writing is called *onomatopoeia* /on'ə mat'ə pē'ə/.

The blade whizzed past his head and hit the target with a thump.

imminent, eminent   See **eminent, imminent.**

Imperative mood   A verb in the imperative mood is used to give commands or to make requests:

Keep this under your hat
Take a number, please.

(See also **Commands and requests, Mood.**)

Imperative sentences   Sentences that give commands or make requests:

Pick up your shoes.
Please don't touch the display.

(See also **Commands and requests.**)

Impersonal it   In talking about weather and time, *it* is used as an impersonal subject in sentences like these:

It always rains a lot in September.
It will be after six o'clock when I get home.

It is called impersonal because it does not refer to a definite person or thing.

Impersonal style   Writing in which the author carefully avoids the personal pronoun *I* or any other direct reference to himself is said to be in the impersonal style. The types of writing that are usually impersonal include editorials, most serious discussions of situations and ideas, academic and professional writing, compilations of facts, and term papers.

Impersonal writing makes use of such words and phrases as the editorial "we," "the writer believes," and "in the opinion of the writer." Used too often, such expressions become tiresome and detract from rather than add to the effectiveness of the writing. Yet they are better than such meaningless phrases as "many believe," "it has been said," "it seems," and the colorless impersonal pronoun "one."

For most student purposes, an informal personal style is more appropriate than a formal impersonal style, with the possible exception of the formal research paper.

imply, infer   Careful speakers and writers distinguish between these two words, using *imply* to mean "indicate without saying outright," and *infer* to mean "draw a conclusion by reasoning."

Every gesture that she made implied that she was extremely vain.
They inferred from my comments that I had never been in Mexico.

However, *infer* has been used so often in the sense of "imply" that many dictionaries record "imply" as a secondary meaning of *infer.*

in, into, in to   *In* generally shows location (in a literal or a figurative sense); *into* generally shows direction:

Amy is in the barn.   Run into the barn and surprise her.
Al is in trouble again.   He got into trouble for fighting.

   Colloquially *in* is often used for *into*:

A bug flew in my eye.   I jumped in the pool.

   Do not confuse the preposition *into* with the adverb *in* followed by the preposition *to*:

Sid ran into the auditorium to show us his costume.
Sid ran in to show us his costume.

in back of   See **back of, in back of.**

Incomplete sentences   See **Sentence fragment.**

incredible, incredulous   *Incredible* means "unbelievable"; *incredulous* means "disinclined to believe; showing disbelief":

He told an incredible story about having been taken for a visit to another planet.
The incredulous expressions of the reporters who listened to his story didn't seem to trouble him.

Indefinite articles   The noun markers *a* and *an*, used to refer to any one of a group of persons, places, or things: *a* box, *a* brush, *an* opera. (See **a, an** and **the.**)

Indefinite it   Formal English and careful informal writing avoid the use of the indefinite *it*:

INDEFINITE: In this book it says that writing well takes practice.
DEFINITE: This book says that writing well takes practice.

(See also **they.**)

Indefinite pronouns   Pronouns used to refer to any one or more of a number of persons or things:

all	everybody	nothing
another	everyone	one, oneself
any	everything	other
anybody	few	several
anyone	many	some
anything	neither	somebody
both	nobody	someone
each	none	something
either	no one	such

(Some of the specific usage problems concerning these pronouns are discussed under separate listings of the words themselves. See also **Agreement,** sections 1g and 2b.)

Indention   Beginning a line in from the left-hand margin. Since an uneven margin makes a page look unsightly, the margin should be kept straight and the indentions consistent.

In longhand copy, paragraphs are indented about an inch; in typewritten copy, from five to ten spaces. These measurements may vary slightly according to the writer's taste or because of special need.

Hanging indention is the setting in of lines below the first line, as in outlines, newspaper headlines, and slant-style headings and addresses of letters. If a line of verse is too long for one line, indent the part brought over to the second line:

> But there is no joy in Mudville—mighty Casey has
> struck out.

Independent clause   (Also called *main* clause.) See **Clause,** section 1.

Indicative mood   The verb forms that are used in ordinary statements and questions about actual things and events are called verbs in the *indicative mood*:

That mean little boy *is throwing* stones at me again.
This time I really *want* to hit him.
Does his mother *know* where he *is*?
She just *punished* him for that yesterday.

(See **Mood; Imperative mood; Subjunctive.**)

Indirect object   A noun or a pronoun (or a phrase or clause used as a noun) that shows to whom or for whom an action is done:

We promised our *parents* a free anniversary dinner.
Craig bought *her* some aspirin for her headache.
The critics gave Gail's *singing* favorable mention.   [Gerund.]
I'll stay and tell *whoever comes* the news about the election.   [Noun clause.]

Notice that the indirect object comes before the direct object and that it is not preceded by *to* or *for*.

Indirect question   A question that is put into the speaker's or writer's own words instead of being quoted as first heard or read. A period, not a question mark, is used after an indirect question:

INDIRECT: Henry asked me if I could read music.
DIRECT: Henry asked me, "Can you read music?"

Indirect quotation   A quotation that is reworded in the speaker's or writer's own words instead of being quoted as first heard or read. Quotation marks are not used to enclose an indirect quotation:

INDIRECT: Laura said that she has fifty dollars in the bank.
DIRECT: Laura said, "I have fifty dollars in the bank."

individual   See **person.**

Inductive and deductive reasoning   1 Inductive reasoning is the process of reasoning from particular instances or individual cases to a generalization. For example, suppose that over a period of time you have met a dozen or more people who were born and raised in the small town of Crestley or in the immediate area around it. In talking with these people, you were struck by their pronunciation of the name *Crestley.* They did not pronounce it /krest′lē/ as you did, but /krez′lē/ — with a /z/ and without a /t/. From these dozen or more "sample" cases, you arrive at a generalization about all natives of Crestley: [If these dozen or more people pronounce *Crestley* the same way, with a /z/ and without a /t/, then it is quite likely that] "All natives of Crestley and the immediate area around it pronounce *Crestley* /krez′lē/ — with a /z/ and without a /t/."

Such a generalization states a probability, of course, not a certainty. To make it a certainty, you would have to hear every Crestley-area native pronounce the name. However, the chances are that your generalization is valid. Even though you have not heard every Crestley native pronounce the town's name, every one you did hear used the same pronunciation, and a dozen or more would be a fairly representative number of natives of a small area.

(See **Generalizations.**)

2 Deductive reasoning is the process of applying a generalization to a particular instance or individual case. For example, suppose that you read in your newspaper that Dr. Paul Jonas, a native of Crestley, will appear on a television panel show that night. This reminds you of the generalization you had reached about Crestley natives, who pronounce *Crestley* with a /z/ and without a /t/. Applying this generalization to Dr. Jonas, you conclude (deduce) that, since he is a native of Crestley, he will also pronounce *Crestley* /krez′lē/ — with a /z/, not a /t/.

This deductive thinking process can be stated in a three-part form, called a **syllogism**. It consists of a *major premise* (the generalization you begin with), a *minor premise* (the particular case), and a *conclusion* (the deductive inference that logically follows from the two premises). For example:

MAJOR PREMISE: [*If it is true that*] all natives of Crestley pronounce *Crestley* /krez′lē/ — with a /z/ and without a /t/,
MINOR PREMISE: [*And if it is also true that*] Dr. Paul Jonas is a native of Crestley,

CONCLUSION: [*Then it must be true that*] Dr. Paul Jonas will pronounce *Crestley* /krez'lē/ — with a /z/ and without a /t/.

Notice the bracketed *if*-clauses before the two premises. They are there to remind us that if either of the premises of a syllogism is not true, the conclusion cannot be true, of course. In any syllogism in which the premises are true and in which the reasoning is valid (as it is here), the conclusion will be valid.

(See **Fallacies in reasoning.**)

infer, imply   See **imply, infer.**

Infinitive   The simple form of the verb, usually preceded by *to*: *to see, to smile, to wiggle, to forget.* Infinitives are used as nouns (subjects, objects, complements), as adjectives, or as adverbs:

SUBJECT: *To criticize* is easy.
OBJECT: He is planning *to resign.*
COMPLEMENT: Rodney's first impulse was *to run.*
ADJECTIVE: The Quinns have a garage *to rent.*
ADVERB: Are you ready *to start?*

After certain verbs (*dare, help, need*) the *to* is sometimes not used:

No one in the room dared [*to*] *object.*
Why don't you help her [*to*] *pack?*

(See also **Split infinitive** and **Tenses of verbs,** section 4.)

Infinitive phrases   **1** Since infinitives are verb forms, they can have objects, complements, and adverb modifiers. Together with the infinitive, these words form an *infinitive phrase* which, like the infinitive alone, can be used as a noun, an adjective, or an adverb. For example:

To go ahead now would be unwise.   [The infinitive is used as a noun, as subject of the verb *would be; ahead* and *now* are adverb modifiers of the infinitive *To go.*]
Harry had always planned *to be a doctor.*   [The phrase is used as a noun, as object of the verb *had planned; doctor* is the complement of the infinitive *to be.*]
No one had any time *to help us.*   [The phrase is used as an adjective modifying the noun *time; us* is the object of the infinitive *to help.*]
The coach dashed over to the referee *to complain about the call.* [The phrase is used as an adverb modifying the verb *dashed; about the call* is an adverb phrase modifying the infinitive *to complain.*]

An infinitive phrase used as a subject may follow the verb:

It would be unwise *to go ahead now.*
Wouldn't it be unwise *to go ahead now?*

It is not the subject in these sentences; the infinitive phrase is. (See **Expletives.**)

2 Objective-case pronouns are used for predicate complements of infinitives that have subjects:

A number of people took Phyllis to be *me.* [*Phyllis* is the subject of the infinitive; *me* is the predicate complement.]

The predicate complement of an infinitive that has no expressed subject may have either the nominative or the objective form. The nominative is generally used in formal English; the objective in informal English:

FORMAL: I certainly would not want to be *he.*
INFORMAL: I certainly wouldn't want to be *him.*

(See also **Split infinitive** and **Tenses of verbs,** section 4.)

Inflection   In grammar *inflection* means a change in the form of a word to show case (*we — us*), number (*cup — cups*), gender (*fiancé — fiancée*), person (*we pay — he pays*), tense (*are — were*), or comparison (*duller — dullest*).

Inflectional endings   See **Endings (of words).**

Informal English   The language that educated people ordinarily use in speech and writing in all but formal situations. For discussion and examples, see **Levels of English usage,** section 2.

ingenious, ingenuous   Because of the similarity in spelling and pronunciation, these words are sometimes confused. *Ingenious* means "clever" or "cleverly planned and made"; *ingenuous* means "frank; open; candid":

Dr. March was a brilliant man, who came up with one ingenious theory after another.
Her ingenuous replies contrasted sharply with the half-truths and evasions of her brother.

Sometimes *ingenuous* carries an added connotation of artlessness and lack of sophistication:

Carl's ingenuous comments on the movie embarrassed his more sophisticated cousins.

inside of   In informal English *inside of* is used in expressions of time:

INFORMAL: He'll be back inside of an hour.   [Or: in an hour.]
FORMAL: He will return within an hour.

The *of* is not necessary in such sentences as:

Once inside [of] the house, we relaxed.

insure, ensure   See **ensure, insure.**

Intensifier   An adverb used to increase or lessen the force of an adjective or another adverb. An intensifier always comes immediately before the word it modifies:

barely warm soup   tapped *very* lightly
a *bitterly* cold day   walked *extremely* fast
was *rather* quiet   came *quite* frequently

Intensive pronouns   Personal pronouns plus the suffix *-self* or *-selves,* used after a noun or pronoun to add emphasis:

The mayor himself gave the order.
He gave the order himself.
They themselves couldn't agree on a fair price.

(See **myself.**)

Interjection   An exclamatory word or phrase: *oh, ouch, hurrah, darn it.* An emphatic interjection is followed by an exclamation point; a mild interjection is followed by a comma:

Unbelievable! We finally won a baseball game.
Oh! How can you say that?   [Or: Oh! how can you say that?]
Oh, it's you again.

Interrogative adjectives   Adjectives used in asking questions: *which, what,* and *whose.*

Interrogative pronouns   Pronouns used in asking questions: *who, whose, whom, which, what,* and sometimes *whoever, whatever.*

Interrogative sentences   Sentences that ask for information:

Who is going to baby-sit?
Which flight are you taking?

When a sentence is phrased as a statement but is meant as a question, it is followed by a question mark:

Your brother will be stationed near Munich?

A polite request phrased as a question for the sake of courtesy is generally followed by a period rather than a question mark:

Will all of the delegates please comment on this decision.

Intransitive verbs   Verbs whose meanings are complete without a direct object:

Jerry's motorcycle almost *crashed* into the side of a truck.
Chet *did* not *answer* for several seconds.

141

Linking verbs are always intransitive, merely connecting a predicate noun, pronoun, or adjective with the subject:

His little brother *is* a pest.
The car *will be* mine soon.
Inez *may have looked* calm, but she *was* very nervous.

(See **Transitive and intransitive verbs.**)

invent, discover   See **discover, invent.**

Inverted sentences   The usual order in sentences is subject—verb, subject—verb—object, or subject—verb—complement. Sentences in which this order is changed are called *inverted sentences*:

Among the evergreens stood a few elms.   [Verb before subject.]
The pink chair she re-covered in red velvet.   [Object first.]
And a very clever scheme it was.   [Complement first.]

By departing from the usual order, you can draw attention to a part of the sentence that you want to stand out as most important.

Irony   A form of expression implying something different, even opposite, from what is actually said:

No, she's not popular at all: she was elected homecoming queen last year, class secretary this year; and you can usually find her with any one of six or seven of the best-looking boys in the senior class.

irregardless   See **regardless.**

Irregular verbs   Verbs whose past tense and past participle are not formed in the regular way (by adding *-ed* to the simple form, as in *jump, jumped, jumped*): *do, did, done; throw, threw, thrown; swim, swam, swum; tear, tore, torn; choose, chose, chosen.*

it   Informal English often uses *it* to refer to the idea of a preceding statement; formal English rarely does so:

INFORMAL: The boys spent the whole afternoon shoveling snow from the sidewalks and driveway. *It* took a lot of stamina.
FORMAL: The boys spent the entire afternoon shoveling snow from the sidewalks and driveway, a task which required much stamina.

(See also **Indefinite it.**)

Italics   In type, letters that slant to the right. (*This sentence is in italic type.*) In longhand and typewritten manuscript, italics are shown by underlining. (For specific uses of italics, see **Underlining.**)

its   The possessive adjective does not have an apostrophe:

The kitten raised *its* head.   No one knew *its* value.

To avoid misspelling, associate *its* with *his* and *hers*.

it's   The contraction of *it is* or *it has*:

It's good to see you.   *It's* been a month since my birthday.

As a contraction, *it's* is always spelled with an apostrophe.

It's me   Formal grammarians explain that the verb *be* should always be followed by the nominative case: *It is I*. But in actual practice *It's me* is so generally used by educated people that it is now acceptable standard usage (even though some users of formal English still prefer *It is I*).

Though *It's me* is acceptable, *It's him, It's her, It's us, It's them* are not.

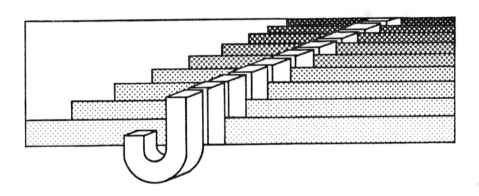

Jargon   Most commonly used in one of these two senses: "confused, meaningless talk or writing" or "the language of a special group, profession, or class":

Mr. Huth's large vocabulary did not help him in teaching; to his students, his lectures were merely jargon.
Using legal jargon to explain the court proceedings to me will only confuse me more.

Linguists use *jargon* to mean "a dialect composed of a mixture of two or more languages." Many non-English-speaking people, in doing business with us, use jargons made up partly of English and partly of their native language. In the Pacific Northwest, for example, the Chinook jargon (a mixture of Chinook, French, and English) was used by Indians and American fur traders in their dealings. Trading between Westerners and Orientals at China ports was carried on in a Chinese-English jargon, commonly called "pidgin English." Though a number of jargons, or pidgin languages, have died out or are dying out, one that is still flourishing is Melanesian pidgin (a mixture of Malay and English). It is used as a trade language in the South Pacific, mainly in New Guinea and the Solomon Islands.

job, position *Job* is the informal word for the formal *position*:

INFORMAL: Miriam wants to apply for a job in advertising.
FORMAL: Miriam wants to apply for a position in advertising.

The two words have different connotations. Though *job* is used informally to apply to any kind of employment, it usually refers to the idea of work to be done for hourly wages. *Position* usually suggests white-collar or professional employment with a fixed salary.

join together The *together* is unnecessary, since *join* means "bring, come, or put together":

Six local groups have joined [together] to work on his campaign.
Joining the six pieces [together] will give us the length we need.

Journalese A style of writing found in some newspapers and magazines. Its chief characteristics (generally considered faults) are the overuse of "big words," roundabout expressions, and trite phrases.

judgment, judgement *Judgment* is the more common spelling in the United States.

just In informal English *just* is often used to mean "very; quite":

This horseradish is just delicious.

Guard against overusing *just* in this sense in your written work.
(For the position of *just*, see **only**.)

kid Informal when used in either of these two senses: (1) as a noun meaning "child" or "young person" ("Tell that kid to stop making so much noise"); (2) as a verb meaning "tease playfully" or "deceive; fool" ("Don't try to kid me").

kind, sort   In formal English the singular adjectives *this* and *that* are used to modify the singular *kind* and *sort*:

This kind of soft drink leaves a bitter aftertaste.
That sort of magazine seldom carries many ads.

Similarly, formal usage requires that the plural adjectives *these* and *those* be used only when *kind* and *sort* are plural:

The leaves on these kinds of trees turn bright red in the fall.
The Security Council decides on those sorts of problems.

In colloquial usage the plural adjectives are often used with *kind* and *sort*:

Beth has three of those kind of posters on her bedroom wall.
We need more of these sort of men to keep our team on top!

In spite of the fact that this usage is common in the speech of educated people, it still has only colloquial standing. You will be wise to avoid it in writing, especially formal writing.

In both speech and writing, avoid the nonstandard *them kind*:

NONSTANDARD: No one wears them kind any more.
STANDARD: No one wears that kind any more.

kind of, sort of   In informal speech *kind of* and *sort of* are often used as adverbs meaning "rather; somewhat; almost; nearly":

Now I'm kind of sorry that I dropped out.
We were sort of worried about leaving Grandfather alone.

In written English the appropriate forms would be:

Now I'm almost sorry that I dropped out.
We were rather worried about leaving Grandfather alone.   [Or: somewhat worried, quite worried.]

kind of a, sort of a   Formal English omits the *a*:

This kind of greeting card is sold only at stationery stores.
Only a bigot would be interested in that sort of book.

But in informal English, especially in speech, *kind of a* and *sort of a* are common:

This kind of a greeting card is sold only at stationery stores.
Only a bigot would be interested in that sort of a book.

lady   See **man, woman.**

last, latest   Formal English makes a distinction between these two words — using *last* to refer to the final item in a series, and *latest* to refer to the most recent item in a series that may or may not continue:

The last biweekly issue of the *Saturday Evening Post* was published on February 8, 1969.
The latest edition of *Sports Car* includes a comparison of the Fiat Spider and the Austin-Healy MGB.
Lulu DeLuca's latest novel received very poor reviews.

In informal English *last* is commonly used in place of *latest*:

The last edition of *Sports Car* includes a comparison of the Fiat Spider and the Austin-Healy MGB.

But this usage should be avoided wherever it might be ambiguous:

AMBIGUOUS: Lulu DeLuca's last novel received very poor reviews.   [This could mean that Miss DeLuca will not write another novel.]

latter, last   See **former, latter; first, last.**

lay   See **lie, lay.**

Lead   /lēd/ The introductory section of a news story, which tells the reader such important facts as *who* is concerned, *what* happened, *when*, *where*, and perhaps *how* or *why*. The lead may vary in length from one sentence to several paragraphs.

lead, led   The present tense of this verb is spelled *lead* and is pronounced to rhyme with *need*. The past tense (and past participle) is spelled *led* and rhymes with *red*:

Three different trails lead to the clearing.
Sir John Hunt led the first expedition to climb Mount Everest.
Ben's sarcastic comments have led to many heated arguments.

Leading question   A question worded in such a way that it suggests the desired or expected answer:

You won't mind if I break our date for Saturday, will you?
You need money, don't you?   [Compare: Do you need money?]

Leading questions are not permitted in a law court.

learn, teach   Nonstandard English often uses *learn* in the sense of *teach*. Standard English (formal and informal) does not:

NONSTANDARD: Janie learned me how to flirt.
STANDARD: Janie taught me how to flirt.
STANDARD: I learned how to flirt from Janie.

leave, let   A common nonstandard idiom is the use of the verb *leave* (*left, left*) where formal and informal English would use the verb *let* (*let, let*). Remember that when you mean "permit" or "allow to pass, go, or come," *let* is the verb to use:

Let him tell you the story.   [Not: *Leave* him tell you.]
My brother *let* me borrow his car.   [Not: *left* me borrow.]
The usher carefully checked our student cards before *letting* us into the museum.   [Not: before *leaving* us into the museum.]
Let me out of here!   [Not: *Leave* me out of here.]
Please *let* Jo come over for lunch today.   [Not: *leave* Jo come.]

With *alone*, however, either word is standard usage: "Leave me alone" or "Let me alone."

lengthways, lengthwise   Mean the same and are used interchangeably.

less, fewer   Formal English usually makes a distinction between these two words, using *fewer* to refer to number (to things that are counted), and *less* to refer to amount or quantity (to things that are measured):

If fewer than ten students enroll, the class will be canceled.
Fewer new cars were purchased last year than ever before.

Mayor Weeks is campaigning for more jobs and less public aid.
The Highway Department will be given less money this biennium.

In informal English *less* is commonly used in place of *fewer*:

If less than ten students enroll, the class will be canceled.
Less new cars were bought last year than ever before.

less, lesser   Both are comparatives of *little*, but they are not used interchangeably. *Less* refers to amount or quantity; *lesser*—a formal word—refers to value or importance:

We had less time than we thought.
Mrs. Gaskell is one of the lesser Victorian novelists.

let's us, let's don't   Since *let's* is a contraction of *let us*, another *us* should not be added to it. "Let's us go" is repetitive—the same as saying "Let us us go." Say "Let's go," "Let's open our presents."

In the negative, either *let's not* or *let's don't* is frequently used: "Let's not tell Mary about it." "Let's don't eat here." Though *do* in the second example is not necessary to the meaning, the expression *let's don't* is a common and well-established idiom. (The expression *don't let's*—"Don't let's get excited"—is also occasionally used; here again, *do* is unnecessary for the meaning.)

Letters   1 The form of business letters. A business letter usually has six parts. Notice the placement and punctuation of the parts:

HEADING	101 Larch Avenue Polo, Illinois 61064 June 6, 19——
INSIDE ADDRESS	Mr. Ollie Bracket Chicago Daily Star 604 N. Picasso Street Chicago, Illinois 60611
SALUTATION	Dear Mr. Bracket:
BODY	Please send me the "Fact Sheet on Home Burglar Alarms," which was offered in your column in the <u>Daily Star</u> of June 4. I am enclosing 25¢ in coin to cover the mailing costs.
CLOSING	Yours truly,
SIGNATURE	*Wendell Marks*

a) If the person to whom the letter is addressed has a title, it is included in the inside address, after his name. A rather long title may be put on a separate line below the name. (Most desk dictionaries have a special section telling the appropriate way to address mail to governors, senators, bishops, and so on.) If the letter is not directed to a particular person, the inside address consists of three lines.

```
Mr. Ferris G. Oaks              Women United, Inc.
Director of Admissions          Box 2001
Simms College                   Bangor, Maine   04401
Sitka, Alaska  99835
```

b) If the letter is not addressed to a particular person by name, one of the following salutations is generally used:

```
Dear Sir:   Dear Madam:   Gentlemen:   Ladies:
```

c) One of the conventional closings is generally used to end the letter:

```
Very truly yours,     Sincerely,     Cordially yours,
```

d) A man does not write the title *Mr.* before his signature, but a woman may write *Miss* in parentheses before her name or add her married name below her signature to indicate how she would like to be addressed in the reply:

```
Very truly yours,          Cordially yours,

(Miss) Dale Foxx           Ruth J. Norris
                           (Mrs. Henry A. Norris)
```

(See also **Ms.**)

2 The envelope.

```
Carol Prattner
211 Taft Road, Apt. 211
Orem, Texas   84057




                    Mr. J. B. Otto, Manager
                    Sugargrove Farm
                    Rural Route 2, Box 27
                    Derby, Vermont   05829
```

3 Folding the letter. A business letter, usually written on paper 8½ x 11 inches, is generally folded in one of two ways, depending on the size of the envelope.

For a long envelope—

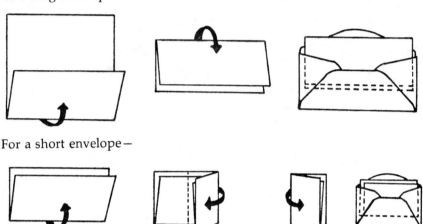

For a short envelope—

4 Kinds of business letters.

a) Letters of request or inquiry. The sample letter on page 148 requests an item; the following letter requests information:

National Conservation Organization
10 Whipple Street, N.W.
Akron, Ohio 44309

Gentlemen:

On a recent radio program I heard a member of your organization state that you were setting up a center which would provide local conservation groups with information about projects being carried on by other, similar groups. Our club has been considering several possible projects for next year. I think it would help us in our planning to study what other groups are doing. How do we go about obtaining information from the center? Is there a fee?

I will appreciate all the information you can give me about the center's services so that I can explain them clearly and completely to the club members.

Sincerely yours,
Willis High Conservation Club

Harry Rosen

Project Chairman

b) Order letters.

Grove Photo Supplies
213–215 Matthews Avenue
Des Moines, Iowa 50318

Gentlemen:

Please send me the following items, advertised in the April issue of *Popular Photography*:

1 developing tank, No. 86902	$ 2.29
1 enlarging timer, No. 73126	7.95
2 safelights, No. 77210, @ $3.95	7.90
	18.14
Postage	2.00
	$20.14

I am enclosing a cashier's check for $20.14.

Very truly yours,

(M)iss) Joann Fisher

An efficient order letter gives clearly and concisely all the information necessary for filling the order promptly and satisfactorily

c) Letters of complaint.

Essex Theater
1210 Desert Boulevard
Reno, Nevada 89502

Gentlemen:

On March 3 I sent you a money order for $10 for two main-floor tickets to *Hamlet*. I asked for seats at any Saturday matinee during the month of April. Today I received two tickets for the matinee of Wednesday, April 27.

Since I am unable to attend an afternoon performance on Wednesday, I am returning the tickets. Please replace them with tickets for a Saturday matinee. If no tickets are available for a Saturday in April, a Saturday in May will be satisfactory.

Yours truly,

Myra Valdez

A letter like this, which explains clearly and courteously what is wrong and what the writer wants done about it, is most likely to receive prompt, efficient attention.

d) Letters of application.

Mr. Joseph R. Still, Director
Camp Mapawanda
Taberg, New York 13471

Dear Mr. Still:

In this month's issue of *Outdoor* you advertised for counselors for Camp Mapawanda this summer. I believe I am qualified and would like to be considered for one of the positions.

I am eighteen years old. I will graduate from Thomas Dooley High School in June and will enter Maximus University this fall. For the past two summers I have been an assistant counselor at the Willow Creek Day Camp here. I supervised craft activities and taught swimming to beginners. I have a senior lifesaving badge and an instructor's certificate. I have been a member of my school tennis team for three years and last spring served as an assistant coach at the YMCA tennis clinic.

The following people have given me permission to use their names as references:

Mr. Morton Heinz, Athletic Director
Thomas Dooley High School
Clifton, New Jersey 07011

Mr. G. R. Griffeths
YMCA Director
4621 Prince Street
Clifton, New Jersey 07013

Miss Naomi Cohen, Principal
Thomas Dooley High School
Clifton, New Jersey 07011

Your advertisement states that you will be holding personal interviews in New York City the first weekend in April. I will be glad to come for an interview at any time that weekend. My telephone number is (201) 668-4210.

Sincerely yours,

Calvin Kurtz

Calvin Kurtz

As you can see, a letter of application should include (1) a sentence or two telling what job you are applying for and how you learned about it; (2) an explanation of your qualifications—age, education, experience, special talents that have a bearing on the work; (3) the names, positions, and addresses of two or three people to be used as references (be sure you ask their permission first); and (4) a request for a personal interview at the employer's convenience.

5 The form of personal letters. Personal letters usually have five parts. Notice the placement and punctuation of the parts:

HEADING	2215 Steger Road Topeka, Kansas 66604 July 12, 19--
SALUTATION	Dear Mrs. Robie,
BODY	You will always be one of my favorite women. When I opened that big box you sent, I let out such a loud yell that the man in the next apartment came over to check. I can't think of any way to thank you adequately for giving me your grand-father's leather-bound set of Sir Arthur Conan Doyle's works. It is one of the greatest presents a Sherlock Holmes buff could get. I promise to give the books the very best care. I have already started building special shelves for them in my room.
CLOSING	Very gratefully,
SIGNATURE	*Herb Polanski*

a) Although most salutations begin with *Dear* followed by a person's name, other salutations can be used, especially in writing to close friends and relatives:

Dearest Bob,   Hi Smarty,   Dear old Curmudgeon,   Greetings,

b) Closings also vary, depending on the writer, the message, and the person the letter is intended for:

With love,   As always,   Sincerely,   Grumpily yours,

c) On a letter to a close friend or relative, a first name—or a nickname —is usually the only signature necessary. But on a letter to someone less well known (a new friend, a teacher, a clergyman, for example), both the first and last names are generally needed.

6 Kinds of personal letters. Most personal letters are written to exchange news and ideas. But occasionally a letter or note is written for one specific purpose—to thank someone for a gift, for example (like the letter on page 153), to invite someone for a visit, to reply to such an invitation, to congratulate someone, to extend sympathy. Since this kind of letter has only one topic, it is generally brief, seldom more than a paragraph or two.

a) A note of congratulation.

Dear Harold,

Randy sent me a newspaper clipping telling about the Junior Achievement Award you won last week. I hope you felt as proud and pleased as you looked in the picture. You ought to be proud, not only of the award but also of that flourishing lamp-kit business of yours. I'm thinking of asking for a distributorship.

I know this is only the first of a long list of successes. And you can be sure that I'll be telling everyone I knew you when.

Sincerely,

James Brady

b) A sympathy note.

Dear Mrs. Randall,

I would like you to know how sorry my family and I were to hear of the death of your son. Nothing I can say can really lighten your grief, but I hope you will find some comfort in knowing that Mark will always have a place in our hearts.

Sincerely yours,

Bruce Miller

Letters of the alphabet The plural of letters of the alphabet is formed by adding either *s* or *'s*, with *'s* being preferred after all small letters and those capital letters that would be confusing if *s* alone were added:

Doesn't she know her ABCs yet?
Americans spell *traveler* with one *l*; the British use two *l*'s.
After all, he is used to getting straight A's.

Notice that a letter used only as a letter (see the second sentence) is italicized—underlined in handwriting and typing.

Levels of English usage The different kinds of English that people use can be sorted out into three major categories: *formal English, informal English,* and *nonstandard English.* Two of these kinds—formal and informal—

belong to what is called the **standard level** of English. The third kind — nonstandard — does not.

FORMAL } STANDARD
INFORMAL }

NONSTANDARD

In the following sections, each of the kinds of English will be discussed in turn. In comparing them, you will find more likenesses than differences. But each kind does have certain characteristics — or *trademarks* — that give it a different flavor and tone from the others.

1 Formal English. Formal English is the kind of English that educated people use on formal occasions. You will occasionally hear it — in sermons, graduation speeches, scholarly addresses, public speeches by government officials, and so on. But it is used more often in writing than in speaking, especially in writing meant for clergymen, doctors, lawyers, scientists, educators, and others whose interests are intellectual. You will find it in academic and technical writing (scholarly magazines, reports of experiments, certain textbooks, theses, legal papers, business reports) and also in certain literature (essays, some fiction and biography, and some poetry).

The following paragraph, discussing the concept of democracy, was written by an American historian, political scientist, and professor. It will give you a good idea of the tone of formal English.

Democracy, like liberty or science or progress, is a word with which we are all so familiar that we rarely take the trouble to ask what we mean by it. It is a term, as the devotees of semantics say, which has no "referent" — there is no precise or palpable thing or object which we all think of when the word is pronounced. On the contrary, it is a word which connotes different things to different people, a kind of conceptual Gladstone bag which, with a little manipulation, can be made to accommodate almost any collection of social facts we may wish to carry about in it. In it we can as easily pack a dictatorship as any other form of government. We have only to stretch the concept to include any form of government supported by a majority of the people, for whatever reasons and by whatever means of expressing assent, and before we know it the empire of Napoleon, the Soviet regime of Stalin, and the fascist systems of Mussolini and Hitler are all safely in the bag. But if this is what we mean by democracy, then virtually all forms of government are democratic, since virtually all governments, except in times of revolution, rest upon the explicit or implicit consent of the people. In order to discuss democracy intelligently it will be necessary, therefore, to define it, to attach to the word a sufficiently precise meaning to avoid the confusion which is not infrequently the chief result of such discussions. — Carl Becker, *Modern Democracy*, Yale University Press.

This passage illustrates many of the trademarks of formal English. The sentences are long and rather involved, as they must be to deal with the complex ideas being presented in it. It also has a scholarly and precise vocabulary: *devotees* instead of the everyday word *followers*, *palpable* instead of *observable*, *conceptual* instead of *imaginary*. Relative pronouns, often omitted in less formal writing, are used in constructions like "a word with *which* we are all so familiar" (instead of "a word we are all so familiar with") and "thing or object *which* we all think of" (instead of "thing or object we all think of"). Contractions are not used: "It is a term" (instead of "It's a term") and "We have only" (instead of "We've only"). There are also allusions (references) to history: Gladstone, the British prime minister whose traveling bag opened into two equal compartments; Napoleon; Stalin; Mussolini; and Hitler.

It is a common mistake to think that formal writing is necessarily stiff and artificial. Good formal writing is not. The example you have just read, for instance, is more dignified, more bookish than ordinary writing. It has to be read more carefully than ordinary writing. But it is not stilted or pompous. Rather, the careful word choice and sentence construction add to the richness and precision of the writer's expression.

Of course, if you use formal English inappropriately—say in a thank-you note for a birthday gift or in a conversation with friends—it will sound unnatural and ridiculously stiff. But it is highly effective where it is appropriate: (1) in discussing difficult, abstract ideas for restricted audiences, as in a literary criticism; (2) in dealing with complex technical and scientific matters, as in a medical report; (3) in speaking or writing on any occasion that calls for a dignified tone, as in a dedication speech.

Few people use formal English in their everyday affairs. In fact, there may be only a few occasions when you will find it necessary to use formal English. (You may possibly need it in an essay for a contest, a research paper, a report for a science class, a debate, a commencement address.) But you will want to be acquainted with it—either as a future member of a profession or business, or simply as a literate person who will often find pleasure in this kind of English.

2 Informal English. Informal English lies between the two extremes of formal and nonstandard English. In speaking, it is the comfortable kind of English that educated people ordinarily use. In writing, it is the speech of educated people tidied up—with an eye to pleasing the reader.

Informal English is all around you. Newspaper reports and columns, many novels and short stories, and most magazine articles are written in informal English. The following paragraph (from the autobiography of the writer) was written by Charles A. Lindbergh, the famous aviator who, in 1927, made the first nonstop flight from New York to Paris. As you read the paragraph, look for its informal trademarks. Some of these are the contractions ("I've," "I'll," "there's," "don't"); the informal vocabulary ("just to be sure" instead of "merely to ascertain," "plenty of speed" instead of "sufficient speed," "come in" instead of "approach"); short sentences, averaging thirteen words; and the conversational tone.

In spite of my speed, the *Spirit of St. Louis* seems about to stall. My lack of feel alarms me. I've never tried to land a plane without feel before. I want to open the throttle wider, to glide faster, to tauten the controls still more. But—I glance at the dial—the needle points to eighty miles an hour. The *Spirit of St. Louis* is lightly loaded, with most of its fuel gone. Even at this speed I'll overshoot the lighted area before my tail skid strikes the ground. No, I'll have to pull the nose higher instead of pushing it down. I'll have to depend on the needle, on judgment more than instinct. I kick the rudder and push the stick to one side, just to be sure— yes, controls are taut, there's plenty of speed. And feeling is not completely gone. I still have a little left. I can feel the skid and slip. But the edge of perception is dull, very dull. It's better to come in fast, even if I roll into that black area after I land. And it's better to come in high—there may be poles or chimneys at the field's edge—Never depend on obstruction lights—especially when you don't see any.—Charles A. Lindbergh, *The Spirit of St. Louis*, Charles Scribner's Sons.

As you can see, Lindbergh wrote his paragraph in about the way he would tell it to you in a conversation. In telling personal experiences, educated people generally use informal English.

Like most people, you have more everyday affairs than special occasions in your life, so you are going to need this kind of English most of the time. It is the normal language of the classroom. It is the appropriate kind of English for almost all of your personal and business letters, and for most of your social affairs. In fact, you will probably never find that informal English is really inappropriate for you (although there may be occasions in your life when formal English would be more effective). Informal English is the most important kind for you to know and to use.

3 Nonstandard English. Nonstandard English is the English used by people who have not had much formal education—or whose education has had little effect on their speech and writing. It is mainly spoken English, because the millions of people who use it do not often find it necessary to write except in personal matters. (When it does appear in print, it is usually in the dialogue of stories and plays or in comic strips.) Here we will consider a sample in print to make it easier to identify the specific characteristics of this kind of English.

The sample passage is from a book that has become a baseball classic, Ring Lardner's *You Know Me Al*. The book, subtitled "A Busher's Letters," consists of letters from a rookie pitcher, Jack Keefe, to his friend Al.

Next morning half the bunch mostly vetrans went to the ball park which isn't no better than the one we got at home. Most of them was vetrans as I say but I was in the bunch. That makes things look pretty good for me don't it Al? We tossed the ball round and hit fungos and run round and then Callahan asks Scott and Russell and I to warm up easy and pitch a few to the batters. It was warm and I felt pretty good so I warmed up pretty good. . . . So I went in and after I lobbed a few over I cut loose my fast one. Lord was to bat and he ducked out of the way and then throwed his bat to the bench. Callahan says What's the matter Harry? Lord says I forgot to pay up my life insurance. He says I ain't ready for Walter Johnson's July stuff. — Ring W. Lardner, *You Know Me Al*, Charles Scribner's Sons.

Anyone familiar with nonstandard English will recognize several colorful trademarks of this kind of English. For example, speakers of nonstandard English often use verb forms like "throwed," "don't it," and "most of them *was*." They also use many double negatives, like the "isn't no better" in this paragraph.

The use of the pronoun *I* in "then Callahan asks Scott and Russell and I to warm up" is common in nonstandard English, though *me* would be used at the standard level. (Jack also writes in other letters, "the game between *we* and the Venice Club," "*him* and I have got to be pretty good pals," and "a big man like *I* needs good food.") The use of the adjectives *easy* and *good* in "to warm up easy" and "I warmed up pretty good" and the use of *ain't* are also typical of nonstandard speech.

Another trademark of nonstandard English, although it is not especially noticeable in the quoted passage, is the overuse of slang. A user of nonstandard English is likely to have in his vocabulary two or three slang expressions of approval or disapproval, which he uses over and over again. Everything he likes is "swell" and everything he dislikes, "lousy" — or whatever the current equivalents may be. In the spoken language, pronunciation may also distinguish the nonstandard level from the standard; you have probably heard such nonstandard pronunciations as "dese," "dem," "southmore," "attackted," "ath-a-letics," and "genu-wine."

Despite what you may have learned, nonstandard English is not necessarily "bad" English. It is simply one kind of English — and it serves a great many people perfectly well. But for most educated people it is both inadequate and inappropriate. Their work and their personal interests usually involve constant use of language. They have to read and write and talk about complex matters. They have to express things exactly, and in a way that meets the approval of other educated people. For them, nonstandard English just would not do the job. So they avoid it.

4 **General usage.** In the preceding discussions of the three main kinds of English, the chief emphasis was on the differences between them — on the trademarks that set each kind off from the others. Yet, as you can see by going back over the example passages, there are actually more similarities than differences between the three kinds. In each example there are only a few words and constructions that mark the passage as nonstandard or informal or formal. The rest of the words and constructions (the major part of each passage) are in **general usage.** Everyone uses such words and

constructions, no matter what kind of English he is speaking or writing. They are always appropriate.

All writers and speakers, for instance, use the ordinary names of things—like *street, cork, house, running, jumping.* Everyone forms the plural of *friend, boy, chair, pencil,* and other regular nouns by adding *s.* All of our sentences fall into a few basic patterns: subject—verb—object, for example. The greater part of our language, then, raises no questions; it can cause you no trouble since it is always appropriate—in any situation.

(See also **Bad grammar** and **Dialect.**)

liable   See **likely, liable, apt.**

Library   See **Card catalog** and **Dewey Decimal System.**

lie, lay   Notice the distinctions between these verbs:

lie, lay, lain—"to recline," intransitive (no object)
lay, laid, laid—"to place," transitive (takes an object)

You *lie* down when you are tired. Your dog *is lying* in the corner. The golf course *lies* just outside town. You *lay* tile, *lay* your paper on the desk, *lay* your proposal before the student-faculty committee. Yesterday you *lay* down when you came home, but you *laid* your coat on a chair. The Colosseum *has lain* in ruins for centuries. Father *has laid* a trap for the fox.

Nonstandard English tends to use only the verb *lay (laid, laid)*—making it do the work of both these verbs. And sometimes in casual informal speech we use *lay* instead of *lie* in such an expression as "Lay still, Woof!" But this usage is inappropriate in careful speech and writing.

lighted, lit   Both of these forms are used as the past tense and past participle of *light:*

Pat lit a match.   We lighted only one lamp.
Tony had lit the lantern.   Everyone has lighted his taper.

When the past participle is used as an adjective preceding a noun, *lighted* is more common:

The lighted oven exploded.   Our lamp was a lighted pine cone.

like, as   **1** In formal speech and writing *as, as if,* and *as though* are used as conjunctions—to introduce clauses:

The jury was deeply moved by his plea, just as he had planned.
Many businessmen acted as if they wanted inflation to persist.
It looked as though it might snow.

Informal English often uses *like* as a conjunction in such sentences:

The jury was deeply moved by his plea, just like he had planned.

Many businessmen acted like they wanted inflation to continue.
It looked like it might snow.

But common as this usage is, it is considered inappropriate by some people. In writing, especially for certain audiences, you may want to avoid it.

   2 In both formal and informal English *like* — not *as* — is used as a preposition in phrases of comparison:

He talks like a lawyer.   This class is like a zoo.   I, like him, objected.

like for   In speech, especially in the South, *like for* is common:

SPOKEN: I'd like for you to meet my parents.

In writing, the *for* is generally omitted:

WRITTEN: The mayor's family would like him to retire at the end of his current term.   [Not: would like for him to retire.]

(See also **want**.)

likely, liable, apt   All three words may be used to suggest that something is probable. Formal English keeps the three distinct, using them with the following shades of meaning: *Likely* is used to mean simply "reasonably to be expected":

Two of the new TV shows are likely to bore the younger viewers.

Liable is used to mean "in danger of something disagreeable":

With this new injury, Eby is liable to be dropped from the team.

Apt is used to mean "tending or inclined to be":

Babies are apt to be attracted to brightly colored objects.

   Colloquially, however, *liable* and *apt* are often used in the ordinary sense of *likely*:

Two of the new TV shows are liable (*or* apt) to bore the younger viewers.

line   Expressions with *line* are often clumsy and roundabout, and should be replaced by simpler, more direct wording:

ROUNDABOUT: His political views ran along the same lines as Warren G. Harding's.
BETTER: His political views were similar to (*or* like) Warren G. Harding's.

Linguistics   The study of language, which includes such branches as phonology (dealing with sounds: phonetics and phonemics), morphology (the forms of words), syntax (the relationships of words and word groups in sentences), lexicography (the making of dictionaries), dialectology (regional and class dialects), semantics (the meaning of words and the relationship between language and thinking), usage (the use of variant word forms), rhetoric (the effective use of words), language history (the origins of words and relationships among languages).

Grammar is concerned mainly with morphology and syntax, though some grammar studies also involve phonology.

Linking verb   A verb used chiefly to connect a subject with an adjective or noun or pronoun that describes or identifies the subject:

Hesse's speech to the delegates *was* quite informative.   [Connects subject *speech* with predicate adjective *informative*.]
Piccadilly Circus *is* an enormous square in London.   [Connects subject *Piccadilly Circus* with predicate noun *square*.]
The next victim *may be* you. [Connects subject *victim* with predicate pronoun *you*.]

Be is the most common linking verb. Other verbs frequently used as linking verbs are *act, appear, become, feel, go, grow, look, run, seem, smell, taste, turn*. Remember that when they are used as linking verbs (rather than as action verbs), they are followed by adjectives, not adverbs:

None of us felt *sad* about his leaving.   [Not: *sadly*.]
We both thought the shrimp tasted *peculiar*.   [Not: *peculiarly*.]

literally   *Literally* means "word for word" (Few idiomatic expressions make sense if taken *literally*) or "without exaggeration or inaccuracy" (The Romans *literally* destroyed the ancient city of Carthage).

Literally is sometimes also used as an intensifier ("We were *literally* walking on air"; "He was *literally* petrified with fright"). But careful speakers and writers avoid this usage, especially before a figurative expression ("We were walking on air"; "He was petrified with fright").

Litotes   /lī'tə tēz'/ A type of understatement in which the writer or speaker says in negative form the opposite of what he really means:

He described his new job with no little enthusiasm.   [Meaning: He described his new job with much enthusiasm.]
Finding worthwhile items at a sale is no minor task.   [Meaning: Finding worthwhile items at a sale is a major task.]

Loaded words   Words that have strong (favorable or unfavorable) connotations for almost everyone—or for almost everyone in a particular group or area. The word *bureaucrat* is a good example. Its denotation—its basic meaning—is simply "an official of a government department." But to many people the word suggests an official who is self-important, unimaginative, lacking in initiative, indifferent to the public's welfare or opinion, and likely to delay action with endless red tape. In fact, these connotations are so strong that it is almost impossible to use the word in its strictly denotative sense.

Some other words that have acquired strongly unfavorable connotations for many people are *politician, reactionary, fascist,* and *leftist.* On the other hand, words like *peace, liberty, love, justice, democracy, underdog, loyalty,* and *freedom* are loaded with favorable connotations.

Loaded words can be dangerous. They are emotion-arousing words, and emotions can block clear thinking. Take the word *radical.* At one time it meant only "a person who holds rather extreme views on political reform." But for many people *radical* has come to suggest someone dangerous, someone who advocates violence, revolution, and even anarchy. When these people hear someone referred to as a "radical," they may unthinkingly react to the connotations of the word and view that person with extreme dislike. They forget for the moment that because a person is called a radical does not necessarily mean that he advocates violence and revolution. He may simply hold more liberal views than the person who labeled him radical.

Since loaded words can have such a strong effect on people's thinking, writers and speakers (scrupulous and unscrupulous) make frequent, and often effective, use of them in promoting various causes. For your own protection, then, it is a good idea to be on the alert for loaded words. If you are aware that they are being used, you will have a better chance of keeping them from blocking your thinking and tricking you into doing or believing something you would not otherwise do or believe.

loan　For many years considered to be only a noun (If I go to a private school, I'll have to take out a loan), *loan* is now generally used as a verb as well. In formal writing, however, many people still prefer the verb *lend*:

GENERAL:　Our country loans its allies billions of dollars yearly.
FORMAL:　Our country lends it allies billions of dollars yearly.

Localism　A word or expression used regularly in one section of a country, but not in other sections. Localisms are also called *provincialisms* or *dialectal expressions.* (See **Dialect.**)

locate　Often used to mean "settle":

My grandfather originally located in northern Kentucky.

However, this usage is generally avoided by careful writers.

Long variants　Needlessly long forms of words. Amateur writers sometimes add an extra prefix or suffix to a word that already carries the meaning they intend. They write *transportational systems,* although *transportation systems* would be clear and acceptable. They write *pacificate,* although *pacify* expresses the meaning just as completely. Some other unnecessarily long variants are:

162

bestrew for *strew*	*simplistic* when only *simple* is meant
denunciate for *denounce*	*hotness* for *heat*
quietude for *quiet*	*hesitative* for *hesitant*
orientate for *orient*	*interrelated* when only *related* is meant

Loose sentence   A sentence in which the grammatical form and the essential meaning are complete before the end:

Every day Ed practiced making basketball shots, waiting until the gym was empty at five o'clock so that no one could make fun of his awkward movements on the court.

This sentence could be stopped after "shots," "empty," "o'clock," or "movements" without destroying the sense of the main statement.

Loose sentences are typical of conversation. Used too consistently in writing, without an occasional *periodic sentence* for variety, they are likely to produce a roundabout and unemphatic style. (See **Periodic sentence.**)

lose, loose   These two words are frequently confused. Try to associate the spelling of each word with its pronunciation and meaning:

lose /lüz/ — lose your watch, lose interest in
loose /lüs/ — loose wiring, loose-fitting, come loose

lot of, lots of   Informal expressions meaning "a great number or amount":

INFORMAL: A lot of students think that to impress their teachers they have to ask lots of questions in class.
FORMAL: Many students believe that to impress their teachers they must ask a great number of questions in class.

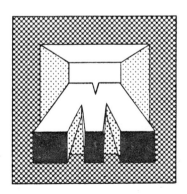

mad   Used in informal English to mean "angry":

INFORMAL: Mr. Rio is mad because no magazine will print his story.
FORMAL: Mr. Rio is angry because no magazine will print his story.

madam   A polite title used in speaking to either a married or an unmarried woman. It is often shortened to *ma'am*:

"Was your dinner satisfactory, madam?"
"Your packages will be delivered on Thursday, ma'am."

Dear Madam: is the usual salutation in a business letter to a woman whose name is not known to the writer. If the letter is to a group of women, either *Mesdames:* or *Ladies:* is used.

majority, plurality   The words *majority* and *plurality* are most frequently used in reporting voting results. When referring to a total divided into two parts, *majority*, in its original and strictest sense, means "the number of votes over half." But the word is now very often used to mean "the number by which votes cast on one side exceeds those on the other." If of 76 votes cast 45 are for a motion and 31 against, the motion is passed by a majority of 7 in the strict sense, but by a majority of 14 in the more ordinary sense.

When referring to a total divided into three or more parts, *majority* usually means "an excess of votes over all others cast"; *plurality* means "the difference between the largest number of votes and the next largest." If 5000 votes are cast, and A gets 3500, B gets 1000, and C gets 500, candidate A has a majority of 2000 and a plurality of 2500.

Majority applies only to numbers; it should not be used to mean "the greater part" of a thing:

A *majority* of the auto workers voted to strike.
Most (or *The greater part*) of the test was taken directly from the textbook. [Not: The *majority* of the test.]

Malapropism   A ridiculous misuse of words, caused by confusing two words that are similar in sound but different in meaning:

Aunt Lou said that you must be sure to visit the Leaning Tower of Pizza. [the Leaning Tower of Pisa]
This morning two hundred volunteers were abducted into the Army.   [inducted into the Army]
In 1936, Edward VIII fabricated the throne of England.   [abdicated the throne of England]
Among the auctioned items were a dozen crystal brandy sniffers. [brandy snifters]

Malapropisms are named after Mrs. Malaprop, a character in Sheridan's comedy *The Rivals*, whose amusing misuse of words has made her one of the best-known comic characters in literature.

Malapropisms are sometimes used intentionally, particularly by certain TV personalities—for humorous effect. But used unintentionally, because of not knowing the meaning of the words, they make the user seem ridiculous. Guard against them in your speech and writing by checking unfamiliar words in a dictionary to make sure of their meanings. And listen carefully to expressions you pick up from others, to make sure of the words. *Shrewd* may sound like *rude*, but the expression is "a rude awakening"—not "a shrewd awakening."

man, woman Now generally preferred to the more pretentious *gentleman* and *lady*, unless a note of special courtesy or respect is wanted. The original social distinctions between *man* and *gentleman*, *woman* and *lady* seem to have practically disappeared in general American usage. At times, in fact, it seems that the distinctions have been reversed; statements like "The women in the club need a lady to clean up after the party" and "The gentleman who owns the vegetable stand said that this man tried to help the injured child" are quite common.

Ladies and gentlemen is the customary formal expression in addressing an audience.

Mass nouns, count nouns Nouns referring to things that can be measured or weighed, like sugar, oil, coal, are sometimes called *mass* nouns. Nouns referring to things that can be counted, like coins, eggs, coats, are called *count* nouns.

(See **amount, number.**)

math A colloquial clip for *mathematics*. Like other clipped words (*flu* for *influenza*, *taxi* or *cab* for *taxicab*, *copter* for *helicopter*), *math* is written without an apostrophe or period. In formal English the full form should be used.

may, can See **can, may.**

may be, maybe *May be* is a verb form; *maybe* (a shortening of *it may be*) is an adverb meaning "possibly; perhaps":

VERB: Winslow may be right for once.
ADVERB: Maybe Nancy will lend you her flapper costume.

may of In speech the words *may have* are often spoken so rapidly that they sound like *may of*. In writing, they should be spelled correctly: *may have* or *may've*—never *may of*.

The same is true of all other verb phrases with *have*. Write *should have* or *should've* (not *should of*), *would have* or *would've*, etc.

me See **It's me** and **between you and me.**

measles Plural in form, but generally used with a singular verb:

Measles *is* a common childhood disease.

Mechanics of writing   The technical part of writing, including such things as spelling, punctuation, forms of words, order of words, and sentence structure (as distinguished from the style, content, and organization).

medium   The singular is *medium*; the plural is *mediums* or *media*. The plural *media* is generally used in scientific writing and in referring to the *mass media* (the various forms of mass communication taken together).

You will occasionally see and hear the form *medias* used as the plural. But careful writers and speakers avoid this usage:

Television and radio were the primary *media* used.   [Not: *medias.*]

They also avoid the use of *media* as a singular:

Television was the only *medium* he mentioned.   [Not: *media.*]

Messrs.   The abbreviation of the French *messieurs* (meaning "men; gentlemen") is generally pronounced as English /mes'ərz/. It is now chiefly used as the plural of *Mr.*:

As of Monday, Messrs. Kneer and Hull will be working with us.

Metaphor   A figure of speech in which a comparison is implied rather than distinctly stated:

To our right lay the pond, *a swatch of shimmering black satin.*   [The writer means that the pond resembled a small piece of smooth, shiny, black satin cloth.]

(Compare **Simile.**)

Metonymy   /mə ton'ə mē/ A figure of speech in which the name of something closely associated with a thing is substituted for its name:

At an early age, he felt drawn to the *pulpit.*   [That is, he felt drawn to a career in the ministry.]
Buckingham Palace is not expected to issue a statement on the matter. [That is, the British monarch is not.]

(Compare **Synecdoche.**)

Misplaced modifiers   Sometimes a modifier is put in such a position in a sentence that the reader misunderstands what the writer is trying to say. For example, in "Jess decided to apologize for insulting Phil yesterday morning," *yesterday morning* seems to modify *insulting* — that is, that Phil had been insulted yesterday morning. But the meaning the writer intended was that Jess had decided to apologize yesterday morning, not that he had insulted Phil then. To make this meaning clear, the writer should move the modifying phrase away from the wrong word and closer to the word it does modify: "Yesterday morning Jess decided to apologize for insulting Phil."

Sometimes a modifier seems to modify a word it could not sensibly modify:

Swaying to and fro on a silken thread suspended from the ceiling, Millie saw the spider.

To most readers this sentence would sound a bit ridiculous; they would be amused at the thought of Millie "swaying to and fro on a silken thread." Though the writer's intended meaning is obvious even with the misplaced modifier, the sentence could easily be improved by moving the phrase closer to the word that it is clearly intended to modify:

Millie saw the spider swaying to and fro on a silken thread suspended from the ceiling.

(For further examples, see **Ambiguity**, section 2; **Dangling modifiers**; and **Squinting modifiers**.)

miss, misses   The title *Miss* (with a capital M) is always used with a name: *Miss Jenkins, Miss Emily Butler*. The noun *miss* (spelled with a small *m*) is used without a name as a term of address: "Have you been waited on, miss?"

Misses is the plural title: *the Misses Swanson and Wright*. When the misses are from the same family, formal English refers to them as *the Misses Rausch;* informal English often uses *the Miss Rausches*.

Mixed figure of speech   Combining two figures of speech that are inconsistent or incongruous produces a "mixed figure." More often than not, such a figure ruins the effect of what otherwise might be a colorful piece of writing:

That morning his motorcycle, purring with pleasure, raced across the beach like a wild stallion.   [A stallion does not purr.]

Modals   The auxiliary verbs *can, could, may, might, shall, should, will, would, must* (used with a main verb to express certain shades of meaning) are sometimes called *modals*. (See **Auxiliary verb**.)

Modifiers   Words or groups of words that restrict, limit, or make more exact the meaning of other words. In the following examples the italicized words modify the words in small capitals:

a nervous, high-pitched GIGGLE   *a royal* PURPLE
the BOY *in the first row*   *sickeningly* SWEET
TIME *to kill*   *scorching* HOT

Jim *frequently* USHERS *at the band concerts*.
Pleased by Miss Walter's compliment, my little SISTER *blushed*.

We'd welcome ANYONE *who is willing to roll up his sleeves and work.*
THINK *twice before you make such a serious accusation.*

The modifiers of nouns and pronouns are usually adjectives, participles, adjective phrases, and adjective clauses. The modifiers of verbs, adjectives, and adverbs are adverbs, adverb phrases, and adverb clauses. (For discussions of the different modifiers, see the various entries.)

Money   1 In ordinary writing (especially in a formal style), sums of money that can be expressed in two words are usually spelled out; others are put in figures:

A few years ago, paperbacks never cost more than fifty cents.
On a twenty-four dollar item, the sales tax is ninety-six cents.
That same coat sells for $39.95 at the wholesale store in town.
My brother's new car cost $3250.

If two or more sums are used in a sentence and only one can be expressed in two words, all are written in figures:

Ned has saved only $35, but he plans to have $125 by Easter.

In technical, statistical, or business writing, exact sums are written in figures (even if they could be expressed in one or two words):

42 cents   42¢ $.42
Burlap curtains are on sale for $6 a pair.
The metal containers are $7.00; the wooden ones are $3.98.

Round sums (approximate sums in even units of hundreds or thousands) are usually spelled out:

The Koan Company grosses almost six million dollars a year.
A round-trip ticket to Denver costs about two hundred dollars.

2 When the sum is used as an adjective modifier, it is generally spelled out (with a hyphen):

Burns College has given Liz a nine-hundred-dollar scholarship.
My brother needed a thousand-dollar loan to buy his car.
No one has ever guessed that this is a three-dollar ring.

(See **Numbers.**)

Months   Except in reference books (where saving space is important) and in the headings of informal letters (where abbreviations may be used), the preferred usage is to write out in full the names of months:

Both Thomas Jefferson and John Adams died on July 4, 1826.
Mrs. Willoughby will be in Paris from August 1 to November 30.
His first book was published in May 1967.   [Or: in May, 1967.]

(See **Dates.**)

Mood   The form of a verb that indicates how the speaker or writer regards the sentence. A verb in the indicative mood shows that the sentence is regarded as a statement or question about an actuality: "Ted *bought* seven candy bars." A verb in the imperative mood shows that the statement is regarded as a command: "*Share* that candy with your little brother, Ted." A verb in the subjunctive mood shows that the statement (or clause) is regarded as doubtful, improbable, or contrary to fact: "If I *were feeling* better, I'd have a piece myself." (See also **Indicative mood, Imperative mood, Commands and requests, Subjunctive.**)

morale, moral   Watch the spelling of these words when you use them. *Morale* (with an *e*) refers to mental and emotional attitudes of cheerfulness, confidence, courage, enthusiasm, etc.:

As the number of casualties dropped, the morale of the troops climbed.

As a noun, *moral* (without an *e*) refers to the teaching or lesson to be learned from a story, experience, or event:

The moral of Aesop's fable about the sun and the wind is "Persuasion is better than force."

Morals—used in the plural only—refers to habits or principles with respect to right or wrong conduct.

Morpheme   A linguistic term used to refer to any of the smallest meaningful units of language. A morpheme may be a word like *war* or *boy* or *walk*. Or it may be a word part or word element that can be combined with other elements or words, like the *anti-* of *antiwar*, the *-ish* and *-ness* of *boyishness*, or the *-ed* and *-ing* of *walked* and *walking*.

most, almost   In colloquial English *most* is commonly used as a clipped form of *almost*:

This year the Bocks made most every ornament for their tree.
Mr. Lutz most always has time to listen to our problems.

Though common in speech, this usage is inappropriate in writing, except in reporting conversation. Otherwise, use *almost*: *almost every, almost always, almost anyone, almost all*

mostly   An adverb meaning "for the most part; mainly; chiefly":

The members of the tour, mostly middle-aged women, were thrilled with everything they saw.

It is not appropriate as a substitute for *most* meaning "in or to the highest degree":

The people *most* affected by the new tax are the owners of small businesses. [Not: The people *mostly* affected.]

Mr., mister   The title *Mr.* (generally abbreviated) is always used with a man's name or the name of his office: *Mr. Ellis, Mr. G. Fitzgerald Higgins, Mr. Mayor, Mr. Chairman.* The noun *mister*, meaning "sir," is a colloquial form of address. It is written out in full and not capitalized: "Check your oil, mister?" In formal English *sir* would be used instead. (See **Messrs.**)

Mrs., missis   The title *Mrs.* is always used with a name: *Mrs. Omachi, Mrs. Jeffrey Woodruff, Mrs. Ruth Cohen.* The noun *missis* (or *missus*), meaning "wife" or "woman in charge of a household," is not appropriate in writing except to represent dialectal usage: "My missis sings in the church choir." "You'll have to ask the missis."

The title *Mrs.* should not be combined with a husband's title. Good usage calls for *Mrs. Lynch*, not *Mrs. Professor Lynch* or *Mrs. Dr. Lynch.* (See **madam** and **Ms.**)

MS.   *MS.* (also written *Ms.* and *ms.*) is the conventional abbreviation for *manuscript* — an author's copy of his work in handwriting or typewriting. (The plural forms are *MSS., Mss.,* and *mss.*)

Ms.   *Ms.* (generally pronounced /miz/) has started to appear before women's names in addresses. Like *Mr.*, which is used before the names of married and unmarried men, *Ms.* is used before the names of both married and unmarried women. Not surprisingly, the use of *Ms.* has been promoted by the movement for increased women's rights and adopted by business firms who find it useful when they do not know the marital status of a woman they are addressing.

must   Ordinarily used as an auxiliary verb (I must call Jane today), *must* is also used as a noun meaning "something necessary or vital" and as an adjective meaning "demanding attention or doing; necessary":

NOUN: The ad said Acme's Keyhole Cleaner is a must for every home.
ADJECTIVE: For a college student, typing is virtually a must skill.

mutual, common   Many careful speakers and writers distinguish between these two words, using *mutual* to mean "each to the other; done, said, or felt by each toward the other" and *common* to mean "shared equally by each or all of a group":

The first time they met, Barbara and Ellen felt a strong mutual dislike. [Each disliked the other.]
Only their common interest in history kept the two men from becoming enemies.   [Each was interested in history; it was an interest they shared in common.]

But in general usage *mutual* is used not only to mean "each to the other" but also "shared in common":

Only their mutual interest in history kept the two men from becoming enemies.

I keep track of Marv's whereabouts through our mutual friends.

myself   **1** As a reflexive pronoun, *myself* is used as the object of the verb or of a preposition in a sentence whose subject is *I*:

I congratulated myself.   [Direct object.]
I made myself a new dress.   [Indirect object.]
There I sat, muttering to myself.   [Object of preposition.]

2 As an intensive pronoun, *myself* is used for emphasis:

I myself saw Marty hit Phil.
I suppose I'll have to mail the invitations myself.

Note: The usage facts above apply as well to other reflexive pronouns — *yourself, himself, herself*, etc.

3 In nonstandard and some colloquial English *myself* is used instead of *I* as the second part of a compound subject, but not in good written style:

NONSTANDARD AND COLLOQUIAL: Henry and *myself* volunteered to help.
WRITTEN: Henry and *I* volunteered to help.

In informal English *myself* is sometimes used instead of *me* as the second part of a compound object:

The police questioned Nancy and *myself* about the accident.
No one was in the lobby except the janitor and *myself*.

Though this usage is common in both speech and writing, many people avoid it and would use *me* instead:

The police questioned Nancy and *me* about the accident.
No one was in the lobby except the janitor and *me*.

namely and other introductory words   **1** Introductory expressions like *namely, viz., i.e., e.g.* are found chiefly in reference books and in rather formal expository writing. They are out of place in other kinds of writing, where less formal expressions — *for example, for instance, that is,* and *such as* — would be more appropriate. Often in informal writing it is most effective to omit a specific introductory word and simply give the examples, setting them off with a colon or a dash:

His shelves held a wide assortment of books: [such as] historical novels, biographies of famous athletes, collections of works on surrealist painters, the comedies of Shakespeare.
There is only one way to impress Matt — [namely,] by beating him in a game of chess.

2 The punctuation used with these introductory words varies, depending on the kind of construction the words introduce. When the introductory word is followed by a clause, a semicolon or a colon is used:

Tom's knowledge of Spanish is rather limited; that is, he can understand it but cannot speak it.
After three hours of discussion, the officers could agree on only one thing: namely, that no one with less than a C+ average would be eligible for membership.

When the introductory word is not followed by a clause, either a dash or a comma is used:

A number of adjectives with the negative prefix *un-* have no affirmative counterparts in current usage — for example, *uncouth, unkempt, unscathed,* and *unspeakable.*
The local zoo recently acquired a wallaby, that is, a miniature kangaroo.

The introductory expression *such as* is not followed by a comma:

Many of their daily necessities, such as [ ] flour and rice, had to be imported.

Names   In factual writing — for instance, in news items for the school paper — you should be careful to have the right names for people, places, and titles. Common courtesy demands that you spell the names correctly.
But in imaginative writing, you should use made-up names rather than the names of real people (except, of course, if you use them by accident). Here care must be taken to choose names to fit the characters, names that sound like real names of people. The names should be interesting, but not conspicuously odd. If you have trouble thinking of names, look through newspapers and books, and study the names of people around you. (See **Cities** and **Given names**.)

nature   Often deadwood that could be omitted with no loss in meaning:

Many hamsters are [of an] affectionate [nature].
To succeed in business, a person must be ambitious [by nature].

N.B., n.b. An abbreviation of the Latin *nota bene,* meaning "note well (what follows)." It is used mainly in technical and scholarly writing, although even there the English word *note* ("Note that . . ." or "Note:") is becoming more common.

necessary Verbs like *must* and *have to* are often more direct and emphatic (though sometimes less courteous) than a construction with *necessary*:

INDIRECT: It is necessary that all graduating seniors be measured for their caps and gowns by the end of this week.
DIRECT: All graduating seniors must be measured for their caps and gowns by the end of this week.

necessity The idiom is *necessity of doing* (or *for doing*) something — not *necessity to do* something:

Until the accident, I did not see the necessity *of* (or *for*) driving slowly on icy streets.

Need is more concise than *necessity*:

Until the accident, I did not see the need of driving slowly on icy streets.

need, needs Although these are both third person singular forms of the verb *need,* they are used in different ways. *Needs* is the form in affirmative statements:

She needs to practice her lines a few more times.

Need not and *does not need* are used in negative statements:

FORMAL: She need not practice her lines any more.
INFORMAL: She does not need to practice her lines any more.

In questions *need* or *does . . . need* is used:

FORMAL: Need he tell the same dull stories every time we see him?
INFORMAL: Does he need to tell the same dull stories every time we see him?

negotiate Generally used to mean "arrange terms for":

They finally agreed to negotiate a treaty in Istanbul.

Negotiate is also used to mean "get past or over":

He put the car in low gear to negotiate the steep hill.

Although this usage is generally acceptable, many careful users of English would avoid it.

neither See **either, neither** and **Correlative conjunctions.**

never *Never* means "not ever; at no time." It should not be used when you simply mean *not*:

Poor Dad didn't even have time to read the sports page this morning. [Not: Dad never even had time.]

(See also **Double negative.**)

Newspaper English Good newspaper English is simply informal English applied to the recording and interpreting of events. It places a premium on accuracy and directness in telling a story, and is written to be read easily and quickly. The essential information — who, what, when, where, why — is usually given first, with details coming later. (See **Lead.**)

Sensationalism, oversimplification, and the overuse of "big words" and trite expressions are characteristic of a careless style of newswriting called *journalese*.

nice In formal English *nice* means "exact; discriminating":

A tightrope walker must have a nice sense of balance.

Nice is also used as a counter word showing approval, with such a wide range of possible meanings that it is of little use in writing. In your written work, substitute a more exact modifier wherever you can. (See **Adjective,** section 3.)

Nicknames Nicknames are generally out of place in formal writing. In informal writing — where they are appropriate, especially in narratives — they should be used naturally, without quotation marks or other signs of apology.

no-account Colloquially used as a compound adjective: her *no-account* brother-in-law. In formal English, *worthless* or *shiftless* would be used: her *worthless* brother-in-law.

nohow Used as an adverb in nonstandard English:

NONSTANDARD: I tried hard, but I couldn't impress her nohow.
STANDARD: I tried hard, but I couldn't impress her at all.

Nominative absolute See **Absolute phrases.**

Nominative case A noun or pronoun that is used as the subject or predicate complement of a verb is said to be in the nominative case:

Becky and *I* collected twenty dollars this afternoon.
Mrs. Lewis, who gave five hundred dollars last year, is this year's *chairman*.

I, you, he, she, it, we, you, they are the nominative forms of the personal pronouns; *who, which,* and *that,* of the relative pronouns.

174

Nonce word   A word that is made up for a particular occasion and is not used again. If, in telling about an acquaintance who habitually repeated the last few words of anything said to him, you remarked that he "suffered from echoitis," *echoitis* would be a nonce word.

none, no one   *None* may be either singular or plural, depending on the meaning intended:

None of her work *is* satisfactory.   [No part of it is.]
There were twenty questions, and none of them *were* easy.   [No questions in the group were easy.]
None of the horses in the show *was* as good a jumper as Royal Turk. [Not a single one was as good.]

When *none* tells how many, a plural verb is generally used, unless the idea of "not a single one" is to be emphasized (as in the third example).
    No one is singular. It is often used instead of *none*, for emphasis:

No one of them really *understands* the problems.
No one of those clerks *deserves* a promotion.

Nonrestrictive modifiers   Modifiers that are used not to identify the word they modify but merely to add a descriptive or explanatory detail. Nonrestrictive modifiers are set off from the word they modify:

The twins, *scared by Uncle Ed's ghost story*, didn't sleep a wink.
Kitty, *who can't remember dates*, wants to be a history teacher.
The hamburgers, *which were covered with grease*, made Jim sick.

(For discussion, see **Restrictive and nonrestrictive.**)

Nonstandard English   The kind of English used by people who do not have much formal education or have not been much affected by the schooling they did have. For examples and an explanation of why this kind of English is not appropriate for general use, see **Levels of English usage,** section 3.

no place   Colloquially used for *nowhere*:

COLLOQUIAL: My coat was no place in sight, but I did find my tie.
WRITTEN: My coat was nowhere in sight, but I did find my tie.

not hardly, not scarcely   See **Double negative.**

not only . . . but also   See **Correlative conjunctions.**

notorious, famous   *Notorious* means "widely known, but in an unfavorable way" (a notorious jewel thief); *famous* means "widely known for accomplishment or excellence" (a famous explorer).

Noun   A word used as the name of a person, place, thing, quality, action, or idea:

COMMON NOUNS: chemist, garden, nail, width, revolution, truth
PROPER NOUNS: Pablo Casals, Idaho, Lake Superior, the Alamo

Noun clause   A group of words with a subject and verb that is used in a sentence in the same way **as** a noun is used:

SUBJECT: *What we need now* is something to distract her attention.
PREDICATE COMPLEMENT: That is not *what you said the first time.*
DIRECT OBJECT: Mike promised *that he would drive more carefully.*
INDIRECT OBJECT: Give *whoever volunteers* a pamphlet and a badge.
OBJECT OF PREPOSITION: Terry will be satisfied with *whatever you can afford to pay him.*
APPOSITIVE: Linda's suggestion, *that we sponsor a bake sale*, was voted down by the boys.

Noun markers   The words *a, an,* and *the* are sometimes called "noun markers" or "noun determiners" because they signal that a noun is coming:

A *committee* of tenants drew up **an** eight-page *list* of **the** most urgently needed *repairs.*

Other words—for example, *my, your, his, our, their, this, that, some, few*—can also serve as noun markers: **his** *schedule,* **this** important *matter,* **some** rather disappointing *results.*

no use   An informal idiom for *of no use:*

INFORMAL: Since I can't swim, scuba gear is no use to me.
FORMAL: Since I cannot swim, scuba gear is of no use to me.

nowhere near   Used mainly in informal English, especially in speech:

INFORMAL: His second book was nowhere near as good as his first.
FORMAL: His second book was not nearly as good as his first.

nowheres   A nonstandard form of *nowhere.*

Number   The form of a noun, pronoun, or verb that shows it to be singular or plural in meaning. (See **Plurals of nouns.**)

number   *A number,* meaning "several" or "many," takes a plural verb; *the number* takes a singular verb:

A number of valuable rings *were missing* from the display.
The number of birds approaching extinction *is* frightening.

(See also **amount, number.**)

Numbers   **1** In ordinary writing, numbers that can be expressed in one or two words are generally spelled out; other numbers are usually written in figures:

Jean and Larry bought four quarts of eggnog for the party.
Despite the snow, thirty-one members of the class were in school.
Martin had memorized 252 definitions for the geography test.
We expect to cycle 175 miles over the weekend.

The form in which numbers are written should be consistent. If one of two or more numbers in a sentence cannot be expressed in two words or less, figures should be used for all:

When my uncle returned from Europe, he gave me 132 English pennies, 47 Belgian francs, and 8 German marks.

2 In statistical, technical, or business writing, figures are generally used, since expressing dimensions, weights, totals, distances, sums, and measures in figures makes it easier for the reader to work with the numbers:

8 ounces	68 percent	10 barrels
74 long tons	98.6 degrees	7 gallons
18 carats	2 by 4 feet	52 pecks
5 cups	125 meters	548 m.p.h.
36 yards	18 acres	29 knots

3 A number at the beginning of a sentence should be written out:

Six hundred twenty-seven children signed up for swimming lessons.
Seventy percent of the children are beginners.

If writing out the number is awkward, rephrase the sentence so as to change the position of the number:

AWKWARD: Fifty-two thousand, nine hundred and twenty-six people attended the final game of this year's World Series.
IMPROVED: The attendance at the final game of this year's World Series was 52,926.

4 The plural of figures is made by adding either an apostrophe and *s* or an *s* alone:

Were those funny squiggles really 3's?
Those aren't 6s; they're 8s.

5 *Arabic numerals* (1, 54, 326) are generally used when numbers are written in figures rather than in words. But there are a few instances in which *Roman numerals* (I, LIV, CCCXXVI) are preferred—for example, to differentiate kings, emperors, and popes with the same names (Louis XIV, Henry V, John XXIII); to differentiate male members of the same family with identical names (Adlai E. Stevenson III, John D. Rockefeller

IV); to differentiate the preliminary pages of a book from the body, which is numbered separately in Arabic numerals; and occasionally to number the sections of an outline, the chapters of a book, or the acts of a play. Otherwise Roman numerals are seldom used today; Arabic numerals are preferred.

6 *Cardinal numbers*, numbers used to tell how many, are written either in figures or in words (1, 2, 3, 15, twenty-five, fifty-six). *Ordinal numbers*, numbers used to indicate order or position, are generally written out (first, second, third, twenty-fifth) rather than abbreviated (1st, 2nd, 3rd, etc.).

The *-ly* adverb forms of the ordinals (firstly, secondly, etc.) are considered rather old-fashioned and are seldom used. The simple forms — without the *-ly* — are used both as adjectives (the first man) and as adverbs (First open the door).

(See also **Dates, Fractions, Money.**)

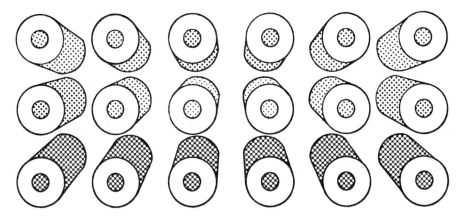

O, oh   *O* is ordinarily used with a noun in direct address. It is always capitalized; but since it is so closely related to the words used with it, it is not followed by a mark of punctuation:

Do not be angry with us, O noble prince.

Oh is an independent exclamation that may be followed by either a comma or an exclamation mark, depending on the stress wanted. It is capitalized at the beginning of a sentence, but not when used within the sentence:

Oh, why worry about it now?   Oh! My wallet is gone!
I kept quiet but, oh, how I longed to tell him off.

Object   See **Direct object, Indirect object, Object of preposition.**

Objective and subjective writing   A writer whose purpose is mainly to present facts about a topic and who does not let emotion or personal prejudice influence his statements is said to have an *objective* point of view and to be writing *objectively*. Good scientific and technical writing — most serious exposition, in fact — is objective.

If the writer's purpose is to present the topic from a personal point of view, and he emphasizes his feelings and opinions instead of presenting only the plain facts, he is said to have a *subjective* point of view and to be writing *subjectively*. Lyric poetry, informal essays, and autobiographies are almost always subjective.

Objective case   A noun (or its equivalent) that is used as the direct or indirect object of a verb, as the object of a preposition, or as an objective complement is said to be in the objective case:

DIRECT OBJECT: You had better take his *temperature*.
INDIRECT OBJECT: Gordon left the *waiter* a big tip.
OBJECT OF PREPOSITION: The man on the *roof* shouted at *us*.
OBJECTIVE COMPLEMENT: They named the baby *Samantha*.

Nouns do not have a special form for the objective case; the same form is used for both the nominative and the objective case. The personal pronouns (*I, he, she, we, they*) and the relative and interrogative pronoun *who* have separate forms for the objective case: *me, him, her, us, them*, and *whom*.

Objective complement   The direct object of certain verbs — *think, find, consider, elect, name*, and *paint*, for example — is often followed by an adjective or another noun. This word, the *objective complement*, explains or describes the direct object:

Most music critics found the new opera *dull*.   [Tells what the critics found the opera to be.]
Her parents thought her a *genius*.   [Tells what her parents thought her to be.]

Object of preposition   A noun or pronoun (or a phrase or clause used as a noun) whose relationship to some other word in the sentence is shown by the preposition:

Bart draped one leg over the *end table*.   [Noun — object of *over*.]
Pat felt he could save money by *buying a used car*.   [Gerund phrase — object of *by*.]
Just pretend to agree with *whatever he says*.   [Noun clause — object of *with*.]

oblivious of, oblivious to   When used to mean "forgetful; lacking remembrance," *oblivious* is followed by *of*:

The doctor predicted that when Kay regained consciousness, she would be oblivious of the accident.

When used to mean "unmindful; heedless; unaware," *oblivious* is followed by either *of* or *to*:

An unsociable man himself, Mr. Armand was oblivious of the neighbors' snubs.
He was oblivious to their dislike.

Obsolete   Dictionaries use the label *Obsolete* (often abbreviated *Obs.*) for a word or a particular meaning of a word that is no longer used in ordinary speech or writing, but exists in earlier writings: *hardiment* meaning "a bold deed," *wanhope* meaning "despair," *wlatsom* meaning "disgusting," *gleek* meaning "sneer," *smoterlich* meaning "disreputable," *to transport* in the sense of "to kill."

o'clock   Usually added only to the actual hour: *nine o'clock*, but *ten to seven, two-fifteen, a quarter to twelve, half-past one*. Do not forget the apostrophe in spelling *o'clock*. *O'clock* is generally not used with the abbreviations *a.m.* and *p.m.* or after figures.

-oe-   See **-ae-, -oe-.**

of   1 *Of* is often used to show possession: property *of* the state (the *state's* property), the jewels *of* the queen (the *queen's* jewels). (See **Possessive case.**)
   2 In colloquial English *of* is often used in the unnecessary doubling of prepositions: *inside of, outside of, off of. Inside of* and *outside of* also are used in informal writing, but not *off of*:

Mr. Wetzel got off [of] the bus at State and Main.

(See also **inside of,** for its use as applied to time.)
   3 The colloquial contraction *'ve* (for *have*) is sometimes carelessly written *of*:

He *should've* apologized at once.   [Not: *should of.*]
I *must've* misunderstood her directions.   [Not: *must of.*]

off of   Nonstandard for *from* in a sentence like this:

NONSTANDARD: Rex borrowed ten dollars *off of* me this morning.
STANDARD: Rex borrowed ten dollars *from* me this morning.

oh   See **O, oh.**

OK, O.K.   Business and informal English for "correct; all right" and "approval":

Everything he said sounded OK to me.
We have Coach Smith's OK to use the gym this Monday.

The verb forms are *OK, OK'd, OK'ing* (or *O.K.'d,* etc.):

Since the manager was not in, his secretary OK'd the requisition.

OK is sometimes spelled *okay. Oke* and *okeydoke* are slang.

Omission in a quotation   Indicated by marks of ellipsis (. . .). (See **Ellipsis,** section 1.)

on account of   Used colloquially in some localities for *because*:

LOCAL: Harvey was annoyed on account of we were late.
GENERAL AND WRITTEN: Harvey was annoyed because we were late.

one   1 In formal speech and writing the pronoun *one* is used to mean people in general:

At times *one* should keep *one's* thoughts to *oneself.*

But to avoid the unpleasant repetition of *one* within a sentence, *he, his, him* (or *she, her*) are often used:

At times *one* should keep *his* thoughts to *himself.*

2 General usage prefers *we* or *you* to the impersonal and more formal *one*:

At times *we* should keep *our* thoughts to *ourselves.*
You never know when *your* words will return to haunt *you.*

(For further discussion, see **you.**)
3 *One* and *ones* are often used to avoid repeating a preceding noun:

I can get you either a new copy or a used one.
Fill out three pink forms and two yellow ones.

4 In many sentences *one* is deadwood, taking attention away from the important word, and should be omitted in writing:

The story of his life is [a] fascinating [one].

(See also **every and its compounds,** section 2.)

one another   See **each other, one another.**

one of those who   The verb in the relative clause following *one of those who* (or *which* or *that*) agrees in number with the antecedent of the pronoun *who*:

She is the only one of those cheerleaders who *understands* football. [Singular verb; the antecedent of *who* is *one.*]
Lenny is one of those people who *take* offense at the slightest criticism. [Plural verb; the antecedent of *who* is *people.*]

181

In informal speech a singular verb is sometimes used in sentences like the second, since the idea uppermost in the speaker's mind is singular: "Lenny is one of those people who *takes* offense at the slightest criticism."

(For further examples, see **Agreement,** section 1j.)

only   Careful users of English put *only* (and adverbs like *almost, even, hardly, scarcely, just, nearly*) right before the word or words it modifies:

I had only ten minutes to rewrite the entire speech.

In general usage, however, *only* is often placed before the verb:

I only had ten minutes to rewrite the entire speech.

Whenever the intended meaning of a written sentence might not be clear because of the position of the adverb, it should be moved or the sentence should be rewritten:

AMBIGUOUS: The spy almost fooled everyone with his clever disguise.
CLEAR: The spy fooled almost everyone with his clever disguise.
CLEAR: Everyone was almost fooled by the spy's clever disguise.

Onomatopoeia   See **Imitative words.**

onto, on to   *Onto*, written solid, is a preposition:

The cat leaped onto the table and inspected the cake.
Alice drove the car onto the ferry.

When *on* is an adverb and *to* a preposition, they are written as two words:

The next day the expedition continued on to Nepal.
Ignoring the hecklers, the speaker went on to his next point.

or   A coordinating conjunction that connects words, phrases, or clauses of equal grammatical value:

WORDS: Send us a check or money order for $5.98.
PHRASES: I don't know whether they are for him or against him.
CLAUSES: Put up or shut up!

Two subjects joined by *or* take a singular verb when each is singular, a plural verb when both are plural:

An aspirin or a cold tablet often *helps* me stop sneezing.
Aspirins or cold tablets often *help* me stop sneezing.

When one subject is plural and the other singular, the verb agrees with the one standing nearer:

A green salad or mixed vegetables *go* well with roast beef.

Mixed vegetables or a green salad *goes* well with roast beef.

(For further examples, see **Agreement**, section 1c.)

-or, -our   American spelling prefers *-or* in words like *honor* and *vigor*; British spelling, *-our* (*honour*, *vigour*). In your writing, use the American spelling except when quoting from British writings or referring to British institutions like the Ministry of Labour. (See also **American and British usage.**)

oral, verbal   Strictly, *oral* means "spoken," and *verbal* means "in words, spoken or written." But *verbal* has been used so often in the limited sense of "spoken words" that dictionaries list "oral" as one meaning of *verbal*: *an oral agreement* and *a verbal agreement* mean the same.

The opposite of both *oral* and *verbal* is *written*:

The sales department will accept verbal orders, but they prefer written ones.

Ordinal numbers   See **Numbers,** section 6.

Originality   Originality in writing means saying something new or saying something old in a new way.

Since you are an individual and differ in your thinking and observations, even if slightly, from all other people, saying something new is merely a matter of presenting your own ideas, rather than someone else's. If you say or write what you yourself believe, have observed, or think, instead of copying what other people before you have reported, you are bound to obtain a degree of originality.

Saying something in a new way is difficult; it may often seem to you that every possible effective expression has already been used numberless times by others. It is perhaps best not to try too hard to be original, for doing so generally results in strained, affected language. Concentrate instead on an accurate choice of words and the use of figures of speech based on your own observations, and you will find that originality often appears as a by-product. (See also **Figures of speech.**)

In general, do not let the feeling that you should be original worry you unduly in your writing. Let originality come naturally, as the result of clear thinking and accurate observation, rather than trying to force it to appear.

other   *Other* is used in a comparison of things in the same class, but not in a comparison of things of different classes:

We spent more money in New York *than in any other* city we visited. [Same class.]
My pet skunk is more loyal *than any* dog.   [Different classes.]

183

If *other* were omitted in the first sentence, the statement would be illogical, since "any city" would include New York itself.

Other is not used with a superlative:

Backing up was the hardest of all the things I had to learn about driving. [Not: of *all the other* things; of *any other* thing.]

(See also **Faulty comparisons.**)

ought　See **had ought.**

Outline form　An outline is a general plan of the material that has been or is to be presented in a speech or paper. The outline shows the order of the various topics, the relative importance of each, and the relationship between the various parts. Outlines are useful in studying material assigned for reading, since in an outline you can give in a clear, concise form an overall view of the subject. But the chief value of outlines is to help you in planning talks or papers of your own.

There are three main types of outlines that you will find useful in preparing papers and talks of various kinds:

1 Work outline. For most of the papers you write or talks you give, an elaborate outline with parallel heads and subheads is not necessary. For a short paper, it is often sufficient merely to list the main topic to be discussed in each paragraph. This type of outline helps you to remember paragraph divisions as well as the main ideas you wish to cover; the details can be filled in as you write the paper itself. Or, if you are planning a longer paper or talk, you may wish to include both topics and subtopics in your outline. Since a work outline is not a showpiece, but merely a rough map to guide you in writing or speaking, the form in which it is written is not important. As long as the points are listed in an order that helps you present your ideas clearly, any outline form that you use is acceptable.

2 Topic outline. For some papers, you may have to submit a formal outline as part of your work. The most common type of formal outline required is the topic outline. The headings are given in brief phrases, clauses, or single words, and are numbered and lettered consistently, as in this example:

Regional Dialects in the United States (Title)

I. Work of the linguistic geographer (Main head)
   A. To determine specific dialect regions (Subhead)
   B. To discover the reasons for dialect differences
      1. By studying the make-up of early settlements (Sub-subhead)
         a. Regional and/or national origin of the settlers
         b. Location of the early settlements
      2. By tracing the migration routes of settlers

3. By noting the physical geography of various regions
    a. Natural boundaries that isolate dialect areas
    b. Natural phenomena that characterize the areas
4. By considering social forces
    a. Development of industry
    b. Growth of cities as cultural centers
    c. Spread of education
        (1) Through mass media
        (2) Through travel
C. To examine specific dialect differences
    1. In pronunciation
    2. In vocabulary
    3. In grammar
II. Procedure followed in obtaining linguistic data
    A. Study made of background of region
        1. Geographical features
        2. Economic and cultural history
    B. Communities representative of region selected
    C. Informants chosen representing cross section of community
        1. Old-fashioned speakers with elementary-school training
        2. More modern speakers with high-school background
        3. Cultured speakers with college education
    D. Regional speech data obtained from informants
        1. By interviewing in person
        2. By mailing out checklist questionnaires
    E. Data compiled and recorded
III. Significant accomplishments of linguistic geographers
    A. Recognition of three main dialect areas in the United States
        1. Northern
        2. Midland
        3. Southern
    B. Description of various minor dialect areas
    C. Publication of findings
        1. *Linguistic Atlas of New England* completed
        2. Atlases for several other regions under way
        3. Increasing number of articles and books in print

Notice the system used in a formal topic outline, the way numbers and letters are alternated—and indented—to show which items are of equal importance and how the various items are related. All items labeled with Roman numerals are main heads, giving the main divisions of the subject. All items marked by capital letters are equally important divisions of a main head, and so on.

Notice, too, that items in the different groups are parallel in form. In the outline shown above, all the main heads are nouns modified by phrases. The A, B, and C subheads under I are infinitive phrases. The four numbered items under B are prepositional phrases. The first item in any group determines the form; all following items in that group should be phrased the same way.

3 Sentence outline. A sentence outline is like a formal topic outline except that each head and subhead is expanded into a complete sentence. A sentence outline demands more thought than a topic outline because it requires you to put your ideas into specific, rather detailed statements. But for this very reason it can be more valuable to you than the sketchier topic outline.

out loud   Informal expression for the formal *aloud*:

She asked me to read the letter out loud.   [Formal: aloud.]

out of date   Expressions like *out of date, out of doors, out of town* are hyphened when they are used as compound adjectives preceding the noun they modify. Otherwise, they are written as separate words:

The mayor accused the aldermen of out-of-date thinking.
Their new zoning proposal is certainly out of date.

over with   Used colloquially to mean "over" or "finished":

COLLOQUIAL: The play should be over with by ten o'clock.
WRITTEN: The play should be over by ten o'clock.

paid, payed   *Paid* is the spelling of the past tense and the past participle of *pay* in all its senses except "to let out (a rope, line, etc.)." In that sense, the form is *payed*.

His patience finally paid off.   We paid our bill in advance.
They payed out the line, and we swung clear of the dock.

186

pair   The usual plural of *pair* is *pairs*:

He has been known to lose five pairs of gloves in one winter.

In business usage and in some informal speech the plural is often *pair* when it follows a number:

We have only three pair of lined gloves left in stock.

pants, trousers   *Pants* is the informal word, *trousers* the formal.

Paradox   See **Epigram.**

Paragraphs   A paragraph — in expository writing — is a group of sentences developing one point, usually one phase of a larger topic. Since the number of sentences needed to make a particular phase clear will vary, paragraph length will vary, ranging from quite short to quite long. However, if a neatly developed paragraph turns out to be formidably long, modern writers are likely to split it into two (or more) parts, making the break between subpoints, where there is a natural break in the thought.

In narrative writing, details are not grouped around main points or phases but follow one another like links in a chain. Deciding where the paragraph breaks should come is largely a matter of judgment. Most writers begin a new paragraph to emphasize a particular action or scene or to show a change in time, in place, in mood. (It is also a general practice to start a new paragraph every time the speaker changes.) In most narratives the paragraphs are fairly short, since long paragraphs tend to slow the action down.

Parallel constructions   Items in a sentence that are of equal importance should be expressed in parallel (or similar) forms:

NOT PARALLEL: His book is *timely, well written,* and *a real challenge.*
PARALLEL: His book is *timely, well written,* and *challenging.*

NOT PARALLEL: The car needs *to be tuned up, air* in the tires, and *the oil needs to be changed.*
PARALLEL: The car needs a *tune-up, air* in the tires, and an *oil change.*

(For further discussion and examples, see **Shifted constructions.**)

Paraphrase   In reading, especially in studying, you may occasionally come across a passage that takes some time and effort to understand because the writer has used involved or figurative or technical language or has packed a great many ideas into a few concise sentences. An excellent way to make sure you get all the author's intended meaning is to write a paraphrase — to restate in your own words the ideas in the passage.

As you compare the following paraphrase with the original, notice that the meaning is the same in each. All that differs is the wording. In the paraphrase it is simpler, more familiar, easier to understand on one reading.

ORIGINAL

ORIGINAL

The disposition of mankind, whether as rulers or as fellow citizens, to impose their own opinions and inclinations as a rule of conduct on others, is so energetically supported by some of the best and by some of the worst feelings incident to human nature, that it is hardly ever kept under restraint by anything but want of power. —John Stuart Mill, *On Liberty*.

PARAPHRASE

Every man, whether in a position of authority or not, has a tendency to try to make others act as he thinks they should or as he would like them to. And this tendency is so strongly supported by his emotions, both noble and base, that about the only thing which keeps it in check is not having the power to enforce it.

In paraphrasing difficult material, you will find it helpful to follow these three steps:

a) Read the passage through several times, until you are sure you have found and understood all the ideas included. Look up any words you are unfamiliar with or that seem to be used in an unfamiliar way.

b) Write your paraphrase, sentence by sentence, restating the author's ideas in words that are clear and meaningful to you. Some of the words, of course, will be the same as those in the original, since there is no point in substituting synonyms for words you are familiar with.

c) When you have completed your paraphrase, check it against the original to make sure that you have included every idea it contains and that you have not added any ideas or meanings the author did not intend.

Once you become skilled at paraphrasing, you may not always bother to write out your restatement. Sometimes you will be able to work out the meaning of a difficult passage just by restating it in your mind.

You are sure to find any time you spend paraphrasing well worth the investment. It will not only help you to understand and remember a writer's (or speaker's) ideas, but also make you better able to judge the value of those ideas.

Parentheses ( )   1 Parentheses are used to enclose added explanations or comments that the writer does not want to stand out conspicuously in a sentence. When the material in parentheses comes within a sentence, it is not begun with a capital letter or followed by a period, even if it is a sentence itself. But commas and semicolons are used, just as they would be in any sentence:

There are even some plants (butterworts, pitcher plants, sundews) that trap insects for food.

We traveled all night (he drove for the first five hours; I took over at midnight) and reached New Orleans by dawn.

If the material enclosed in parentheses is a question or an exclamation, a question mark or an exclamation mark is used within the parentheses:

I smiled politely (what else could I do?) and said, "Don't worry. The chair can easily be repaired."
Poor Ann (how frightened she looked!) was the last one questioned.

Punctuation marks (commas, periods, semicolons, etc.) that belong to the sentence come after the parentheses, not before:

While we were sitting in the warming house (it was much too cold to skate), we noticed a small dog trying to walk on the ice.
No one did well on the French test (except Jacques, of course).
I offered to pay for the damage (the bill came to $12.80); Mr. Lewis, however, absolutely refused to take my money.

2 Parenthetical material that is not in the body of a sentence begins with a capital letter and ends with a period (or question mark or exclamation mark):

I turned off the alarm and crawled back into bed. (That was my first mistake for the day.) An hour and a half later, the ringing of the telephone waked me out of a sound sleep.

3 Parentheses are often used to enclose letters or figures that mark items in a series:

We were offered three alternatives: (1) having a dinner dance in the school gym, (2) holding a dance only—at the Park Hotel, or (3) taking a class trip.

4 Parentheses, dashes, and commas are all used to set off explanatory comments. In the sentence "Though the house is old (built in 1910), it is in very good condition," the parentheses make the explanatory comment inconspicuous and show that it has only a slight bearing on the rest of the sentence. Dashes tend to emphasize an explanatory comment, while commas show that the writer wants it to be more closely related to other words in the sentence.

Parentheses are effective when they are used only occasionally. Used too often, they become tiresome and may distract the reader.

5 Parentheses should not be used to enclose words that you want omitted from a sentence. Draw a straight line through such words.

part   Used with *from* when it means "go away from; leave" and with *with* when it means "give up; let go":

Jean-Claude parted from us sadly, promising to write often.
Though his old jalopy barely ran, he still hated to part with it.

part (on the part of)   Often a clumsy substitute for *by, among, for,* and the like:

CLUMSY: The feeling on the part of the local merchants was that no two stores should have bargain days at the same time.
BETTER: The feeling among the local merchants was that no two stores should have bargain days at the same time.

partake of   A pretentious expression for *eat:*

AFFECTED: Not one tourist suspected he had partaken of raw fish.
NATURAL: Not one tourist suspected he had eaten raw fish.

Participial phrase   A modifying phrase made up of a participle and its objects (or complements) and modifiers:

Tapping his foot impatiently, Ned waited for the clerk to return.   [Modifies the noun *Ned.*]
All items *purchased by December 15* will be delivered before Christmas. [Modifies the noun *items.*]

   Sometimes the phrase also contains the word modified:

She tore open the telegram, *her hands trembling with excitement.* [Participle *trembling* modifies noun *hands.*]

This kind of phrase is called an *absolute phrase.* (For further examples and discussion, see **Absolute phrases.**)

Participle   **1 Forms.** The present participle ends in *-ing: crying, trimming, debating.* The past participle usually ends in *-ed, -t, -d, -en,* or *-n: ordered, lit, held, fallen, flown.*
   2 Uses. (a) Participles are used in forming various tenses of verbs:

I am thinking.   It was forbidden.
They have been practicing.   Al should be invited.

   b) When not part of a verb form, participles are used (alone or in phrases) as verbal adjectives modifying nouns or pronouns:

the *whimpering* baby   the *stolen* merchandise
The girl *playing the vibes* looked familiar.   [Modifies *girl.*]
Born in Syria, he came to this country in 1950.   [Modifies *he.*]
We heard a voice *calling for help.*   [Modifies *voice.*]

   c) Though generally used to modify a particular noun or pronoun, participles are sometimes used in phrases that relate to the whole sentence (to the situation) rather than a particular word:

Speaking of money, can you lend me a quarter?
Considering the damage, it's a miracle that no one was hurt.

Phrases like these are equivalent to subordinate clauses ("Since we are speaking of money, can you lend me a quarter?"). Because they are not intended as modifiers of a particular word, they are not considered "dangling" modifiers. (See **Dangling modifiers.**)

party   See **person.**

passed   The past-tense form of the verb *pass* is *passed*:

On the way back we *passed* two overturned tank trucks.   [Not: On the way back we *past* two overturned tank trucks.]

Passive voice   See **Active and passive voice.**

Past tense, past perfect tense   See **Tenses of verbs.**

peeve   Used informally for *annoy* or *annoyance*:

She was peeved at their going without her.
My pet peeve is recorded messages.

per   *Per* (Latin, "through; by; for") is chiefly used in business and technical English: *six hours per diem, $3 per capita, $8500 per annum, $12 per ounce, 28 miles per gallon.*

In general usage an equivalent English expression is usually more appropriate: *six hours a day, $3 for each person, $8500 a year, $12 an ounce, 28 miles to a gallon.*

percent, per cent   More commonly written as one word than as two, and not followed by a period: *a 5 percent loss, a 10 percent service charge.*

Colloquially *percent* is used in place of *percentage*:

COLLOQUIAL: A large percent of once-fatal diseases are now curable.
WRITTEN: A large percentage of once-fatal diseases are now curable.

perfect   See **Comparison of adjectives and adverbs,** section 2.

Perfect tenses   The *present perfect tense* suggests an action begun at some point in the past and completed at the time of the statement: The phone *has rung* five times in the last hour.

The *past perfect tense* shows that the action had been completed before a specific time or happening in the past: They apparently *had ransacked* the building before the night watchman went on duty.

The *future perfect tense* shows that the action will have been completed at some time in the future: By this time next year, Mayor Loy *will have been* in office for two full terms.

(See **Tenses of verbs.**)

Period **1** The chief function of a period is to mark the end of a sentence that is not regarded as a question or an exclamation:

Then Emily asked Ron where he was going.
I wondered what they were thinking.
Don't take *no* for an answer.
Will you kindly pay the balance immediately. [Intended as a polite request, not as a question.]

2 Periods have several conventional uses:
a) After abbreviations and initials:

Oct.   Inc.   N.Y.   Mr. J. J. Bryant, Jr.

b) Between dollars and cents when the dollar sign is used:

$1.39 $4893.37 $.42 [But: 42 cents or 42¢]

c) Before decimals or between the whole number and the decimal:

.4   3.14159   53.2%

3 Three spaced periods (. . .) are used to show the omission of words in a quotation. (See **Ellipsis.**)
4 A period coming at the end of a quotation is generally placed inside the quotation marks:

"I told only one person," Sam said, "but he told everyone else."

(For the use of periods with parentheses, see **Parentheses,** sections 1 and 2.)

Periodic sentence   A sentence in which the main thought is not complete until the end:

Thirty days after sentence of death had been passed on him at Charles Town, on the morning of December 2, 1859, John Brown was hanged.

Because the reader has to wait for the main idea until after he has read all the minor details upon which it is based, the effect of a periodic sentence is one of suspense.

Used occasionally, periodic sentences add a pleasant variety and emphasis to writing. Used too often, though, they give an unnatural, stilted tone.

(See **Loose sentence.**)

Person   Personal pronouns change form to indicate person:

FIRST PERSON, THE ONE SPEAKING: I, me, mine; we, us, ours
SECOND PERSON, THE ONE SPOKEN TO: you, yours
THIRD PERSON, THE ONE SPOKEN OF: he, him, his; she, her, hers; it, its; they, them, theirs

In English the only change in the form of verbs to indicate person occurs in the third person singular: I write, you write, he *writes*; we, you, they write.

The verb *be* is exceptional: I *am*, you *are*, he *is*; we, you, they *are*.

person   *Person* is the word generally used to refer to a human being. Many people use *individual* interchangeably with *person*; but *individual* is a rather heavy and pretentious word to use unless the person referred to is being contrasted with others, or his distinctiveness is being emphasized:

PRETENTIOUS: He was an extremely generous individual.
BETTER: He was an extremely generous person.

Though *party* is used colloquially to mean "person" (He is looking for the *party* who pulled the fire alarm), this use is not generally considered acceptable. *Party*, used in legal English, means "each of the persons or sides in a contract or lawsuit."

personal, personnel   *Personal* means "private; individual":

Her personal affairs are no concern of mine.

It should not be confused with *personnel*, which refers to employees or employee matters:

Only military personnel are allowed to enter the building.
Return the insurance forms to the personnel department by Friday.

Personal letters   See **Letters,** sections 5 and 6.

Personal pronouns   Pronouns whose forms show person; that is, the forms show whether the speaker (first person), the one spoken to (second person), or the one spoken of (third person) is meant: *I, we; you; he, she, it, they.* (See **Case,** section 1.)

Personification   A figure of speech in which a lifeless thing or quality is spoken of as if alive:

The mother, father, and two sons had scurried into a cellar while the twister tucked their shanty under its arm and raced like a monstrous halfback over a gigantic field. —Gene Fowler, *Timber Line.*

perspire, sweat   The once-popular distinction between these words— "Horses sweat; men perspire"—is not now generally observed. In fact, many people prefer the simpler, more direct word *sweat* to its polite substitutes *perspire* and *perspiration*, and always use *sweat* except in situations where it might offend more sensitive people (as in commercials for deodorants, where even the word *perspiration* is often avoided).

phenomenon   The usual meaning is "an observable fact, event, or circumstance": The simple phenomenon of water becoming ice can cause many accidents on the highway. The plural is *phenomena*: The aurora borealis is one of the most beautiful of nature's phenomena.

   Phenomenon is also used to mean "something or someone extraordinary." Used in this sense, the plural is generally *phenomenons*.

phone   See **telephone, phone.**

Phoneme   A linguistic term used to refer to one of the basic units of sound in a language, one of the sounds that serve to distinguish meaning. In English, for example, we know that *got* and *cot* are two different words because their beginning sounds—the phonemes /g/ and /k/—are different. The different ending sounds of *tap* and *tab*—the phonemes /p/ and /b/—and the different vowel sounds of *hat*, *hot*, and *hut*—the phonemes /a/, /o/, /u/—show that they are different words.

photo   An informal clipped word for *photograph*, similar to *phone* but not so widely used, since *picture* is a handy substitute.

Phrases   A phrase is a group of words without a subject and verb, used as a single word in a sentence:

PREPOSITIONAL PHRASE: Laura cut the pizza *with a scissors.*   [Used as an adverb modifying *cut.*]

PARTICIPIAL PHRASE: *Following Doug's example*, everyone stood up and cheered.   [Used as an adjective modifying *everyone.*]

GERUND PHRASE: *Parking alongside the road* is not permitted.   [Used as a noun, as the subject of *is.*]

INFINITIVE PHRASE: Beatrice asked *to be excused from the table.*   [Used as a noun, as the direct object of *asked.*]

Plagiarism   A person who knowingly takes the ideas, expressions, or writings of others and passes them off as his own is just as dishonest as if he took money, clothing, or anything else belonging to another. A writer's ideas and his way of expressing them are his own property, and using them without permission is called *plagiarism.*

   When a writer has established a thought as his own in writing, common honesty requires all others to respect his ownership rights. This does not mean that you are not to use his material. It simply means that you must not use his words, facts, or ideas without giving him credit (see **Footnotes**), and in writing intended for publication you should not use more than a sentence or two of his without getting his permission.

plenty   *Plenty* is colloquial when used as an adverb or as an adjective modifier preceding a noun:

ADVERB: I'll bet you were plenty scared.
           The back seat is plenty big enough for three.
ADJECTIVE: He always has plenty money for clothes.
           She can get plenty volunteers to help.

These modifier uses are avoided in formal English.

plurality   See **majority, plurality.**

Plurals of nouns   **1** Most nouns are regular, forming their plurals with *s*:

tent — tents	alibi — alibis	jersey — jerseys
Aztec — Aztecs	bowl — bowls	Mr. Ray — the Rays

2 Nouns ending in *sh, s, z, x,* or *ch* (when pronounced /ch/ and not /k/) add *es*:

wish — wishes	waltz — waltzes	Mr. Marx — the Marxes
atlas — atlases	quiz — quizzes	Mrs. Jones — the Joneses
class — classes	hoax — hoaxes	sketch — sketches

3 Nouns ending in *y* preceded by a consonant change the *y* to *i* and add *es*:

spy — spies	penny — pennies	Gypsy — Gypsies
duty — duties	daisy — daisies	dictionary — dictionaries

Names of people are exceptions to this rule:

The *Bradys* often go camping with us.   [Not: *Bradies.*]
There are five *Sherrys* in my history class.   [Not: *Sherries.*]

4 Nouns ending in *o* preceded by a vowel add *s*:

ratio — ratios	stereo — stereos	kangaroo — kangaroos
curio — curios	rodeo — rodeos	shampoo — shampoos

But nouns ending in *o* preceded by a consonant vary. Some add *s*, others *es*, and still others either *s* or *es*:

WITH *s*:   avocado — avocados   pinto — pintos   silo — silos
WITH *es*:   hero — heroes   Negro — Negroes   potato — potatoes
WITH *s* OR *es*:   zero — zeros or zeroes   cargo — cargoes or cargos

5 Nouns ending in *f* and *fe* also vary:

WITH *s*:   reef — reefs   safe — safes   sheriff — sheriffs
WITH *ves*:   thief — thieves   life — lives   half — halves
WITH *s* OR *ves*:   hoof — hoofs or hooves   scarf — scarfs or scarves

6 A few nouns form their plurals by a change in spelling:

woman — women	die — dice	goose — geese
mouse — mice	ox — oxen	child — children

195

7 Some nouns borrowed from foreign languages have English endings, others foreign endings, and still others have both:

ENGLISH PLURALS: encyclopedia — encyclopedias   bonus — bonuses
asylum — asylums   imbroglio — imbroglios
FOREIGN PLURALS: crisis — crises   bacterium — bacteria
alumna — alumnae   stimulus — stimuli
BOTH: formula — formulas or formulae   index — indexes or indices
virtuoso — virtuosos or virtuosi   fulcrum — fulcrums or fulcra

In scientific and formal writing the foreign plurals of words that have both forms are more likely to be used. But in other situations the English plurals are more common and are the appropriate forms to use.

8 Compound words generally form their plural by adding *s* or *es* to the end:

onlooker — onlookers   get-together — get-togethers
rosebush — rosebushes   trade-in — trade-ins
stepsister — stepsisters   ten-year-old — ten-year-olds
disk jockey — disk jockeys   chief justice — chief justices

But there are exceptions. When a compound is composed of a noun followed by a modifying word or phrase, the noun — the most important word — is usually made plural:

attorney general — attorneys general
bill of sale — bills of sale
hanger-on — hangers-on
son-in-law — sons-in-law

9 Either *s* or *'s* is added to numbers, signs, letters, and words discussed as words. The *'s* is preferred after all lower-case letters and those capital letters that would be confusing if *s* alone were added:

three 5s *or* three 5's   the 1940s *or* the 1940's
four #s *or* four #'s   several +s *or* several +'s
knows his ABCs   put two *a*'s in *grammar*   got straight A's
too many *so*'s   too many *if*'s

10 A few nouns have the same form for both singular and plural:

one Iroquois — ten Iroquois   a Portuguese — many Portuguese
one sheep — twenty sheep   one bellows — a dozen bellows

p.m.   Abbreviation for the Latin *post meridiem*, "after noon." (See **a.m., p.m.**)

Poetry (quoted)   When quoting poetry in your writing, copy it exactly as it was originally written, keeping each line, capital letter, indention, spelling, and punctuation mark. If the quotation consists of only one line or part of a line, it is put in quotation marks and written into the text. If two lines or more are quoted, they are usually set below the text and indented from each margin. When they are set off in this way, no quotation marks are needed. (If, because of lack of space, more than one line is incorporated in the text, the end of each line is usually indicated by a short diagonal mark [/] separating it from the following line.)

When possible, a line of poetry should be written complete on one line of your paper. If a long line has to be carried over, it should be indented deeper than the other lines. (See **Indention**.)

politics   Usually singular, but plural when it means "political principles or opinions":

Once again, politics *has influenced* the school-board elections.
Mr. Fahey stated that his politics *were* no one else's business.

position   See **job, position.**

Possessive adjectives   *My, your, his, her, its, our, your,* and *their,* possessive forms of the personal pronouns, are called *possessive adjectives* when they modify a noun:

my error   his courage   our uncle   their axe

Possessive case   **1 Forms.** The possessive case (sometimes called the genitive case) is formed in various ways:

a) Singular nouns and indefinite pronouns generally add an apostrophe and *s:*

my sister's cat   the mayor-elect's wife   Dickens's novels
everybody's loss   the Attorney General's speech   Frank's grin

With singular proper names ending in *s,* usage is divided. Sometimes only an apostrophe is added: Dickens' novels. But most often both an apostrophe and *s* are used except with the names *Jesus* and *Moses* and Greek names of more than one syllable ending in *es:* Moses' leadership, Aristophanes' plays.

b) Plural nouns ending in *s* add only the apostrophe:

his pals' voices   three doctors' offices   their babies' toys
the Darbys' yard   some foxes' dens   the Burnses' ranch

But plural nouns not ending in *s* add both the apostrophe and *s:*

their children's nursery   his henchmen's loyalty
the alumni's votes   several moose's tracks

c) To show joint ownership, the last noun is made possessive:

Tom and Jerry's room   [They share it.]
Mr. Lee and Mr. Wild's drugstore   [They own it together.]
her mother and father's vacation   [They went together.]

But to show separate ownership, each noun is made possessive:

Tom's and Jerry's report cards
Mr. Lee's and Mr. Wild's salaries
her mother's and father's suntans

d) The personal pronouns and the relative and interrogative *who* have special possessive forms, spelled without the apostrophe:

USED BEFORE NOUNS: my, your, his, her, its, our, their; whose
USED ALONE: mine, yours, his, hers, its, ours, theirs; whose

e) The possessive may also be formed by using a phrase with *of*:

the wings of the plane (the plane's wings)
the research of Dr. Peabody (Dr. Peabody's research)

The *of*-possessive is more common with names of inanimate objects than the 's-form, but both are used. The 's-form is more common with names of people, although both are used:

the lining of my coat   my coat's lining
Abe Lincoln's wit   the wit of Abe Lincoln

In general, choose the form that sounds best in the sentence.

f) The 's-form and the *of*-form are often combined, especially with *this* or *that*:

this junk of Ted's   these trophies of my brother's
that bicycle of Judy's   those wild stories of Peter's

2 Uses. Although the principal use of the possessive case is to show ownership (the boy's freckles, Ed's stamp collection, their bicycles), it is also used to show a number of other relationships:

DESCRIPTION: a children's program, the taste of nutmeg
DOER OF AN ACT: Walter's teasing, the jury's verdict, the verdict of the jury
RECIPIENT OF AN ACT: the team's defeat, the President's critics
AUTHORSHIP: Pinter's plays, the plays of Pinter
MEASURE: a week's work, arm's length, a quarter's worth

Possessive pronouns   The possessive forms of the personal pronouns and of *who* are *mine, yours, his, hers, its, ours, theirs; whose.* (Compare **Possessive adjectives** and **Pronominal adjectives**.)

Post hoc fallacy   See **Fallacies in reasoning,** section 2.

pre-   Prefix meaning "before in place, time, or rank." Generally words with *pre-* are written without a hyphen: *predetermine, preshrink, precook, prearrange, preschool, prefabricated.* But a hyphen is usually used when the part following *pre-* is a proper name: *pre-Roman, pre-Civil War.*

Usage varies when the part following *pre-* begins with an *e*. Such words are sometimes hyphened or written with a dieresis (*pre-exist, preëxist; pre-endorse, preëndorse*), but it is becoming more common to write them as solid words (*preexist, preendorse*).

precede, proceed   *Precede*, meaning "to go or come before," is often confused in spelling with *proceed*, meaning "to go on after having stopped" or "to move forward":

Len politely let Nora precede him into the room.
After a short lunch break, the cast proceeded with the rehearsal.

Précis   You may often want to give the gist of something you have read or heard: a book, a magazine article, a speech, a movie, a discussion, or a conversation. If you write an accurate and brief summary of such material in your own words, keeping the author's or speaker's original point of view, you are writing a précis. (*Précis*, pronounced /prā'sē/ or /prā sē'/, is spelled the same in the singular and plural, but the plural is pronounced with a final /z/ sound — /prā'sēz/.)

For an average paragraph the précis might be only a sentence, or it may run to half the length of the passage summarized. The important thing is to include in a clear, brief statement all the major ideas expressed by the author or speaker without distorting his point of view. For an example, compare the following paragraph — taken from Robert Louis Stevenson's "An Apology for Idlers" — with the précis given below it:

It is surely beyond a doubt that people should be a good deal idle in youth. For though here and there a Lord Macaulay may escape from school honors with all his wits about him, most boys pay so dear for their medals that they never afterward have a shot in their locker, and begin the world bankrupt. And the same holds true during all the time a lad is educating himself, or suffering others to educate him. It must have been a very foolish old gentleman who addressed Johnson at Oxford in these words: "Young man, ply your book diligently now, and acquire a stock of knowledge; for when years come upon you, you will find that poring upon books will be but an irksome task." The old gentleman seems to have been unaware that many other things besides reading grow irksome, and not a few become impossible by the time a man has to use spectacles and cannot walk without a stick. Books are good enough in their own way, but they are a mighty bloodless substitute for life. It seems a pity to sit, like the Lady of Shalott, peering into a mirror, with your back turned on all the bustle and glamour of reality. And if a man reads very hard, as the old anecdote reminds us, he will have little time for thoughts. (228 words)

It is not wise to force young people to spend all their time on their studies. There should be a time for idleness as well, for free time gives a young person a chance to experience life at first hand before he grows too old. (45 words)

Some passages are more difficult to summarize than others, depending on the material and the author's style. Until you master the technique, it may be best to follow these steps:

a) Read the passage carefully, but as quickly as possible, for the overall meaning. If necessary, reread the difficult parts.

b) Reread the passage, focusing your attention on key words and connectives, and checking the meaning of those you do not know.

c) List mentally or on paper the major ideas of the passage.

d) In your own words, write a summary of these ideas. As far as possible, avoid the words and phrasing used by the author or speaker, though you will have to use certain key words because they are essential to the meaning. Usually all details, figures of speech, and examples are omitted.

e) Reread the passage and your précis to see where you can further compress the meaning or economize on words. Check carefully to see that you have not changed the point of view of the passage or otherwise changed the author's intended meaning.

Once you have become skilled in writing précis, you can combine or even omit some of these steps, especially in summarizing simple material. In dealing with more complex material, though, you will find that following these steps will bring the best results. The time you spend practicing précis-writing will be repaid in increased ability to understand what you read and to express clearly and compactly what you learn.

Predicate   The verb and the words used with it to make a statement about the subject of a sentence or clause:

The elephants *stampeded.*
The man in the end seat *hurriedly got to his feet.*
The wind *carried the kite high into the air.*
A year later she *became president of the firm.*

Two or more verbs used with one subject are known as a *compound predicate:*

The guru *sat* cross-legged on the ground, *meditated* for a long while, and finally *began* to speak in a singsong voice.

Predicate complement   A word that completes the meaning of a linking verb or of a transitive verb in the passive voice. The predicate complement is usually a noun or a pronoun that refers to the same person or thing as the subject, or an adjective that modifies the subject:

PREDICATE NOUN: The lead guitarist was a ten-year-old *girl.*
PREDICATE NOUN: Joel Goldberger was made *editor in chief* of the paper.
PREDICATE PRONOUN: So it was *you* ringing the doorbell!
PREDICATE ADJECTIVE: To put it nicely, his haircut was *unique.*

prefer   The better idiom is *prefer . . . to:*

I'd prefer a piece of pie *to* another helping of meat.   [Not: I'd prefer a piece of pie *more than* another helping of meat.]
Phil prefers reading *to* watching television.

With infinitives, in order to avoid repetition of *to, rather than* is used:

She prefers to take the bus *rather than* [to] drive with them.

Prefix   A word, syllable, or syllables put at the beginning of a word to change its meaning or to form a new word. For example, adding *dis-* (meaning "not") to *honest* makes *dishonest,* meaning "not honest."

Knowing the meaning of the common prefixes is often a help in figuring out the meaning of new words you run across. The following list gives just a few of the more common prefixes and illustrates one meaning of each:

a- (not):   amoral, aperiodic, asocial
ante- (before):   antedate, anteroom, antemortem
bi- (two):   bilingual, bihourly, bimotor, bicolored
circum- (around):   circumnavigation, circumlunar, circumlocution
co- (together):   coeducational, coexist, co-worker
contra- (against):   contraindicate, contraorbital
dis- (not):   disagreement, discomfort, discredit, disregard
extra- (beyond):   extracurricular, extrasensory, extralegal
fore- (before):   foregone, forenoon, forerunner
hyper- (excessively):   hyperacid, hypercritical, hypersensitive
in- (not):   inexhaustible, indecisive, insecure
inter- (between; among):   interlock, interplay, intertribal
mal- (bad):   maladjustment, malnutrition, malpractice
mis- (wrong):   misuse, misguided, misinterpret, misspent
non- (not):   noneffective, nonrigid, nonunion
pseudo- (false):   pseudoscience, pseudoprofessional, pseudoheroic
re- (again):   reeducate, rerun, reheat, reinforce
retro- (backward; back):   retrorocket, retroactive
semi- (half):   semiconscious, semiprivate, seminormal
super- (over; above):   superheat, supernatural, supersaturate
trans- (across):   transalpine, transcontinental, transpacific
tri- (three):   triangle, tricolor, tricycle, trilinear

(See also **anti-, ex-, pre-, re-,** and **semi-.**)

Preposition   **1** A preposition is a word used to show the relationship between a noun or its equivalent (called the *object of the preposition*) and some other word in the sentence:

The magazines *behind* the door should be given away.   [Shows the relationship between *door* and the noun *magazines.*]

We swam *under* the bridge.   [Shows the relationship between *bridge* and the verb *swam.*]

The man standing *over* the body proved to be the murderer.   [Shows the relationship between *body* and the participle *standing.*]

2 Among the most common prepositions are:

above	before	down	in spite of	since
across	behind	except	of	to
against	below	for	on	under
at	between	from	out of	until
because of	by	in	past	with

But remember that it is the use of a word, not its form, that determines what part of speech it is. *Before*, for example, is often a preposition (Everyone was nervous *before* the test); but it may also be a subordinating conjunction (Give me your new address *before* you leave) or an adverb (Ann had never played pinochle *before*).

3 The right preposition to use after certain words depends sometimes on the meaning intended. We say, for example, "agree *with* his ideas," "agree *to* take the responsibility," "agree *on* a method of attack," "agree *in* number and gender." At other times, the right preposition is a matter of idiom. We say "comply *with* regulations," not "comply *to*"; "pleased *with* the results," not "pleased *by*"; "engrossed *in* his book," not "engrossed *with* his book."

Ordinarily you learn the idiomatic prepositions to use with common words by hearing or seeing them in phrases. Words not in your everyday vocabulary may raise questions. Here is a list of such words and the idiomatic prepositions to use with them:

an *abhorrence of* violence	*enveloped in* clouds
accused of cheating	his *familiarity with* Swahili
acquit of the charges	*impervious to* criticism
adept at skiing	*incompatible with* the facts
adept in music	*independent of* her family
an event *analogous to* this	*meddle in* their affairs
appreciative of his help	*meddle with* the lock
compare my plan *with* yours	lines *parallel to* each other
complied with our request	a *partiality for* sweets
conducive to good thinking	*prejudiced against* doctors
too *confident of* success	a strong *resemblance to* Mary
totally *devoid of* warmth	an idea *similar to* mine
dissent from the majority	held under *suspicion of* arson
a *distaste for* violence	*tolerant of* his opinions
encumbered with debts	at *variance with* his beliefs

(For words not in this list or not covered in separate entries, consult a dictionary.)

Keep in mind that when two words requiring different prepositions are used with a single object, both prepositions should be given:

Eva was aware *of* but indifferent *to* their troubles. [Not: Eva was aware but indifferent to their troubles.]

But when the two words require the same preposition, it need not be repeated:

We appreciated his *interest* and *belief in* us.

4 It was once a general practice for textbooks to warn against ending a sentence with a preposition—and many writers, as a result, wrote quite awkward and unnatural sentences in an effort to avoid doing so. The taboo against the final preposition holds only in certain cases: (1) in sentences like "Where is my coat at?" and "Where do you think you're going to?"—in which the prepositions are not needed; (2) in sentences like "Our candidate, John Q. Doe, is a man on whom you can rely on"—in which either the second *on* or the first should be dropped; (3) in sentences like "What did you give him something to complain about for?"—in which the two prepositions at the end sound awkward.

Except for cases like these three, there is no reason for hesitating to end sentences with prepositions. "What are you so happy about?" is far more natural and less awkward than "About what are you so happy?" Except in very formal writing, a sentence like "These are the blueprints you were asking about" is preferable to "These are the blueprints about which you were asking." And in a sentence like "All of the missing papers have been accounted for" the preposition not only fits smoothly and naturally at the end, but would be impossible to shift from that position without rewording the sentence.

Prepositional phrase   A preposition and its object, which together serve as a modifier—either adjective or adverb:

The girl *in the green coat* stamped her foot.   [Used as an adjective modifying *girl*.]
We planted the tree *behind the house*.   [Used as an adverb modifying *planted*.]

Present tense   See **Tenses of verbs**.

pretty   In informal English *pretty* is often used to mean "somewhat; moderately; quite":

He was pretty sleepy.   They were pretty upset.

Avoid overusing *pretty* in this sense in your written work.

principal, principle   Let the *a* in *principal* remind you that the adjective *principal* (meaning "chief") ends in *al: her principal concern, the principal* *idea*. Then if you remember that the *principal* of a school is the "principal person," that the *principal* in your bank is the "principal sum," and that the *principals* in a play or movie are the "principal actors," you will spell all these nouns correctly with an *a*.

To spell the noun *principle* right, remember that it means "a rule of conduct" and, like *rule*, ends in *le*.

Principal parts of verbs   The various tenses of a verb are formed from its principal parts: the infinitive (*jump*), the past tense (*jumped*), and the past participle (*jumped*). Most verbs are "regular"—that is, both the past tense and past participle are formed by adding *-ed* to the infinitive (*call, called, called*). But there are some verbs—"irregular verbs"—whose principal parts are formed in other ways. Because of their irregularity, the forms of these verbs sometimes cause trouble for speakers and writers.

Here is a list of the more common troublesome verbs:

INFINITIVE	PAST TENSE	PAST PARTICIPLE
arise	arose	arisen
awake	awoke, awaked	awaked, awoke
be	was	been
bear	bore	borne (born: "given birth to")
beat	beat	beaten, beat
become	became	become
begin	began	begun
bend	bent	bent
bid ("offer")	bid	bid
bid ("order")	bade, bid	bidden, bid
bind	bound	bound
bite	bit	bitten, bit
bleed	bled	bled
blow	blew	blown
break	broke	broken
bring	brought	brought
broadcast	broadcast, broadcasted	broadcast, broadcasted
build	built	built
burn	burned, burnt	burned, burnt
burst	burst	burst
buy	bought	bought
catch	caught	caught
choose	chose	chosen
cling	clung	clung
come	came	come
cost	cost	cost
creep	crept	crept

deal	dealt	dealt
dig	dug	dug
dive	dived, dove	dived
do	did	done
draw	drew	drawn
dream	dreamed, dreamt	dreamed, dreamt
drink	drank	drunk
drive	drove	driven
eat	ate	eaten
fall	fell	fallen
feed	fed	fed
fight	fought	fought
find	found	found
flee	fled	fled
fling	flung	flung
fly	flew	flown
forbid	forbade, forbad	forbidden, forbid
forget	forgot	forgotten, forgot
freeze	froze	frozen
get	got	got, gotten
give	gave	given
go	went	gone
grind	ground	ground
grow	grew	grown
hang ("put to death")	hanged	hanged
hang ("suspend")	hung	hung
hear	heard	heard
hide	hid	hidden, hid
hold	held	held
hurt	hurt	hurt
kneel	knelt, kneeled	knelt, kneeled
knit	knitted, knit	knitted, knit
know	knew	known
lead	led	led
lean	leaned	leaned
leap	leaped, leapt	leaped, leapt
leave	left	left
lend	lent	lent
let	let	let
light	lighted, lit	lighted, lit
lose	lost	lost
mean	meant	meant
mistake	mistook	mistaken
pay	paid (of ropes: payed)	paid (payed)
plead	pleaded, pled	pleaded, pled

prove	proved	proved, proven
put	put	put
read	read	read
ride	rode	ridden
ring	rang	rung
rise	rose	risen
run	ran	run
say	said	said
see	saw	seen
seek	sought	sought
sew	sewed	sewn, sewed
shake	shook	shaken
shine ("glow; gleam")	shone, shined	shone, shined
shine ("polish")	shined	shined
show	showed	shown, showed
shrink	shrank, shrunk	shrunk, shrunken
sing	sang, sung	sung
sink	sank, sunk	sunk
slay	slew	slain
sleep	slept	slept
slide	slid	slid, slidden
sling	slung	slung
slink	slunk	slunk
sow	sowed	sown, sowed
speak	spoke	spoken
speed	sped, speeded	sped, speeded
spell	spelled, spelt	spelled, spelt
spit	spit, spat	spit, spat
spring	sprang, sprung	sprung
stand	stood	stood
steal	stole	stolen
stick	stuck	stuck
sting	stung	stung
stink	stank, stunk	stunk
stride	strode	stridden
strike	struck	struck, stricken
string	strung	strung
strive	strived, strove	strived, strove
swear	swore	sworn
sweat	sweat, sweated	sweat, sweated
swell	swelled	swelled, swollen
swim	swam	swum
swing	swung	swung
take	took	taken
teach	taught	taught
tear	tore	torn

tell	told	told
throw	threw	thrown
tread	trod	trodden, trod
understand	understood	understood
wake	woke, waked	waked, woken
wear	wore	worn
weave	weaved	weaved
weave (of cloth)	wove	woven, wove
weep	wept	wept
win	won	won
wind	wound	wound
wring	wrung	wrung
write	wrote	written

prior to   Sometimes used when the simpler word *before* would be better:

HEAVY: Prior to moving here, he lived in Ohio.
BETTER: Before moving here, he lived in Ohio.

proceed   See **precede, proceed.**

Progressive verb forms   See **Tenses of verbs,** section 2g.

prohibited   Followed by *from*, not *against*:

As a matter of fact, underclassmen are prohibited from having cars on campus.

The noun *prohibition* is followed by *against*:

The prohibition against camping in the park is usually ignored.

Pronominal adjectives   In the sentence "Rhoda has the key; I gave it to her," *her* is a pronoun used as the object of the preposition *to*. In the sentence "Rhoda forgot her glasses," *her* has two uses — as a pronoun referring to Rhoda and as an adjective modifier of *glasses*. Pronouns that are used also as adjectives are sometimes called *pronominal adjectives.*

Pronouns   Words that represent persons, places, or things without naming them. There are several kinds of pronouns: demonstrative, indefinite, intensive, interrogative, personal, possessive, reflexive, relative.
   For more detailed information on the various kinds and uses of pronouns, see the entry for each kind, as well as **Agreement,** section 2; **Case,** section 1; **Reference of pronouns;** and entries on particular pronouns (for example, **every and its compounds; who, whom, whose**).

Pronunciation   When a pronunciation is given in this book, it is enclosed by two slanted lines: /prə nun'sē ā'shən/. The symbols used in the pronunciation respellings are those of the Thorndike-Barnhart dictionaries. A key to the symbols is given below:

a	hat, cap	o	hot, rock	ə	represents:
ā	age, face	ō	open, go		a in about
ä	father, far	ô	order, all		e in taken
					i in April
b	bad, rob	oi	oil, voice		o in lemon
ch	child, much	ou	house, out		u in circus
d	did, red				
		p	paper, cup		
e	let, best	r	run, try		FOREIGN SOUNDS
ē	equal, see	s	say, yes	Y	as in French *du*. Pro-
ėr	term, learn	sh	she, rush		nounce ē with the lips
		t	tell, it		rounded as for ü in *rule*.
f	fat, if				
g	go, bag	th	thin, both	œ	as in French *peu*. Pro-
h	he, how	ᴛʜ	then, smooth		nounce ā with the lips
					rounded as for ō.
i	it, pin	u	cup, butter		
ī	ice, five	u̇	full, put	N	as in French *bon*. The
		ü	rule, move		N is not pronounced,
j	jam, enjoy				but shows that the vow-
k	kind, seek	v	very, save		el before it is nasal.
l	land, coal	w	will, woman		
m	me, am	y	young, yet	H	as in German *ach*. Pro-
n	no, in	z	zero, breeze		nounce k without clos-
ng	long, bring	zh	measure, seizure		ing the breath passage.

Propaganda   *Propaganda* is the systematic attempt of a person or a group to lead others to accept certain opinions, principles, or beliefs. Since words are the chief medium of propaganda, readers (and listeners) must be constantly alert. Facts and even statistics can be presented in such ways that they lose their true significance and seem to prove what the propagandist wants them to prove—unless readers can see through any attempts to mislead and can think clearly for themselves.

Propaganda may be present in any form of writing—in novels, adver-tising, and poetry—and in various kinds of oral expression—radio and TV addresses, political speeches, drama, motion pictures. It may be used to advance a good cause by truthful and legitimate means, but in general the term is applied to writing or speaking that resorts to deceit and dis-torting facts to achieve its purpose.

Some of the more common methods used by propagandists which you should learn to detect are:

a) *Emotionalizing*, appealing to such emotions in the reader or hearer as hate, fear, greed, jealousy, etc.

b) *Generalizing*, making broad statements that permit a wide variety of interpretations or that are true in only a few exceptional instances: "Young people in America want to destroy the judicial system," "The democracies are decadent," "Europeans are better educated than Americans," "The thinking man reads the Chicago *Banner*," and so on. (See also **Generalizations.**)

c) *Name-calling*, labeling a person or idea with a term of unfair or unpleasant connotations: "fascist," "radical," "effete snob," and the like.

d) *Distorting facts*, giving only one side of a picture or so confusing an issue that the average person will get only the aspect the propagandist wants.

As a good reader or listener you must try to separate facts and honest opinion from propaganda and to arrive at your own opinions uninfluenced by the deceptions that are hidden in many of the words that you read and hear. As an intelligent person you will want to arrive at convictions through your own reasoning power. (See also **Fallacies in reasoning.**)

Proper adjectives Adjectives that are formed from proper nouns and proper nouns that are used as adjectives are capitalized:

French perfume	Shakespearean actor
Salk vaccine	Venetian lace

When a proper adjective no longer suggests its origin, it is treated as a simple adjective and is not capitalized:

herculean tasks	diesel engine
bowie knife	quixotic ideas

Proper noun The name of a particular person, place, or thing. Proper nouns are always capitalized: *Ralph, John D. Rockefeller, Finland, the Gulf of Mexico, the Statue of Liberty, Brooklyn Bridge.*
(See **Common noun.**)

prophecy, prophesy *Prophecy* /prof'ə sē/ is the noun, and *prophesy* /prof'ə sī/ is the verb:

NOUN: His prophecy was fulfilled shortly after his death.
VERB: The oracle at Delphi prophesied the tragic fate of Oedipus.

proved, proven *Proved* is the usual past participle of *prove*, but *proven* is also used, especially as an adjective:

She has proved her point.
His theories are now proven facts.

Proverb See **Epigram.**

provided, providing   Both are used (often with *that*) as conjunctions meaning "on the condition that":

Your money will be refunded provided you return the damaged merchandise.   [Or: provided that, providing (that).]

Provincialism   See **Localism.**

Pun   A figure of speech in which a word is used humorously in two senses at the same time:

Max Beerbohm once declined an invitation to go for a hike in the Swiss Alps by saying, "Put me down as an anti-climb Max."
Nunswear firm bows to new habits   [A newspaper headline.]
May we have the next dents?   [Sign outside a car-repair shop.]

The best puns play on both sound and meaning. A reasonable amount of punning adds variety to writing. Overdone, puns lose their effectiveness.

Punctuation   For help in punctuation, see the entries on the various marks of punctuation: **Colon, Comma, Dash, Ellipsis, Exclamation mark, Parentheses, Period, Question mark, Quotation marks, Semicolon.**

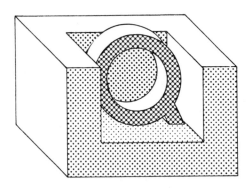

quay   Place where ships load and unload. The standard pronunciation is /kē/, though some people, misled by the spelling, pronounce the word /kwā/ or /kā/.

Question   See **Interrogative sentences, Question mark.**

Question mark (?)   **1 Uses.** (a) A question mark is used at the end of a sentence that the writer intends as a question:

Did they hire a lawyer?   What does an emulsifier do?
The final exam was canceled?   You were joking, weren't you?

210

b) A question mark may be used after each item in a series of interrogative expressions, for emphasis:

Has anyone bothered to consider the cost of renting costumes? of paying royalties? of buying sheet music? of hiring musicians?

c) A question mark, generally in parentheses, may be used as an editorial mark to show that a statement of fact is questionable or a date is only approximate:

Edward the Confessor (1002?–1066) was the last English king descended from Alfred the Great.

2 With other punctuation. (a) When a question mark and a quotation mark fall together, the question mark is placed inside the closing quotation mark if it applies to the quoted sentence, and outside if it applies to the complete sentence:

She read the poem a second time and then asked, "Who wrote this?"
How did you keep from laughing when he said, "Like cool, man"?

When both the complete sentence and the quoted sentence are questions, only one question mark is used—inside the closing quotation mark:

Does he have to answer the phone by saying, "Who intrudes?"
Which cartoon character always says, "What's up, doc?"

b) When a parenthetical question within a sentence is set off by dashes or enclosed in parentheses, the question mark is put before the second dash or inside the parentheses:

I've heard the Apes' new album—did you know they're not going to record together any more?—but I don't really like it.
Jim Peters (he sat behind you in typing, didn't he?) and Brad Ulrich are my campaign managers.

c) When a question mark and parenthesis fall together at the end of a sentence, the question mark goes inside the parenthesis if it applies only to the parenthetical material, outside if it applies only to the rest of the sentence:

Steve offered to sell me his motorcycle for ten dollars (doesn't that sound suspicious?).   [Notice that another punctuation mark must be used to end the complete sentence.]
How many hockey games have you seen this winter (I mean live, not on television)?

When both the complete sentence and the parenthetical material are questions, only one mark is used—outside the parentheses:

Is Don Washington a good debater (that is, is he good enough to substitute for Willy at the tournament next weekend)?

3 Unnecessary question marks. (a) A question mark is not used after indirect questions or after polite requests phrased as questions:

Mr. Pratt asked Mary Anne when her report would be ready.
Will you please settle your account by the end of next month.

b) A question mark in parentheses used to indicate sarcasm or irony is a weak, amateurish device and is better omitted:

We all fell asleep watching that hilarious new situation comedy.   [Not: that hilarious (?) new situation comedy.]

Quotation marks (" ")   **1** Quotation marks are used to enclose the exact words of the speaker:

"Why didn't you call me last night?" Judy asked.
"I did," Steve answered, "but your line was always busy."
"It couldn't have been," she objected. "No one called all evening."
"The line was busy," he insisted. Then, beginning to look suspicious, he asked, "Are you sure you weren't using the phone?"
"Well, I did make one or two calls," she admitted. "But I called only Therese and Pat and Sandy, and I didn't talk to any of them for more than forty-five minutes. You should have been able to get me between calls."

a) Notice that introductory and explanatory expressions (*Judy asked*, *Steve answered*, *she objected*) are set off by a comma or, if they interrupt the quoted sentence, by two commas. If a quoted sentence ends with a question mark or an exclamation point, though, that mark serves; no comma is added.

b) All sentences belonging to one uninterrupted quotation are put in one set of quotation marks. (See the last two sentences in the example conversation.)

c) Periods and commas are put inside the closing quotation mark:

After thinking a moment, he said, "I'll give you another chance."
I answered, "That's very good of you," but I didn't mean it.

d) Semicolons are always put outside the closing quotation mark:

Uncle Art looked up and snapped, "It's time you learned to be accurate"; then he went back to checking the columns of figures.

e) A question mark or an exclamation point is put inside the quotation mark if it applies only to the quoted matter, outside if it applies to the complete sentence that contains the quotation:

Closing the back door, Dad asked me, "Were you born in a barn?"
Michael screamed at his sister, "Turn off that radio!"
Wasn't it Julius Caesar who said, "I came, I saw, I conquered"?
How tired I got of her saying, "That's not my problem"!

When both the sentence and the quotation ending the sentence are questions or exclamations, only one mark is used — inside the closing quotation mark:

Don't you know it annoys him every time you ask, "How's tricks?"
What a relief it was to hear him yell, "They're safe!"

f) A new paragraph is generally used for each change of speaker, as in the example conversation at the beginning of this article. But when short bits of conversation are given to illustrate a point, rather than for their own sake, they may be put together in one paragraph:

The best stories told about Calvin Coolidge illustrate not only his laconic speech but also his ready wit. One evening at a dinner in Washington a matron boasted to a group of friends, "I'll bet *I* can get him to talk." With this, she went up to Coolidge and said, "Mr. President, I've just bet that I can make you say at least three words." "You lose," he replied.

When a quoted passage is made up of more than one paragraph, an opening quotation mark is put at the beginning of each paragraph, but a closing quotation mark is put only at the end of the last paragraph.

2 Quotation marks are used to enclose any direct quotation from another writer. Before such quotations, which are not part of a conversation, a colon rather than a comma is generally used, especially if the quotation is more than one sentence:

Though Ralph Waldo Emerson urged nonconformity, he did not pretend it was an easy course to follow: "What I must do is all that concerns me, not what people think. This rule, equally arduous in actual and in intellectual life, may serve for the whole distinction between greatness and meanness. It is the harder because you will always find those who think they know what is your duty better than you know it."

Above the shelf of delicate, expensive china hung this warning: "If you break it, it's yours."

A very long quoted passage is often presented without quotation marks, especially in typed and printed material. Then the whole passage is indented, and in typed matter single-spaced, in printed matter often set in smaller type than the rest of the text.

3 Quotation marks are generally used to enclose titles of chapters of books, magazine articles, essays, short stories, short poems, and songs:

He began by reading "The Harbor" from Sandburg's *Chicago Poems*.
She gave Jo a silver music box that plays "Beautiful Dreamer."

(See **Titles of books, articles, etc.**)

4 Quotation marks may be used to call the reader's attention to words that the writer is defining or explaining, and to special or technical terms that may be new to a reader:

This report will use the word "aborigine" to refer only to the primitive tribes now living in Australia.
The last letter of the alphabet is called "zed" in England.

(Many writers prefer to italicize such words. See **Underlining.**)

5 A quotation within a quotation is enclosed in single quotation marks:

Ed asked anxiously, "Didn't you just hear someone call 'Help'?"
"Then," Roy continued, "he shook his fist and yelled, 'I'll get you yet, Red Baron!'"
"It was John Donne who first used the phrase 'for whom the bell tolls,'" Lucy informed us.

6 Unnecessary quotation marks. (a) Quotation marks are not used to enclose *indirect* quotations:

He said that Judge Coffey is strict but fair.   [Not: He said that "Judge Coffey is strict but fair."]

However, even when you are reporting someone's speech indirectly, you may want to emphasize the fact that certain of the words you use are the exact words spoken; then you may put those words in quotation marks. If you have no particular reason for emphasizing that they are the exact words, there is no need to use quotation marks:

Rivers pointed to the failure of the President's "divide and conquer" campaign in the previous election.
Joe never bothered with names; every man was "mate" and every woman "lady."   [If the quotation marks were omitted here, the words would be italicized. See **Underlining,** section 3.]

b) It is rarely a good idea to enclose in quotation marks words or phrases that seem a little informal or slangy for the context. If a word is appropriate, using it requires no apology; if it isn't appropriate, it should not be used at all:

After listening to their insulting remarks for over an hour, Ted finally "blew his top."   [Omit the quotation marks; the phrase is perfectly appropriate in this informal context.]
Although O'Neill's *Strange Interlude* was considered "way out" when it was first produced, compared with today's experimental theater it is quite conventional.   [*Way out* is clearly inappropriate in this formal context. Either substitute a phrase like *extremely innovative*, or rewrite the sentence.]

c) Quotation marks are occasionally used to indicate sarcasm or irony. But a too frequent use of this device is considered a mark of weak, amateurish writing and should be avoided:

The only five-syllable word in Marvin's extensive vocabulary is *delicatessen*.   [Not: Marvin's "extensive" vocabulary.]

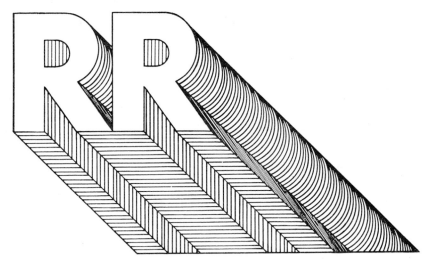

radio   The verb and noun forms are regular. *radioed, radioing; radios, radio's.*

raise   See **rise, raise.**

raise, rear   *Raise* is the term generally used to mean "bring up"; *rear* is the formal term:

GENERAL: David was raised (*or* brought up) by his older sister.
FORMAL: The author was reared by education-minded parents.

re-   Words made with the prefix *re-*, meaning "again," are usually written as solid — or single — words: *reorder, relive, reread.* But the prefix is hyphened: (1) When the form without the hyphen has a different meaning:

release the prisoners	re-lease the apartment
reform a criminal	re-form your opinions
retreat from battle	re-treat the wood

2) When the prefix is to be especially emphasized:

He re-stated the question a fourth time.

Usage varies when the part following *re-* begins with an *e.* Such words are sometimes hyphened or written with a dieresis (*re-employ, reëmploy; re-explain, reëxplain*), but it is becoming more common to write them as solid words (*reemploy, reexplain*).

real, really   In formal English and informal writing *real* is used only as an adjective, and *really* as an adverb:

The real purpose of the expedition was to locate enemy bases.
Is it really necessary to raise taxes again this year?

In colloquial usage *real* is often used as an adverb meaning "very," but this use is not appropriate in writing:

COLLOQUIAL: He was real nervous about having to speak first.
WRITTEN: He was very nervous about having to speak first. [Or: He was really nervous about having to speak first.]

reason is because   In formal English the expression "the reason is" is followed by a noun or a noun clause beginning with *that*:

The reason he refused is his *shyness*. [Noun.]
The reason he refused is *that he is shy*. [Noun clause.]

In informal speech and frequently in informal writing, many people use the connective *because*, which more obviously stresses the idea of reason:

The reason he refused is *because of his shyness*.
The reason he refused is *because he is shy*.

receipt, recipe   At one time these words were used interchangeably to mean "a set of directions for preparing something." Today *receipt* is seldom used in this sense except in certain regional dialects. It is used mainly to mean "a written statement that something has been received."

reckon   A localism for *think* or *suppose*:

LOCALISM: I reckon I should have studied more.
GENERAL: I suppose I should have studied more.

Redundancy   The use of unnecessary words, especially of words that repeat an idea expressed elsewhere in the sentence:

And then the man in the trench coat [he] started to run, too.
None of the congressmen to whom I wrote [to] answered my letter.
Your appointment is for 3:30 p.m. Monday [afternoon].
Entry into the building was restricted to military personnel [and no civilians were allowed].

(For further examples, see **Tautology.**)

refer   See **allude, refer.**

refer back   Though *refer back* is commonly used, the *back* is unnecessary in most sentences:

The summary on page 572 refers [back] to the chart on page 568.

Reference of pronouns   A pronoun has little specific meaning of its own; it gets its exact meaning from the word or words to which it refers — its *antecedent.* Generally the antecedent of a pronoun is made clear by the context. In the sentence "Al would have bought the boots, but they were too small," the antecedent of the pronoun *they* is clearly *boots.* But if a sentence is so phrased that the antecedent is not clear or if the antecedent is omitted, confusion may result.

1 Ambiguous reference. Sometimes a pronoun is so placed that it might refer to either of two antecedents. There are three ways to avoid this ambiguity: (a) replace the pronoun with a noun, (b) move the pronoun closer to the intended antecedent, or (c) rephrase the sentence:

FAULTY: The partnership between Katz and Riley was dissolved when *he* retired.
CLEAR: The partnership between Katz and Riley was dissolved when *Riley* retired.

FAULTY: Anita seldom wrote to her sister when *she* was away at college.
CLEAR: When *she* was away at college, Anita seldom wrote to her sister. [Or: When her sister was away at college, Anita seldom wrote to *her.*]

FAULTY: Ted doesn't enjoy playing chess with Ralph because *he* is a much better player.
CLEAR: Ted, *who* is a much better player, doesn't enjoy playing chess with Ralph. [Or: Ted doesn't enjoy playing chess with Ralph, *who* is a much better player.]

A sentence containing two or more pronouns referring to different antecedents may also be ambiguous. Often the only way to remove the ambiguity is by rewriting the sentence:

FAULTY: Sam continued to work for Mr. Fuller, even though *he* disliked *him.*
CLEAR: Even though he disliked Mr. Fuller, Sam continued to work for him. [Or: Even though Mr. Fuller disliked him, Sam continued to work for him.]

(See also **Ambiguity,** section 1.)

2 Vague reference. The intended antecedent of a pronoun should be stated, not merely implied:

ANTECEDENT MISSING: Ed thinks flying is the best way to travel, although he has never been on *one.*
CLEAR: Ed thinks flying is the best way to travel, although he has never been on a *plane.*

ANTECEDENT MISSING: She said that a library is a pleasant place to work but *they* have to be on their feet a good deal.
CLEAR: She said that a library is a pleasant place to work but *librarians* have to be on their feet a good deal.

If the antecedent is a noun used as a modifier or possessive, the reference will also be vague and perhaps confusing:

FAULTY: We stopped at one or two souvenir stands but didn't see *any* worth buying.
CLEAR: We stopped at one or two souvenir stands but didn't see any *souvenirs* worth buying. [Or: . . . but didn't see *anything* worth buying.]

FAULTY: When Frank's father left, *he* gave the dog away.
CLEAR: When his father left, *Frank* gave the dog away.

The pronouns *which*, *this*, and *that* are often used to refer to the whole idea expressed in a preceding group of words:

She didn't offer to help, *which* was unusual for her.

But this use should be avoided if there is any danger that a reader may think the pronoun refers to a noun in the group:

FAULTY: Grandfather was always bringing us presents, *which* Dad disapproved of.
CLEAR: Dad disapproved of Grandfather's always bringing us presents. [Or: Grandfather was always bringing us presents—a practice Dad disapproved of.]

3 Indefinite reference. The use of *it* and *they* without a definite antecedent is common in everyday speech. But in writing this use is better avoided:

FAULTY: When I read Helen Hayes's autobiography, *it* made me realize what hard work acting is.
CLEAR: Reading Helen Hayes's autobiography made me realize what hard work acting is.

FAULTY: Since the world's supply of food is decreasing as the population is increasing, *they* are looking for new sources of food.
CLEAR: Since the world's supply of food is decreasing as the population is increasing, scientists are looking for new sources of food. [Or: . . . new sources of food are being sought.]

(For further examples, see **Indefinite it** and **they**.)

Referent   The meaning of any word lies in what the word stands for—or "refers" to. Whatever person or thing the word refers to is called its *referent* /ref'ər ənt/.

Reflexive pronouns   Pronouns ending with *self* or *selves*: *myself, yourself, himself, herself, itself, oneself, ourselves, yourselves, themselves.* They are called *reflexive* pronouns because the action of the verb is turned back on the subject:

She burned *herself.*   [Direct object.]
The cat was giving *itself* a bath.   [Indirect object.]
We were proud of *ourselves.*   [Object of preposition.]

The forms *hisself, ourself, theirself,* and *theirselves* are nonstandard. (For further discussion, see **myself.**)

regard, regards   The standard idioms are *in regard to* and *with regard to* ("In regard to your request, we are sending you our new catalog and our revised price list"). In nonstandard English *in regards to* and *with regards to* are often used ("In regards to your question").

regardless   The ending *-less* gives *regardless* a negative meaning: "without regard to." Adding the prefix *ir- — irregardless —* makes a double negative. Though *irregardless* is often heard, it is not considered good usage and should be avoided in writing:

STANDARD: They will come regardless of the expense.

In colloquial usage *regardless* is used as an adverb meaning "anyway": They will sell the stock, *regardless.*

Regular verbs   Verbs whose past tense and past participle are formed in the regular way — by adding *-ed* to the simple form: *stamp, stamped, stamped; play, played, played.* (See **Irregular verbs.**)

Relative adverb   When an adverb like *when, where, why, since, before,* or *after* is used to introduce an adjective clause, it is called a *relative adverb:*

Grandmother remembers the days *when* only the very rich had cars.
A plaque now marks the spot *where* the guillotine stood.

Relative clause   Since adjective clauses are usually introduced by a relative pronoun (*who, which, that*) or a relative adverb (*where, when, why, after*) that refers, or "relates," to an antecedent, they are often called *relative clauses:*

His coming twenty minutes late was the straw *that broke the camel's back.* [Modifies the antecedent *straw.*]
A month *after she retired* the company went bankrupt.   [Modifies the antecedent *month.*]

A succession of relative clauses in one sentence is likely to be awkward. In revising first drafts, watch out for sentences that follow a "house that Jack built" pattern:

AWKWARD: The artifacts that were found in the clearing that lies between the two extinct volcanoes that are located due north of the town proved conclusively that a tribe that was far more advanced than its neighbors had lived there.

BETTER: The artifacts found in the clearing between the two extinct volcanoes due north of the town proved conclusively that a tribe far more advanced than its neighbors had lived there.

(For punctuation of relative clauses, see **Comma**, section 5.)

Relative pronouns   The pronouns *who*, *whose*, *whom*, *which*, and *that* — used to introduce adjective clauses. Ordinarily *who* is used to refer to persons, *which* to refer to things, and *that* to refer to persons or things:

Sometimes people that (*or* who) know the most say the least.
The team that (*or* which) scores first has the advantage.

remember   Standard English does not use *of* after the verb *remember*:

NONSTANDARD: Dad couldn't remember of where he'd parked the car.
STANDARD: Dad couldn't remember where he'd parked the car.

Repetition   The *unnecessary* repetition of the same word (or the use of the same word in two different senses) in a short space is likely to be annoying and distracting to readers:

The potatoes had been *baked* long enough to be thoroughly *baked*, but they turned out to be only partly *baked*.

But *intentional* repetition, if not overused, can be an effective device for gaining emphasis. Repeating key words or key ideas in different words or repeating a particular construction can make your ideas more forceful and more memorable:

WITHOUT REPETITION: What he remembered most about the prison camp was the gray buildings, uniforms, meals, and days.
EFFECTIVE REPETITION: What he remembered most about the prison camp was the grayness — the gray buildings, the gray uniforms, the gray meals, the gray days.

WITHOUT REPETITION: The steady thumping of the antiaircraft guns soon got on her nerves.
EFFECTIVE REPETITION: The thump, thump, thump of the antiaircraft guns soon got on her nerves.

WITHOUT REPETITION: The bowl slid off the tray, and the hot gravy splashed on the table, the rug, the wall, and Mrs. Morton's dress.
EFFECTIVE REPETITION: The bowl slid off the tray, and the hot gravy splashed on the table, on the rug, on the wall, and on Mrs. Morton's dress.

Reports   Business, technical, and official reports should be impersonal and businesslike in tone. They should be complete, of course, but also as concise as possible. When you are writing such reports, go straight to the point. Set down all facts, opinions, and recommendations briefly and clearly. Be sure also to distinguish between facts and opinions. Wherever you express a personal opinion, make clear that it is one, and back up your judgment with sound reasons.

Mechanical devices—like putting information into the form of tables, diagrams, graphs; and listing, labeling, or numbering ideas or steps—are often useful. This is especially true in committee reports, where the ideas of several people have to be combined into a clear, concise piece of writing. For example:

REPORT OF THE COMMITTEE ON IMPROVING SCHOOL-BUS SERVICE

Date: October 15, 19—

To: Dunbar High School Student Council

Subject: Ways to provide adequate and prompt school-bus service.

   This report was requested by the Student Council following complaints from students and parents about the overcrowding on some of the buses and the frequent lateness of most of the buses.

   Our committee was appointed by the Council president on September 15, 19—.

Procedure: The committee investigated the situation and conferred with Mr. Felix Kerl, assistant superintendent and director of school services; Mr. Harvey Matz, our principal; Mrs. Carol Zeller, assistant principal of Burnside Junior High School; and Mrs. Marvin Grorby, PTA representative.

Recommendations: The recommendations of the committee are as follows:

1. New bus routes should be worked out so that no bus will carry more students than it can seat. Mr. Kerl agrees, and his staff is already working on new routes and schedules.

2. Dunbar and Burnside students should insofar as possible be assigned to separate buses so that a bus will not need to make two school stops, which lengthens each run by at least fifteen minutes, and so that the bus schedules can conform better to the different opening and closing times of the two schools. Mr. Kerl, Mr. Matz, and Mrs. Zeller will support this request.

3. Classes going on field trips should not use school buses if they will not return to school by 2:45 p.m., in time for the buses to begin their regular afternoon runs. Classes going on field trips that extend beyond school hours should apply

to the PTA Enrichment Program for funds to charter a bus. Mr. Matz and Mrs. Grorby concur and will help work out the necessary procedures.

4. The Student Council should help relieve congestion at the afternoon departure time by working out an assigned place for each bus to load and by providing signs identifying the buses.

The committee urges the Council to accept these recommendations and take action at once.

Respectfully submitted,

Stanley Nizer, Chairman
Philip Brantingham
Ruth Jensen
Howard Casey

Research paper   A research paper (also called a term paper, library paper, reference paper) is a report, usually of from 1000 to 2000 words, of the writer's conclusions after a systematic investigation of a subject. Generally much of the writer's information comes through reading, and the facts and ideas that he derives from his reading are acknowledged in footnotes.

Most research papers consist of four parts: (1) a title page (giving the title of the paper, the writer's name, the name of the course, and the date the paper is submitted), (2) an outline of the paper (which serves as a table of contents), (3) the paper itself, and (4) a bibliography (a list of all books, magazine articles, and other materials used in preparing the paper). A writer sometimes also includes a *preface*, following the title page, in which he comments on any special problems involved in his research or acknowledges any special help received during his investigation. Additional information that he thinks readers might find interesting — maps, charts, tables, diagrams, pictures — is put in an *appendix*, after the bibliography.

(See also **Bibliography; Footnotes.**)

residence   See **home, house, residence.**

resign   Usually followed by *from*, though sometimes immediately by the object:

The ambassador to Ghana has resigned from his post.   [Or: The ambassador has resigned his post.]

Resolution   A formal statement of opinion or intent adopted by a committee, club, or other organization. It is used typically for group expres-

222

sions of sympathy, thanks, and so on, and for recommendations of action. The style is formal and impersonal, and the wording is standardized:

WHEREAS, The Student Association of King High School has received a great deal of cooperation and support from the merchants of Harperville in conducting its annual Spring Bazaar; and

WHEREAS, The association has also received a great deal of financial assistance from these merchants in the past, specifically through their buying advertising space in various programs printed for association activities, therefore be it

Resolved, That a letter of appreciation be sent to each of the merchants who has worked with us; and be it further

Resolved, That a copy of each of these letters be sent to the Harperville Chamber of Commerce.

Arthur Daniels, Secretary

respectively, respectfully   Avoid confusing these words. *Respectively* means "each in the order given":

Gold, silver, and bronze medals are awarded to the first-, second-, and third-place winners *respectively*.

Respectfully means "in a respectful or deferential manner":

Angry though he was, the attorney was careful to speak *respectfully* to the judge.

Restrictive and nonrestrictive   A *restrictive* modifier—one that is used to tell which particular person or thing is meant—is not set off by commas from the word it modifies:

Only the people *in the front row* could hear him.
Anyone *wearing a Bunker-for-President button* got in free.
A house *built in 1530* would not be centrally heated, of course.
The only other person *who knew Jack's lines* was my brother.
A deciduous tree is a tree *that sheds its leaves annually*.
The evils of Reconstruction became particularly obvious during the years *when Grant was President*.

But a *nonrestrictive* modifier—which is used merely to add a descriptive or explanatory detail—is set off from the word it modifies:

We sat in our usual place, *in the front row*.
Bob, *wearing a Go-for-Garvey button*, was passing out leaflets.
The White Horse Inn, *built in 1530*, is still in operation.
My brother, *who had registered for the drama course only because his girl friend was taking it*, has the lead in the play.
Elms and oaks are deciduous trees, *which shed their leaves annually*.
We spent the day in Galena, *where Ulysses S. Grant once lived*.

Adverb clauses that tell the particular time, place, reason, purpose, manner, condition, etc., are *restrictive* and are not set off:

He had started to run *before the signal was given.*
Terry put the key *where he thought you'd be sure to find it.*
I helped her *only because I couldn't think of a way to refuse.*
He wrote himself a note *so that he wouldn't forget anything.*
Clyde acted *as though he owned the place.*
His coat got *so wet that it took three days to dry.*

Those that merely add explanatory details or comments (which could be omitted without changing the basic meaning of the sentence) are *nonrestrictive* and should be set off from the rest of the sentence:

He had started to run too soon, *before the signal was given.*
Jan wanted to stand near the back, *where no one would notice her.*
He finally ate at El Diner, *because it was the only place open.*
The note was written in code, *so that it was meaningless to me.*
Ellie acted surprised, *as though she hadn't expected a present.*
We sent them complimentary tickets, *though we hated to do it*
Be sure to call us, *no matter how late it is.*

(For further discussion and examples, see **Comma,** section 5; **Dash,** section 3; and **Parentheses,** sections 1 and 4.)

Reverend   A term of respect for clergymen. In formal English it is preceded by *the,* and must be followed by the first name, initials, or title of the person as well as his last name:

the Reverend Thomas Crewe   the Rev. Thomas Crewe
the Reverend T. J. Crewe   the Rev. Thomas J. Crewe
the Reverend Mr. Crewe   the Rev. Dr. Crewe

In informal English *Reverend* is sometimes used with only the last name:

Reverend Crewe   the Reverend Crewe

The use of *reverend* as a noun meaning "clergyman" (Ask the reverend to stay for dinner) is increasingly found in informal English.

Rhetoric   *Rhetoric* is sometimes used as a disparaging term for inflated, wordy, insincere speech or writing. But used by linguists, the term refers to the study and practice of the effective use of language. It deals with the selection of those words and constructions that will most clearly and effectively convey a writer's or speaker's meaning on a particular subject, to a particular audience, for a particular purpose.

Rhetorical question   A question asked only for effect—usually to emphasize a point, to suggest an opinion, or to introduce a topic. No direct answer is expected (though it is, of course, obvious):

There is hardly a person who does not go around proclaiming that we must do something about pollution. Yet despite all our talk, clouds of smog still hang over our cities. The number of polluted lakes and rivers keeps increasing. Our streets and highways continue to be littered. Few antipollution laws are passed. And those that are, are either too lenient or too casually enforced. Is counteracting pollution nothing more than a popular topic for discussion?

rise, arise   In referring to people, *arise* is formal and poetic; *rise* is rather formal; *get up* is general.

rise, raise   *Rise* (*rose, risen, rising*) is intransitive and does not take an object; *raise* (*raised, raised, raising*) is transitive and takes an object:

The cost of a college education *is rising* rapidly.
He *raised* the rent again last month.

rôle, role   In formal writing the circumflex accent is sometimes kept; in informal, it is usually dropped.

Roman numerals   See **Numbers,** section 5.

Root   A word or part of a word that is used as a base for forming other words, as *new* is the root of *renew, newly; ject* is the root of *reject, object, projectile, injection.*

round   See **around, round.**

route   Generally pronounced /rüt/ (rhymes with *suit*), but /rout/ (rhymes with *trout*) is used in the Army and for newspaper and delivery routes.

Run-together sentence   When you put two independent statements into one sentence, you ordinarily join them with a conjunction and a comma or separate them with a semicolon. If you use a comma alone between the clauses or no punctuation at all, you have a run-together sentence (sometimes called a *comma fault*). There are four ways in which a run-together sentence can be corrected:
   1 Repunctuate with a period:

RUN-TOGETHER: Mr. and Mrs. Avery are moving to Texas, he's going to manage his company's branch office in Dallas.
REVISED: Mr. and Mrs. Avery are moving to Texas. He's going to manage his company's branch office in Dallas.

   2 Repunctuate with a semicolon:

RUN-TOGETHER: O'Hare is probably the world's busiest airport, it handles over 1900 flights a day.

REVISED: O'Hare is probably the world's busiest airport; it handles over 1900 flights a day.

RUN-TOGETHER: Dr. Frant must have approved of the plan, otherwise he would have spoken out against it.
REVISED: Dr. Frant must have approved of the plan; otherwise he would have spoken out against it.

3 Insert a coordinating conjunction (*and, but, for, or, nor, yet*) to make a compound sentence:

RUN-TOGETHER: The hi-fi was thumping in one room, the TV was blasting in another.
REVISED: The hi-fi was thumping in one room, and the TV was blasting in another.

4 Rephrase the run-together, using a subordinate clause or a verbal phrase to show the exact relationship between the ideas:

RUN-TOGETHER: I had to read the menu to Grandma, she had forgotten her glasses.
REVISED: I had to read the menu to Grandma, who had forgotten her glasses.

RUN-TOGETHER: We got two more runs in the seventh inning, this gave us a four-run lead.
REVISED: We got two more runs in the seventh inning, giving us a four-run lead.

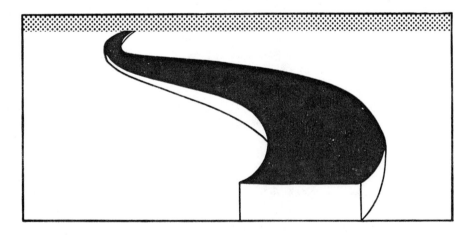

saint   *Saint* is abbreviated with proper names (*St. Augustine, St. Helena*). The plural form is abbreviated *SS.* or *Sts.* (*SS. Cyril and Methodius, Sts. Matthew and Mark*). Sometimes the French feminine form *Sainte* is used (*Sault Sainte Marie*) with the abbreviation *Ste.*

salary, wages   *Salary* is used to refer to a fixed compensation paid at regular intervals (often monthly or semimonthly) for clerical or professional work. *Wages* is used for money paid an employee at relatively short intervals, often daily or weekly, especially for manual or mechanical work.

same   *Same* as a pronoun is no longer used in such business expressions as "Enclosed find payment for same." Current usage prefers *it* or *them*:

Please complete the enclosed application, and return *it* by Thursday. [Not: return *same*.]

Sarcasm   A remark made with the intention of hurting someone's feelings by taunting, ridiculing, mocking at, or sneering at him. Sarcastic remarks are often ironical (saying one thing but meaning another):

When Arnold finally arrived, after getting lost twice following my directions, the first thing he said was, "You make a great navigator!"

But sarcasm may also be direct:

After seeing Sarah's performance in the class play, her brother told her sarcastically, "There is certainly a place for you in the theater—in the audience."

Since sarcasm is often indicated by the tone of the voice, it sometimes passes unnoticed in writing. In dialogue, if it is not unmistakably indicated by the context, writers often label it, as in the second example. But usually the sarcasm is obvious. (See also **Irony**.)

Satire   The use of ridicule, irony, or sarcasm to make fun of a person, a custom, an idea, or an institution. This "fun-making" may be harmless, intended only to amuse the reader or listener, or it may be a bitter attack intended to discredit by ridicule the person or thing at which it is aimed. It may be concerned with a trivial and laughter-provoking subject, such as the latest in wearing apparel for dogs; or it may expose the weaknesses of the social and political customs and policies of a nation.

say, state, talk   *Say* is a general word for speaking: Bob *said* that he was planning to quit. *State* implies a more formal, orderly communication: The chairman *stated* his objections at the City Council meeting. *Talk* implies conversation, especially of an informal kind: My mother and the woman next door *were talking* about the difficulties of raising children. (For the use of *say* in reporting conversation, see **Conversation**.)

scarcely   See **Double negative**.

scarcely . . . when   The idiom is *scarcely . . . when*, not *scarcely . . . than*:

The class had *scarcely* begun *when* the fire bell rang.

227

School subjects   The name of a school or college course is not capitalized unless it is the name of a language or a specific numbered course:

I wish I had taken French or Algebra 2 instead of botany.

Schwa (ə)   The *schwa* /shwä/ is the symbol used in this book and in most recent dictionaries to simplify the system of showing pronunciation: *prominent* — /prom'ə nənt/, *surveillance* — /sər vā'ləns/. The schwa represents the neutral vowel sound of many unstressed syllables:

a as in *about*	*i* as in *April*	*u* as in *circus*
e as in *taken*	*o* as in *lemon*	*y* as in *martyr*

Seasons   The names of the seasons — *spring, summer, fall, winter, midsummer*, and so on — are not capitalized except for emphasis in some poetry or nature essays.

secretive   There are two different words with this spelling: one derived from the word *SEcret* and generally pronounced /sē'krə tiv/; another derived from the word *seCRETE* and always pronounced /si krē'tiv/.

seem   *Can't seem* is a useful informal idiom for the more formal and logical *seem unable*:

INFORMAL: Lenny can't seem to overcome his shyness.
FORMAL: Lenny seems unable to overcome his shyness.

self   As a prefix *self-* is usually hyphened to the root word:

self-interest   self-evident   self-cleaning

But there is no hyphen in words like *selfish* and *selfless*, in which *self* is the root to which the endings *-ish* and *-less* have been added.
For the use of pronouns ending in *self* (*myself, yourself, himself*, etc.), see **Intensive pronouns** and **Reflexive pronouns.**

Semantics   The scientific study of the meanings and the changes in meaning of words. Some entries in this Handbook that deal with points of semantics are **Abstract and concrete words, Connotation, Generalizations, Loaded words,** and **Words: formation of.**

semi-   Prefix meaning "half" (*semicircle*), "occurring twice within a certain period" (*semiannually*), or "partially" (*semiconscious*). Before a word beginning with a capital letter or with *i*, a hyphen is used: *semi-Norman, semi-industrial.*

Semicolon (;)   **1** A semicolon is used to separate the clauses of a compound sentence when they are not joined by a coordinating conjunction (*and, but, for, or, nor, yet*):

I'm not good at telling jokes; I always forget the punch line.
Mary confessed her part in the plot; Karen denied everything.
The almanac is mine; the other books are Wynn's.

Remember that connectives like *then, still, however, moreover, neverthe-less, consequently* are not coordinating conjunctions but conjunctive adverbs. Main clauses joined by these adverbs are separated by a semicolon:

Leo started to answer back; then he remembered his promise.
Most of the congressmen disliked raising taxes in an election year; however, they had no choice.

2 A semicolon is generally used (instead of a comma) between main clauses joined by *and, but*, etc., if either clause contains a comma:

Paula, who loses at least three things a week, lost another wallet this morning; and her mother was furious.
During the campaign of 1896 the Democratic candidate, William Jennings Bryan, traveled thousands of miles speaking to voters; but the Republican candidate, William McKinley, who made all his speeches from his own front porch, won.

3 A semicolon is used (instead of a comma) between items of a series if the items contain commas:

My aunt's tour included overnight stops in San Sebastian, Spain; Antibes, France; and San Remo, Italy.
Only three people didn't attend the class picnic: Ed Arnold, who was in Beloit visiting relatives; Rochelle Hudson, who was at her sister's graduation; and John Boles, who had a bad case of poison ivy.

Sentence fragment   A piece of a sentence that has been detached from the sentence to which it belongs and punctuated as a separate sentence:

FRAGMENT: John suddenly disappeared around the corner of the house. *Leaving me to make peace with Mrs. Gorstop.*   [Participial phrase.]

A sentence fragment can easily be corrected by joining it to the sentence it was cut off from:

CORRECTED: John suddenly disappeared around the corner of the house, leaving me to make peace with Mrs. Gorstop.

Here are some other common types of fragments:

FRAGMENT: In extremely hot weather the demand for electric power increases sharply. *Because so many air conditioners are in use.*   [Adverb clause.]
CORRECTED: In extremely hot weather the demand for electric power increases sharply, because so many air conditioners are in use.

FRAGMENT: The current strike is expected to go on longer than the previous one. *Which lasted 119 days.*   [Adjective clause.]
CORRECTED: The current strike is expected to go on longer than the previous one, which lasted 119 days.

FRAGMENT: Joe has been going from used-car lot to used-car lot looking for a car. *One that costs less than a hundred dollars.*   [Appositive.]
CORRECTED: Joe has been going from used-car lot to used-car lot looking for a car, one that costs less than a hundred dollars.

FRAGMENT: She tried on every pair of boots in her size. *And then bought the first pair she had been shown.*   [Part of a compound verb.]
CORRECTED: She tried on every pair of boots in her size and then bought the first pair she had been shown.

   (Compare **Sentences: major and minor types,** section 2.)

Sentences: classifications   English sentences can be sorted, or "classified," in several different ways. Here we will review three common ones:
   1 By pattern. Sentences can be classified by their basic patterns. Most English sentences are built on just a few basic patterns. For example:
   a) SUBJECT — VERB   [S — V]:

Henry bowed.
A book fell off the shelf.
Help will arrive soon.

   b) SUBJECT — VERB — OBJECT   [S — V — O]:

Doug was chasing Larry.
Someone threw a snowball at me.

   c) SUBJECT — VERB — INDIRECT OBJECT — OBJECT   [S — V — IO — O]:

A neighbor had told Al the whole story.
She gives me a pain.

   d) SUBJECT — LINKING VERB — COMPLEMENT   [S — LV — C]:

Janos became a citizen.
The snow was dirty.

   e) SUBJECT — VERB — OBJECT — OBJECTIVE COMPLEMENT   [S — V — O — OC]:

Eduardo had dyed his mustache red.
The lodge members elected him Grand Geyser.

(See also the individual entries for the various sentence parts.)
   2 By number and kind of subject-verb units. Classified by this method, sentences fall into four groups:
   a) *Simple sentences* — sentences containing only one subject and one verb — either or both of which may be compound:

The *plane* **landed**.
The *captain* and the *first officer* **congratulated** each other.
Edwin **opened** the refrigerator and **peered** in.
Mark and *I* **borrowed** a ladder, **climbed** to the roof, and **rescued** the cat.

b) *Compound sentences* — sentences made up of two or more simple sentences. The simple sentences may be joined by a comma and coordinating conjunction (*and, but, for, yet, or, nor, so*):

The *meat* **was** dry, and the *gravy* **was** greasy.
The *Maxons* **were** at home, but *they* **wouldn't answer** the door.

Or the simple sentences may be joined by a semicolon:

Because of the fog the *plane* **did** not **land** in Chicago; *it* **went** on to Cincinnati.
At first *Mrs. Root* **looked** annoyed; then *she* **began** to laugh.

c) *Complex sentences* — sentences with one main clause and one or more subordinate clauses:

Has he ever worn the socks *that you knitted for him*?
I wondered *why Gertrude was so upset*.
When Uncle Ted saw us on the station platform, he seemed surprised, *as though he hadn't expected us to meet him*.

d) *Compound-complex sentences* — sentences containing two or more main clauses and one or more subordinate clauses:

The real-estate agent knew that the roof leaked, but he didn't tell us. [Two main clauses joined by *but* and one subordinate clause — *that the roof leaked*.]

(See also **Clause** and the individual entries for the sentences in this classification.)
3 By purpose.
a) *Declarative sentences* are used to make statements:

Squirrels, like rats, are rodents.

b) *Imperative sentences* are used to express commands or requests:

Do not write in this space.

c) *Interrogative sentences* are used to ask questions:

How did he break his arm?

d) *Exclamatory sentences* are used to express strong feeling:

What a fraud he was!

(For further examples, see the individual entries for the sentences in this classification.)

Sentences: major and minor types   Over the centuries that English has been a language it has developed a wide range of sentence patterns for communicating meaning. We express our thoughts, feelings, and ideas by putting words together in groups arranged according to these patterns. We do this without conscious effort, of course, since we learned the sentence patterns by imitation as we were growing up and they are as much a part of us as our vocabulary.

Grammarians classify the sentence patterns in a number of different ways. One way is into *major* and *minor* types.

1 Major-type sentences. The sentence patterns most commonly used belong to the major type. They are sentences like these:

Jennifer giggled.
Until last month Ralph sent money home every payday.
By noon everyone there was ready to scream.
Have they ever given Clyde the credit he deserves?
Up the stairs came Aunt Lu, dragging Sam along by the collar.
The senator termed the charge ridiculous.
You mind your own business, Tony, or you'll be sorry.*
How tall you've grown!
It is not easy to learn a foreign language quickly, especially one as difficult as Russian.
If I get stuck on a calculus problem, I can usually get my brother or my father to help me.
Before leaving the cottage, we turned off the water and drained the pipes so that there would be no danger of their bursting in freezing weather.

These are representative samples of major-type sentences. As you can see, they differ from one another in several respects: The first, for example, has no modifiers; the last (a complex sentence) has many, including an adverb clause. Some have a direct object. In addition, one has an indirect object and one an objective complement. Others have a predicate complement. One is a compound sentence with two coordinate clauses. One has a long appositive at the end, another a participial-phrase modifier. But all of them—long or short—are alike in one respect: All have a *subject* and a *verb*. These are the basic elements, the parts that serve as a framework to which all other parts are related.

2 Minor-type sentences. A common definition of a sentence is "a group of words that contains a subject and a verb and that is grammatically complete." Because the great majority of our sentences are of the major type, centered on a subject and a verb, this definition is a practical and useful guide—nine tenths of the time. But like many definitions that have been simplified for general use, it is not quite accurate, since it does not take into account many sentences that lack a subject or a verb or both, yet are perfectly good sentences. For example:

---

*Usually the subject in a command or request is not expressed: "Mind your own business, Tony. . . . ."

The more, the merrier.
On your way, please.
What a stupid thing for him to do!
Good riddance!

There are two ways of explaining sentences that do not fit the usual definition. A common practice is to explain that the sentences are "elliptical" — that is, words necessary for grammatical completeness but not for meaning have been omitted. For instance, the answer to the question "Where is the key" might be "It is on the table." It is more likely to be simply "On the table" — since the subject *It* and the verb *is* are clearly understood. By supplying the understood words, you can make the elliptical sentence fit the usual definition.

Many modern grammarians prefer another explanation. They point out that though the typical English sentence has a subject and a verb, there are many sentences of a "minor" type, without these elements. Nothing, they explain, is left out of these sentences; and no words need be "understood" in analyzing them. They are natural forms of expression and just as "correct" as the major sentences, though of more limited use. Here are some of the common kinds of minor-type sentences. Notice that the first four groups are forms used primarily in speech and would usually appear in writing only to record conversation.

a) Exclamations and interjections:

Gesundheit.   Help!   Oof!   Good grief!
Good morning.   Bon voyage.   What a mess!

b) Requests and commands:

Two cherry sundaes, two banana shakes, and six tacos to go.
One box of Sunshine birdseed, please.
No smoking.
Quiet, everybody!

c) Specific answers to questions:

["Where did Sam go?"]   "Out."
["Which car is yours?"]   "That red one on the end."
["Have you been waiting long?"]   "About an hour."
["What was Carol doing?"]   "Tie-dyeing a blouse."

d) Questions:

["C. B. DeMille wants to speak with you."]   "Who?"
["I'll meet you right after school."]   "Where?"

e) "Equational" sentences:

Out of sight, out of mind.
Waste not, want not.
The sooner, the better.

f) "Appositional" sentences (in which a predicate complement is set beside the subject without a linking verb):

That character class president?
A good idea, that.

g) Transitional sentences (by which one part of a speech or composition is linked to another):

So much for the history of the problem. Now for some possible solutions.

As you can see, though the sentences differ greatly in form, they all have one thing in common—all are, in their contexts, independent units that stand alone to express the intended meaning.

Sequence of tenses   See **Tenses of verbs,** section 3.

Series   For the punctuation of items in a series, see **Comma,** section 3, and **Semicolon,** section 3.

set   See **sit, set.**

shall, will   For many years the following two-part rule has been taught: To show simple future, use the auxiliary *shall* in the first person and *will* in the second and third ("I shall apply for the job"; "You will need a pencil"; "He will probably be the new editor"). To show determination, reverse the pattern, using *will* in the first person and *shall* in the second and third ("I will pass physics this time"; "You shall pay for this"; "He shall regret it"). But the rule, even though memorized by many, is rarely followed. Speakers of standard English generally use *will* (or its contraction *'ll*) in all persons to show both simple future and determination. *Shall* is seldom used except for special emphasis.

Shifted constructions   Ideas of equal importance in a sentence should be expressed by words in the same grammatical forms; that is, the constructions should be "parallel":

PARALLEL ADJECTIVES: As usual, Gomer's comments were highly *intelligent*, extremely *witty*, and exceedingly *caustic*.
PARALLEL VERBS: The skiers *zigged* to the left, *zagged* to the right, and then *plunged* out of sight behind a line of trees.

Using similar forms for similar ideas not only makes a smoother-sounding sentence, but also helps the reader understand easily how the ideas are related.

In the sentence "He likes swimming, boating, and to fish" the objects of the verb are not parallel; the first two are gerunds, the third an infinitive. In a sentence as simple as this, such an inconsistency does not obscure the meaning, though it does make the sentence sound awkward. However, in longer, more involved sentences, shifts in construction might easily confuse the reader.

In proofreading your papers, be on the alert for shifted constructions like these:

ADJECTIVE – NOUN SHIFT: Camels can be not only *stubborn* and *quarrelsome* but also downright vicious *beasts*.
PARALLEL ADJECTIVES: Camels can be not only *stubborn* and *quarrelsome* but also downright *vicious*.

NOUN – CLAUSE SHIFT: A skillful watchmaker must have sharp *eyes*, a mechanical *mind*, and *his fingers must be sensitive to tiny objects*.
PARALLEL NOUNS: A skillful watchmaker must have sharp *eyes*, a mechanical *mind*, and *fingers* sensitive to tiny objects.

GERUND PHRASE – CLAUSE SHIFT: Dr. Frank said that *using a variety of pesticides* is safer and more effective than *when you use the same one for everything*.
PARALLEL GERUND PHRASES: Dr. Frank said that *using a variety of pesticides* is safer and more effective than *using the same one for everything*.

INFINITIVE PHRASE – CLAUSE SHIFT: Arthur did not know whether *to go on to college* or *if he should start working* after finishing high school.
PARALLEL INFINITIVE PHRASES: Arthur did not know whether *to go on to college* or *to start working* after finishing high school.

Be alert also for shifts in tense, voice, person, and number, like these:

SHIFT IN TENSE: No sooner *had* the police car *pulled* into the drive than a fire engine *comes* tearing around the corner.
PARALLEL: No sooner *had* the police car *pulled* into the drive than a fire engine *came* tearing around the corner.

SHIFT IN VOICE: They *ushered* us to the door and we *were asked* to leave.
PARALLEL: They *ushered* us to the door and *asked* us to leave.   [Or: We *were ushered* to the door and (*were*) *asked* to leave.]

SHIFT IN PERSON: *Anyone* can stop smoking if *you* really want to.
PARALLEL: *Anyone* can stop smoking if *he* really wants to.   [Or: *You* can . . . if *you*. . . .]

SHIFT IN NUMBER: A *blacksnake* usually *runs* away when attacked, but if *they are* cornered, *they fight* back.
PARALLEL: *Blacksnakes* usually *run* away when attacked, but if *they are* cornered, *they fight* back.   [Or: A *blacksnake* . . . , but if *it is* cornered, *it fights* back.]

(See also **Correlative conjunctions**.)

Ships' names   In most books and generally in formal writing, the names of ships (aircraft, submarines, trains, etc.) are capitalized and italicized (underlined in handwriting): the *Titanic* (ship), the *Airacomet* (airplane), the *Super Chief* (train), the *Squalus* (submarine), the *Tinkerbelle* (sailboat). Use this style in your written work.

In some informal writing, especially in newspapers, such names are treated simply as proper names, capitalized but not italicized (or underlined): the Lusitania (ship), the Alouette (airplane), Apollo 14 (spaceship).

In all writing, names indicating the make and class of cars, planes, missiles, helicopters, and so on, are generally capitalized but not italicized: Pontiac Catalina (car), CF-104 Starfighter (plane), Minuteman (missile), Westland Scout (helicopter).

Shoptalk   Shoptalk is the special vocabulary used by people in a certain occupation. Stagehands, for example, use terms like *keystone, proscenium, dutchman, ratchet,* and *to size.* Electricians deal with *cathodes, resistance, circuits,* and *amps.* Hockey players talk about *icing the puck, stick handling, face-offs,* and *hat tricks.* Stockbrokers are concerned with *blue chips, quotations, pay-out ratios,* and *bull and bear markets.*

Shoptalk, then, consists of names for materials, processes, people, and tools in a special job. The names may be technical, like *trephine* in medicine or *parallax* in photography. More often they are clipped or made-up words like *to lip sync* in television, *blurb* in advertising, and *typo* and *cut* in printing.

Hobbies and other special interests of any kind involve shoptalk too. Ham radio operators use terms like *rig, transceiver,* and *patch,* and such expressions as *73* (meaning "regards"), *QSG* ("Have you a doctor nearby?"), and *Calling CQ* ("Does anybody anywhere feel like talking — about anything?"). Coin collectors discuss *galvanos, double-struck coins, cabinet pieces,* and *clad coinage.*

Sometimes shoptalk words move into the general vocabulary. In recent years, for instance, space flights and lunar landings have introduced many terms from the field of space exploration. People have been quick to take over such space shoptalk as *A-OK, go* ("All systems are go"), *to splash down,* and *to scrub.* And they are quite familiar with terms like *blast-off, countdown, launching pad, lunar module, docking,* and *EVA.*

But as a rule, shoptalk is not appropriate in speaking or writing that is intended for a general audience. To such a group it would be meaningless. Unless shoptalk is clearly defined, it is appropriate only for an audience familiar with the field in which it is used.

sic   *Sic* /sik/ (Latin for *thus, so;* underlined in handwriting) is used to show that a mistake has been copied exactly as it appeared in the original: His essay discussed "differances [*sic*] between law and custom."

similar to   A wordy way of saying *like*:

WORDY: His views on segregation are similar to mine.
BETTER: His views on segregation are like mine.

Simile   A figure of speech in which a comparison between two unlike things is introduced by *like* or *as*:

The next morning a light snow lay on the ground like a sprinkling of powdered sugar.

(Compare **Metaphor.**)

Simple sentence   A sentence that has only one subject and one verb, either or both of which may be compound, is called a *simple sentence*:

He bought several posters at the novelty store.
On the first warm day of spring Ted and I hauled out the remains of our bicycles and began to build a tandem from them.

sit, set   *Sit* (*sat, sat, sitting*) is generally intransitive and does not take an object; *set* (*set, set, setting*) is generally transitive and takes an object:

Tom just *sat* there and smiled.
I *had set* my suitcase on the man's foot.

But in certain phrases and constructions, *sit* takes an object and *set* does not:

Sit the baby up.
The sun *sets* in the west.
How many of your hens *are setting*?

situated   Often deadwood that should be pruned away in writing:

Adville is [situated] forty miles north of the state line.
Mr. Atchison runs a gas station [situated] near the highway.

(See **Deadwood.**)

size, sized   In advertising matter, the form *size* is commonly used: small-*size* boxes, a quart-*size* carton, a king-*size* bottle. In general writing the more formal *sized* is usual: a medium-*sized* glass, a large-*sized* sweatshirt. Often the word is better omitted altogether: small boxes, a large sweatshirt.

Slang   The breezy, colorful, timely language we call *slang* can be found in both the standard and nonstandard levels of English. Everyone, young or old, who likes humor and novelty and color also likes slang—especially good slang. Used skillfully, it adds liveliness and sparkle to anyone's speech. Part of its attraction, of course, is that slang gives the people who use it a feeling of being "with it," of being up on the very latest thing.

The chief attraction slang has for people is novelty. It is fun to hear an idea phrased in a new, unusual, streamlined way. But after hundreds of repetitions, the novelty wears off; the slang loses its freshness and sparkle. The history of most slang expressions is that they are born — they are overused — they become stale — and they die an early death.

That is one reason why slang is often ineffective in speech and usually inappropriate in writing — especially in writing that is meant to last for some time. Today a novel filled with the slang of the Roaring Twenties not only sounds dated but is in part meaningless. (Do *sockdolager*, *lounge lizard*, or *cake-eater* mean anything to you? And if you read that "Lydia thought Craig was the cat's pajamas," would you know whether Craig was being complimented or insulted?)

Then too a great many slang expressions are so general that they hardly have any meaning at all beyond a vague indication of approval or disapproval. Using such words adds no more to your speech or writing than does calling everything you like "wonderful" and everything you dislike "awful." Words like *neat*, *dreamy*, *groovy*, and *punk*, *lousy*, *crummy* are slang of this kind and add little to style or meaning.

Occasionally a slang term becomes an accepted part of the language, instead of fading into meaninglessness or oblivion. *Bonus*, for instance, was once stockbrokers' slang. *Carpetbagger* originally was a slang term of disapproval, but today anyone referring to the days in American history when carpetbaggers were active would use that name, even in the most formal context. *Hobo*, *fogy*, *highbrow*, and *killjoy* are some other examples.

Slang is usually more appropriate in speech than in writing. But if not overused, it can be appropriate in informal writing meant for current reading — in a sports column, for example, or a feature article. Slang may also be needed in writing fiction, to make the speech of certain characters in a story seem real and believable.

But slang should always be used with caution. A safe prescription is this: In conversation with friends, use it, but in small doses. Use it even more sparingly in informal writing, making sure that what you use is appropriate to the subject and will not annoy or bore readers. Do not use it at all in formal speech or writing.

If you read a great deal and listen with interest to the speech of people who use language well, you will gradually develop a reliable judgment about the appropriateness of slang. Then, when you feel sure a slang expression is effective, you will probably be right.

slow, slowly   Both *slow* and *slowly* are used as adverbs. Use whichever sounds better in the sentence:

Drive slow; there's a speed trap ahead.
The crippled airplane taxied slowly down the field.

so   **1** In speech *so* is often used to introduce clauses of purpose:

COLLOQUIAL: We left early so we could avoid the rush hour.
WRITTEN: We left early so that we could avoid the rush hour.   [Or: to avoid the rush hour, in order to avoid the rush hour.]

So is common in clauses of result, which written English would usually introduce by *so that* or change to a *because* (or *since*) construction:

COLLOQUIAL: There was a power failure that night, so we had to study for our exam by candlelight.
WRITTEN: There was a power failure that night, so that we had to study for our exam by candlelight.
WRITTEN: Because there was a power failure that night, we had to study for our exam by candlelight.

2 The overuse of *so* to connect sentences is sometimes referred to as the "so-habit." It is especially common in speech, particularly in narrative accounts:

The front door was locked, so we tried the side door, but it was locked too. So then we pulled a crate up to a back window, so we could try to get in that way. The window was open about a foot, so we squeezed little Gary through it.

Sentences like these should be rewritten to avoid the overuse of *so*.

3 The use of *so* as an intensive is mainly colloquial; in written English it is usually avoided or the comparison completed:

COLLOQUIAL: His attitude was so cynical!
WRITTEN: His attitude was so cynical that everyone avoided him.

so-called   When *so-called* is used, quotation marks are not needed, because they would duplicate the idea: *a so-called intellectual*, not *a so-called "intellectual."*

So-called is usually hyphened when it comes before the word it modifies, but not when it follows: His intelligence, *so called*, is really just an ability to talk faster than anyone else.

some and its compounds   1 *Some* is most often used as an adjective or a pronoun:

ADJECTIVE: He had made some changes in the design.
PRONOUN: Some are right, but some are wrong.

Some is also used colloquially as an adverb meaning "somewhat; little":

COLLOQUIAL: Now and then his leg still pains him some.
WRITTEN: Now and then his leg still pains him a little.

2 The pronouns *someone* and *somebody* are grammatically singular; they take singular verbs and are usually referred to by singular pronouns:

When someone *finds* and *returns* a valuable lost item, *he is* usually given a reward.
Is somebody willing to lend you *his* tape recorder?

For further discussion and examples, see **Agreement,** sections 1g and 2b.

3 *Somebody, somehow, something, somewhat,* and *somewhere* are always written as single words. *Someone, sometime,* and *someday* may be written as one word or two, depending on the meaning intended. Pronunciation will give a clue to the right spelling. If the stress is on *some*, the one-word form is used. For example:

STRESS ON *some*:   He will have to retire someday.
STRESS ON *day*:   Make an appointment for some day next week.

4 In informal English *someplace* is often used instead of *somewhere*. *Somewheres* is nonstandard.

sooner . . . than   *Than*, not *when*, is used as a connective after *no sooner*:

We had *no sooner* set up the tent *than* a strong gust of wind blew it over.   [Not: *no sooner* set up the tent *when*.]

sort   See **kind, sort; kind of, sort of; kind of a, sort of a.**

so . . . that   Even though several words come between *so* and *that*, no comma should precede *that*:

He was so busy telling everyone else what to do [ ] that he didn't get his own work done.

species   Has the same form in both singular and plural: a *species*, many *species*. Pronounced /spē'shēz/ or sometimes /spē'sēz/.
    Specie /spē'shē/ or /spē'sē/, meaning "money in the form of coins," is a different word, a collective noun without a plural form.

Spelling   The argument that many of our celebrated writers and great men have been notably poor spellers does not alter the fact that accurate spelling has become a generally applied test of literacy — one of the minimum requirements of an educated person. Not only your future employers, but anyone who reads your writing, will expect you to be able to spell. It would be foolish to disregard this universal respect for accurate spelling, when with a bit of work and practice you could learn to spell well enough to escape unfavorable notice.
    To be a good speller does not mean you have to be a perfect speller, one who without help can spell correctly every word he uses. It does mean that you should master the spelling of simple, everyday words (*coming, often, government, friend, height, nickel*) and should form the habit of referring to a good dictionary for less common words whose spelling you may be unsure of (*amethyst, paraphernalia, peccadillo, charisma, inoculate, desiccated*).
    1 One of the best ways to improve your spelling is to master a few general rules that apply to large groups of common words:

a) **Doubling final consonants.** When a suffix beginning with a vowel is added to a one-syllable word that ends in a single consonant preceded by a single vowel, the final consonant is doubled:

bid + er = bidder	flat + est = flattest
skim + ed = skimmed	prig + ish = priggish
war + ing = warring	can + ery = cannery

If the word has more than one syllable, the final consonant is doubled only if the accent is on the last syllable:

con fer′ + ed = conferred	re gret′ + able = regrettable
be gin′ + er = beginner	oc cur′ + ence = occurrence
re bel′ + ing = rebelling	ad mit′ + ance = admittance

(But: ben′e fit + ed = benefited; de vel′op + ing = developing.)

b) **Final silent e.** A final silent *e* is generally dropped before a suffix that begins with a vowel:

hope + ed = hoped	sense + ible = sensible
write + er = writer	value + able = valuable
dine + ing = dining	grieve + ance = grievance
create + or = creator	desire + ous = desirous

There are a few exceptions: the *e* is kept in words like *dyeing* and *singeing* (to keep them distinct from *dying* and *singing*) and in words like *traceable* and *courageous* (to keep the /s/ sound of the *c* and the /j/ sound of the *g*).

Before a suffix beginning with a consonant, the final *e* is usually kept:

hope + ful = hopeful	blithe + ly = blithely
love + less = loveless	achieve + ment = achievement
white + ness = whiteness	entire + ty = entirety

A number of common words are exceptions: *ninth, truly, duly, argument, wholly.*

c) **Words with y.** A final *y* preceded by a consonant is changed to *i* before a suffix that begins with a consonant:

busy + ly = busily	merry + ment = merriment
greedy + ness = greediness	penny + less = penniless
bounty + ful = bountiful	glory + fy = glorify

The same change is made before the suffixes *-ed, -er, -es, -est*:

spy + ed = spied	terrify + es = terrifies
ugly + er = uglier	showy + est = showiest

But before the suffix *-ing*, the *y* is kept:

spying	hurrying	studying	worrying

d) **Adding prefixes.** The prefixes *dis-*, *mis-*, and *un-* end with a single consonant. When they are attached to a base word beginning with the

241

same letter, there will be two *s*'s or two *n*'s. Otherwise there will be only one:

dis + satisfy = dissatisfy   dis + agree = disagree
dis + service = disservice   dis + respect = disrespect
mis + state = misstate   mis + treat = mistreat
mis + spelling = misspelling   mis + print = misprint
un + nerve = unnerve   un + able = unable
un + numbered = unnumbered   un + usual = unusual

e) Adding suffixes. No letter is dropped from the base word when the suffix -*ness* or -*ly* is added:

even + ness = evenness   final + ly = finally
stubborn + ness = stubbornness   legal + ly = legally

But remember that if the base word ends in *y* preceded by a consonant, the *y* is changed to *i*: *friendliness, wearily*.

f) Ei and ie. Use *ie* when the sound is long *e* (as in *be*):

piece	believer	grief	yield
shriek	relieve	achieve	niece

A few common words are exceptions to the rule: *either, neither, leisure, seize, weird*.

Use *ei* after *c*, or when the sound is not long *e*:

conceive	foreign	neighbor	eighty
receipt	forfeit	weight	sleigh
deceit	vein	skein	heir

The most common exceptions are *friend, mischief, handkerchief, sieve, view, fiery, financier*.

2 Often pronouncing words correctly will help you with the spelling. For example, if you pronounce *arthritis* and *mischievous* and *athletics* correctly as three syllables, you will not put an extra vowel in the words ("artheritis" and "mischievious" and "athaletics"). If you look at *hundred* and *prescribe* carefully and pronounce them correctly, you will not be tempted to transpose letters in them ("hunderd" and "perscribe").

If you remember that *tian* (as in *Christian*) spells a /chən/ sound, you will not use *tian* in spelling words like *mountain, certain, fountain*, and *captain* — which end with a /tən/ sound (not /chən/). If you remember that the /shən/ sound in words like *expression* and *succession* and *admission* is spelled with *ssion*, you will use two *s*'s in these words. But you will use only one *s* in words like *division* and *invasion* and *explosion* — since they end with the sound /zhən/. Make it a practice to compare the way words sound with the way they are spelled. The pronunciations are not always foolproof clues, but they help with many groups of words of similar sound.

3 For single words whose spelling is hard or seems unreasonable or illogical, try to figure out some formula to fix the spelling in your mind.

Notice, for example, the "bullet" in *bulletin* and the "nun" in *pronuncia-tion*. Keep *desert* (a dry, barren region) distinct from *dessert* (food) by letting the single *s* in *Sahara* remind you of the single *s* in *desert*. Remember that a *laboratory* is a place to work—or to "labor." Any device, no matter how nonsensical it may seem, that helps you with the spelling of a difficult word is valuable.

(See also **Homonyms.**)

4 Finally, since many misspellings are due to carelessness or haste rather than ignorance, make it a point to proofread all your written work carefully before handing it in. Keep a list of all words that you habitually misspell and check your papers especially for those. Wanting to be a good speller is half the battle.

5 Following is a list of words frequently misspelled in student papers. (The words are divided into syllables so that you can more easily visual-ize their spelling.) Look over the list carefully, making sure you know the meaning and pronunciation of each word. Check the particular words that cause you trouble and review them from time to time. Refer to the list when you proofread your papers.

ab sence	ap pa ra tus	can di date
ac cept	ap pre ci ate	car i ca ture
ac ci den tal ly	ar gu ment	ca tas tro phe
ac com mo date	ar riv al	cem e ter y
ac cu rate	ar ti cle	char ac ter is tic
ac cus tom	as cend ed	co coa
ac quaint ance	as sent ed	co er cion
ac quired	as so ci a tion	colo nel
a cross	at tacked	co los sal
ad vice (noun)	at tor ney	col umn
ad vise (verb)	au thor i ty	com e dy
aisle	aux il ia ry	com mit tee
all right (2 words)	awk ward	com par a tive
al read y	bach e lor	com pet i tive
al to geth er	bal ance	con cede
a lu mi num	be fore	con science
al ways	bis cuits	con sen sus
am a teur	bound a ries	con sist ent
a mong	breath (noun)	con ven ience
a mount	breathe (verb)	cor rob o rate
a nal y sis	bril liant	cour te ous
an gle	Brit ain	crit i cize
a non y mous	bu reau	cur ric u lum
an swer	busi ness	dair y
ant arc tic	caf e te ri a	dealt
anx ious	cal en dar	debt or
a pol o gize	cam paign	de ceased

de ci sion
de fense
def i nite ly
de scrip tion
de spair
de spise
di a ry
dif fer ent
dis as trous
dis ci pline
dis ease
di vine
di vis i ble
does n't
dom i nant
drowned
du al
ef fi cien cy
el i gi ble
em bar rass
em pha size
en trance
en vi ron ment
es pe cial ly
ex ag ger at ed
ex cel lent
ex cept
ex haust ed
ex ist ence
ex pe ri ence·
ex traor di nar y
ex treme ly
fal la cy
fa mil iar
fas ci nate
fa tigued
Feb ru ar y
fem i nine
for ty
fourth
fu tile
gen er al ly
gen u ine
ghost
gov ern ment
gram mar

guar an tee
guard i an
guid ance
gym na si um
hand some
hin drance
his to ry
hu mor ous
hy giene
hy poc ri sy
il lit er ate
i mag i na tive
im me di ate ly
im mi grant
in ci den tal ly
in cred i ble
in de pend ent
in dict ment
in ev i ta ble
in fi nite
in oc u la tion
in quir y
in stead
in tel li gent
in ter fere
in ter pret ed
ir re sist i ble
ir rev er ent
is land
jeal ous y
jew el ry
knowl edge
knuck les
le git i mate
li a ble
li brar y
li cense
lieu ten ant
light ning
lit er a ture
loose
lux u ry
ly ing
main tain
main te nance
mar riage

math e mat ics
med i cine
min i a ture
min ute
mis cel la ne ous
mis sile
mort gage
mus cles
mus tache
mys te ri ous
nat u ral ly
ne ces si ty
ne go ti ate
nick el
nui sance
o be di ence
ob sta cle
oc ca sion
oc curred
op er ate
o pin ion
op po nent
op por tu ni ty
o rig i nal
pam phlet
par al lel
par a lyzed
pa ren the ses
par lia ment
pas time
pa tience
pe cu liar
per haps
per ma nent
per mis si ble
per se ver ance
per spi ra tion
per suade
phase
phe nom e non
phy si cian
play wright
pleas ant
pos sess
pos si ble
prai rie

244

pre ced ing
prej u diced
pres ence
prim i tive
pri or i ty
priv i lege
prob a bly
pro ce dure
pro ceed
pro fes sor
pro tein
psy chol o gy
pump kin
pur su ing
qual i fied
quan ti ty
quar ter
ques tion naire
qui et
quit
quite
re al ize
re cip i ent
rec og nize
rec om mend
ref er ence
re ferred
rel e vant
rem i nisce
ren dez vous
re pel lent
rep e ti tion
res er voir
res tau rant
rhyme
rhythm
ri dic u lous

sal a ry
sand wich
scen er y
sched ule
scis sors
sec re tar y
sen si ble
sep a rate
ser geant
se vere ly
sim i lar
sol dier
sol emn
so phis ti cat ed
soph o more
sou ve nir
spec i men
speech
spon sor
sta tis tics
stat ue
stat ure
stat ute
stom ach
strat e gy
strength
stretched
sub si dize
sub tle
suc ceed
suf fi cient
sum ma rize
su per sede
sure ly
sur prise
sus cep ti ble
syl la ble

sym met ri cal
sym pho ny
tech nique
tem per a ture
tend en cy
there fore
thor ough ly
to mor row
tour na ment
to ward
trag e dy
trai tor
treas ur er
Tues day
typ i cal
un con scious
un doubt ed ly
un prec e dent ed
un til
u ten sil
va can cies
vac u um
va ri e ty
veg e ta ble
vi cin i ty
vil lain
vi o lence
vis i bil i ty
vis i tors
vol ume
war rant
weath er
Wednes day
wel come
wheth er
wom en
writ ten

Split infinitive   Putting an adverb modifier between *to* and the infinitive form of the verb results in what is called a "split infinitive":

Joe was too confused *to fully realize* what had happened.
My aunt has decided *to completely refurnish* her apartment.

Split infinitives that sound awkward are to be avoided in writing:

AWKWARD: He is supposed to at least once a week call home.

BETTER: He is supposed to call home at least once a week.

But otherwise there is no point in revising a sentence just to avoid splitting an infinitive. Good writers, in fact, prefer using split infinitives in sentences where not doing so would result in ambiguity or awkwardness:

CLEAR: I was too excited to really listen to what she was saying.
UNCLEAR: I was too excited really to listen to what she was saying.
AWKWARD: I was too excited to listen really to what she was saying.

Spoonerism   A (usually accidental) transposition of initial or other sounds of words, like "off the treaten back" for "off the beaten track." The term is derived from the name of William A. Spooner, an English clergyman and educator (1844–1930), famous for his "spoonerisms." For example, Spooner once scolded an Oxford student because he had "hissed a mystery lecture." He expelled another student, telling him, "You have deliberately tasted two worms. . . ."

Squinting modifiers   Modifiers that are ambiguous because they could refer to a preceding or to a following construction:

SQUINTING: Miss Johnson sees sophomores only on Tuesdays.
CLEAR: On Tuesdays Miss Johnson sees only sophomores.
CLEAR: Miss Johnson sees sophomores on Tuesdays only.

SQUINTING: Mr. Porter promised Ellen when we moved to the new office she would get a raise.
CLEAR: When we moved to the new office, Mr. Porter promised Ellen she would get a raise.   [Or: Mr. Porter promised Ellen when we moved to the new office that she would get a raise.]
CLEAR: Mr. Porter promised Ellen she would get a raise when we moved to the new office.   [Or: Mr. Porter promised Ellen that when we moved to the new office she would get a raise.]

Standard English   The language used by educated people. For a discussion and examples, see **Levels of English usage.**

state   See **say, state, talk.**

stationary, stationery   These two words are sometimes confused. *Stationary* (with an *a*) is an adjective meaning "in a fixed position; standing still; not changing in size, number, etc.":

The plant manager placed an order for three stationary cranes.

Stationery (with an *e*) is a noun referring to materials for writing letters—paper, cards, envelopes, etc.:

Business stationery usually has a printed letterhead.

Story The word *story* is most commonly applied to a narrative of imaginary happenings — to a short story or a novel. It is also used to refer to a narrative of actual events — to a newspaper story, for example.

Articles, editorials, reviews, essays, treatises, and so on, are not narratives, but pieces of expository writing — writing that discusses ideas or explains processes. The word *story* should not be applied to them.

street In many newspapers *street* is not capitalized as part of an address: *10 Downing street.* In other forms of writing it is capitalized: *10 Downing Street.*

The abbreviation *St.* or *st.* is not much used except to save space in texts or reference works and occasionally in letter headings.

Structural grammar A grammatical study that is concerned primarily with describing the system of structural signals that help to communicate meaning in a language. In English these signals are word order, derivational endings, inflectional endings, function words, and intonation. The complete meaning of a communication is conveyed by the meaning of the words used (lexical meaning) and the structure signals used (structural meaning).

Subject and verb The basic parts of the standard sentence are the subject and the verb. The *subject* is the word or group of words that names the person or thing about which the *verb* makes a statement or asks a question. In the typical sentence the subject — usually a noun or pronoun — precedes the verb:

A **siren** *wailed* in the distance.   **Who** *called?*
Usually **we** *eat* dinner at six.   **What** *delayed* you?

In some sentences the order is "inverted," and the subject follows or comes between parts of the verb:

Out *rushed* **Gwen**, waving a white scarf.   Why *was* **she** late?
There *was* a big **hole** in the road.   Didn't **he** *know* them?

Either the subject or the verb (or both) may be compound — that is, it may consist of two or more equal parts joined by a conjunction:

Fred AND **Stanley** *picked* the apples.
The **car** *slowed* BUT *did* not *stop.*
Ruth AND **Millicent** *sat* down at the piano AND *began* to play.

(See also **Agreement**, section 1.)

Subjunctive The subjunctive form of the verb is used in certain set phrases and in parliamentary motions:

Heaven *forbid!*   If I *were* you . . .   Far *be* it from me
I move that the meeting *be adjourned.*

In addition, the subjunctive is used in formal English: (1) In wishes:

Olga often wishes she *were* back in Minnesota.
I wish I *were* less timid.

2) In statements or conditions that are highly doubtful or contrary to fact:

If she *were appointed* chairman, we would all resign.
If Claude *were* one year older, he could vote. [But: If Claude *was* at the party, he must have seen her. (Here the subjunctive is not used, since the writer feels it is quite probable that Claude was at the party.)]

3) In *that*-clauses after verbs of *insisting, asking, ordering, requesting,* and such expressions as *it is necessary* and *it was urged*:

Dad insisted that Henry *apologize.*
It is not necessary that the defendant *be* present.

But the subjunctive is far less common than it once was. In informal English the indicative is often used in wishes and in statements contrary to fact:

Olga often wishes she *was* back in Minnesota.
I wish I *was* less timid.
If she *was appointed* chairman, we would all resign.
If Claude *was* one year older, he could vote.

And in both formal and informal English people frequently avoid the subjunctive in *that*-clauses, by expressing the idea in another way:

Dad insisted that Henry *should apologize.*
It is not necessary for the defendant *to be* present.

To show that a wish or condition refers to a past time, the helping word *had*, not *would have*, is used:

I wish you *had been elected.* [Not: *would have been elected.*]
If she *had been appointed* chairman, I would have resigned. [Not: *would have been appointed.*]

(See **Mood.**)

Subordinating conjunctions   Subordinating conjunctions connect dependent, or subordinate, clauses with main clauses:

I don't know *why* Bob hit Al.   Jim left *before* we did.

Among the most common subordinating conjunctions are:

after	because	since	unless
although	before	so that	when
as	how	that	where
as if	if	though	while
as long as	in order that	till	why

248

The relative pronouns (*who, which, that*) and the interrogative pronouns (*who, which, what*) serve as subordinating conjunctions:

RELATIVE: The photographs *that* Linda took are excellent.
INTERROGATIVE: I asked the mechanic *what* was wrong with the car.

such   Colloquially, *such* is used as an intensive:

It was such a ridiculous story.

In writing that is at all formal this use is avoided or the comparison is completed:

It was an extremely ridiculous story.
It was *such* a ridiculous story *that* no one believed it.

such as   When used to introduce examples, *such as* is not followed by a comma:

Dances such as [ ] the mashed potato and the watusi died out quickly.
Certain nineteenth-century playwrights, such as [ ] Strindberg and Ibsen, greatly affected the development of modern drama.

Suffix   An addition made at the end of a word to form another word of different meaning or function:

-able: laughable, agreeable	*-ize*: moralize, humanize
-en: strengthen, harden	*-less*: painless, useless
-er: cleaner, loser	*-ly*: easily, usually
-ful: wonderful, shameful	*-ment*: treatment, government
-fy: classify, simplify	*-ness*: eagerness, awareness
-ish: boyish, fiendish	*-ship*: membership, hardship

Sunday school   Capitalize only the *Sunday* except in names of particular Sunday schools:

Anthony missed Sunday school three weeks in a row.
The Dutch Reformed Sunday School is only a block from our house.

Superlative degree   See **Comparison of adjectives and adverbs.**

sure   *Sure* is used primarily as an adjective:

A crocus is a sure sign of spring.   Are you sure of that?

Sure used as an adverb meaning "yes" or "certainly" is a colloquialism. It is frequently heard in conversation, but is inappropriate in writing (except in dialogue):

"Will you put in a new light bulb for me?"   "Sure."
"That sure isn't the same story he told before."

suspicion   Used as a verb, *suspicion* is nonstandard:

NONSTANDARD: We suspicioned that he was lying.
STANDARD: We suspected that he was lying.

sweat   See **perspire, sweat.**

swell   As an adjective meaning "excellent," *swell* is slang, inappropriate in serious writing and in careful speech. Like many other slang expressions, *swell* is a counter word — used not to express a specific meaning but merely to convey general approval (a swell teacher, a swell party, a swell idea). It has been so badly overworked in conversation that many people find it objectionable.

swim   The principal parts are *swim, swam, swum.* The past-tense form *swum* is archaic or dialectal.

Syllogism   See **Inductive and deductive reasoning,** section 2.

Synecdoche   /si nek′də kē/ A figure of speech in which the writer names (1) a part when he means the whole, or (2) the whole when he means only a part:

The captain ordered all *hands* on deck.   [That is, the members of the crew.]
Montreal won the Stanley Cup that year.   [That is, the Montreal hockey team.]

(Compare **Metonymy.**)

Synonym   Synonyms are words that have the same basic meaning, but suggest slightly different things. That is, they have much the same denotation but different connotations:

famous — renowned — celebrated — illustrious — eminent
praise — extol — eulogize — commend — applaud
predicament — quandary — dilemma — plight — fix — jam

The best way to build up your fund of synonyms is to observe and use the new words that you come across in reading and conversation. But when in your writing you need a synonym for a specific word, it may be necessary to use a special reference book. Some good ones are:

Webster's New Dictionary of Synonyms (Springfield, Mass., 1968)
Modern Guide to Synonyms and Related Words (New York, 1968)
Roget's Thesaurus of English Words and Phrases (New York, 1964)

The first two not only list synonyms but make clear what their different connotations are. The last simply lists the words without making any real distinctions between them.

Remember too that most standard dictionaries contain "synonym studies" that give special help with synonyms.

Syntax   *Syntax* refers to the relationship of words and word groups in sentences. Some entries in this book that deal with matters of syntax are **Clause, Direct object, Predicate complement, Preposition, Subject and verb.**

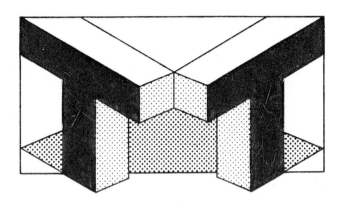

take   See **bring, take.**

talk   See **say, state, talk.**

Tautology   The needless repetition of an idea:

The yellow sweater was too small [in size] for me.
Mrs. Cory kept making irrelevant comments [that had nothing to do with the subject].

(See also **Redundancy.**)

taxi   The plural of the noun is *taxis* or *taxies*. The principal parts of the verb are *taxi, taxied, taxiing* or *taxying*.

teach   See **learn, teach.**

telephone, phone   In informal usage *telephone* is commonly shortened to *phone* (without an apostrophe). Since *phone* is a clipped word, not an abbreviation, it does not have a period: The extension phone is out of order. Why not phone for an appointment today?

Tenses of verbs   **1 Forms.** The form of a verb helps to show the time of the action. Though there are only three divisions of time—present, past, and future—English has six "tenses" to show various distinctions within these divisions. The simple present and past tense forms are single words: he *tells*, he *told*. All other tense forms are phrases in which helping verbs are combined with a part of the main verb. The following table shows the forms most commonly used to show time distinctions:

		Active	*Passive*
PRESENT TENSE		he tells he is telling he does tell	he is told he is being told
PAST TENSES	Past	he told he was telling he did tell	he was told he was being told
	Present perfect	he has told he has been telling	he has been told
	Past perfect	he had told he had been telling	he had been told
FUTURE TENSES	Future	he will tell he will be telling	he will be told
	Future perfect	he will have told he will have been telling	he will have been told

2 Uses. (a) The *present* tense is used not only to show that the action takes place at the present time, but also to make a statement that is generally true, regardless of time:

Five times twelve *equals* sixty.
He said that all mercury compounds *are* poisonous.
The First Amendment *guarantees* the freedom of the press.

Occasionally the present tense is used to tell of things that happened in the past, especially when the speaker or writer wants to make the past events seem more vivid. This use of the present tense is called the *historical present*:

Just then the door *opens*, and in *walks* Mr. Price, looking furious.

b) The simple *past* tense form is used for action completed in the past:

The union management immediately *called* for a strike.
Unfortunately Hal *lost* the address.

To show customary or repeated action in the past, a form with *used to* or *would* is used:

We *used to go* to the movies at least once a week.
On Sundays Dad *would serve* Mother breakfast in bed.

c) The *future* tense, which shows that the action will occur in the future, is usually formed with the helping verb *shall* or *will*. But it can be formed in other ways. The present tense form, used in combination with an adverb of time, is common:

Next week the baseball season *opens*.
He *is leaving* for Buffalo *on Tuesday*.

Phrases with *be* or *go* and an infinitive are also often used to refer to future time:

There *is to be* a discussion afterwards. I *am to lead* it.
Patrick *is going to ask* for a raise.

d) The *present perfect* tense indicates an action begun in the past and extending to the time the statement is made:

Nora *has been* on the telephone for over an hour.
They *have worked* hard on the skit.

e) The *past perfect* tense indicates an action completed earlier than some other past time:

Someone asked him if he *had* ever *raised* chickens.
Before I left, Clara *had changed* her mind again.

f) The *future perfect* tense indicates an action to be completed at some definite time in the future:

By the end of August Ken *will have saved* five hundred dollars.
Before the day is over, she *will have changed* her mind several more times.

g) The *progressive* tense forms (made with the helping verb *be* and the present participle) are used to show continuing action:

They *are plotting* their revenge right now.
At that time Henry *was selling* brushes door to door.
The neighbors *have been complaining* about our dog again.
I'm sure the mayor *will be riding* in the first car.

h) The *emphatic* tense forms (made with the helping verb *do* and the infinitive) are used for emphasis and in negative statements and questions:

I *do like* cauliflower, but not drowned in lukewarm cheese sauce.
They *do not approve* of smoking, drinking, or playing cards.
Does Harold *know* anything about running a pizza parlor?

3 Sequence of tenses. When the verb in the main clause is in the present tense, the verb in the subordinate clause is in whatever tense expresses the intended meaning:

Sara *insists* that he *is* innocent.
The chief *does* not *think* that the fire *was set*.

Few people *doubt* that Zillo *will win* the election.
The Carsons *say* they *may emigrate* to Australia.

When the verb in the main clause is in a past tense, the verb in the subordinate clause is also in a past tense form, except in a sentence like the last in the following group:

Sara *insisted* that he *was* innocent.
The chief *did* not *think* that the fire *had been set.*
Few people *doubted* that Zillo *would win* the election.
The Carsons *said* they *might emigrate* to Australia.
He *explained* that water *is* a good conductor of electricity.   [The subordinate clause states a fact that is generally true.]

4 Tenses of verbals. Participles and infinitives have two tenses, the present (*giving, being given; to give, to be given*) and the perfect (*having given, having been given; to have given, to have been given*).

The perfect tense is used to show action that took place before the action of the main verb:

Having given his word, he felt he couldn't change his mind.
I am sorry *to have missed* your exhibit.

Otherwise the present tense is used:

Wishing that he had not come, he wondered how soon he could leave.
We had intended *to see* the exhibit on Friday.   [Not: *to have seen.* The intention — which we had in the past — was *to see* not *to have seen* it.]

terrible   Colloquial in the sense of "bad; unpleasant; annoying": a *terrible* gossip, a *terrible* headache. Avoid this use in writing. (See also **Counter words.**)

than   1 In formal English the case of the pronoun after *than* in elliptical clauses of comparison depends on the use of the pronoun in the clause. The nominative form is used if the pronoun is the subject; the objective form is used if the pronoun is the object:

Mark is a better tennis player than *I* [am].
No one is more absent-minded about driving than *he* [is].
Coach Swanson gives him much more help than [he gives] *me.*

In colloquial usage the objective form is often used in sentences like the first two ("Mark is a better tennis player than *me*"; "No one is more absent-minded about driving than *him*"). But this usage is not considered appropriate in writing or in formal speech.

Using the right form of the pronoun is often important in avoiding ambiguity. For example, a sentence like "She criticizes Brian more than me" might mean "She criticizes Brian more than I do" or "She criticizes Brian more than she criticizes me." If in your writing you consistently use

I when you mean the first, and *me* when you mean the second, you will make your intended meaning clear.

2 *Than* is the idiomatic conjunction after *no sooner*:

We had *no sooner* parked the car *than* a fire truck raced past.   [Not: *when* a fire truck raced past.]

But *when* — not *than* — is used after *barely*, *hardly*, or *scarcely*:

We had *barely* parked the car *when* a fire truck raced past.

than, then   Since *than*, when spoken rapidly and without stress, is pronounced /ᴛʜən/, careless writers tend to spell it *then*. Remember that *then* is an adverb of time (*Then* he handed us the bill), and *than* a conjunction (Ours cost more *than* theirs did).

than whom   In the phrase *than whom* (meaning "compared to whom"), *than* is a preposition and *whom* the object of the preposition. The phrase is formal and old-fashioned, and many people avoid it as rather awkward.

AWKWARD: Arnold Rosenberg, than whom there is no better debater in the league, got a bad case of laryngitis and had to be replaced.
BETTER: Arnold Rosenberg, the best debater in the league, got a bad case of laryngitis and had to be replaced.

that   **1 Conjunction.** *That* should usually be repeated with each of a series of parallel subordinate clauses:

Their letter stated *that* they had received our order, *that* the truckers' strike was slowing down deliveries only slightly, and *that* we should have our couch within the next two weeks.

But *that* should not be repeated within a single clause:

He said *that* if no one objected [that] he would replay the tape.

2 Adverb. In general usage *that* (or *this*) is commonly used as an adverb modifying adjectives and adverbs of quantity and extent:

He had never seen *that* many people together in one place.
None of the Scouts had ever hiked *that* far before.

In colloquial usage *that* is also used to modify other adjectives and adverbs:

I didn't realize I was *that hungry.*   [Formal: *so hungry.*]
Getting a replacement for him will not be *that easy.*   [Formal: *so easy* or *so easy as that* or *as easy as that.*]

In the speech of some localities *that* is used instead of *so . . . that*:

LOCAL: Marty was that amazed he was speechless — for once.

GENERAL: Marty was so amazed [that] he was speechless—for once.

(For pronoun use, see **this, that,** section 1.)

that, which   *That* is usually preferred as a relative pronoun in restrictive clauses, and *which* in nonrestrictive:

A novel *that he wrote in ten days* was on the best-seller list for nine months.

His first novel, *which he wrote in ten days,* was on the best-seller list for nine months.

that is   A connective used to introduce examples or explanations. When it introduces a clause, it is usually preceded by a semicolon (sometimes a dash) and followed by a comma:

Her calmness in speaking to the parents was amazing; that is, it was amazing to anyone who knew how frightened she really was.

When it introduces words or phrases, commas are used:

The choir will sing the last two selections a cappella, that is, without instrumental accompaniment.

In informal writing the *that is* frequently is omitted before a short construction:

No matter where Peter eats, he always orders the same thing, [that is,] a hamburger and French fries.

the   1 When spoken without stress, *the* is pronounced /ᴛʜə/ before consonants, and /ᴛʜi/ before vowels. When stressed, as in "Bilbo's Basement was *the* campus hangout," it is pronounced /ᴛʜē/.

2 Repeating *the* before the various nouns in a series emphasizes their distinctness:

There were ants in the oatmeal, the flour, and the pudding.   [Compare: in the oatmeal, flour, and pudding.]

3 *The* should always be used before the name of our country: *the* United States.

4 *The* is used as an adverb in expressions like "the more the merrier." In formal writing, a comma is used in such expressions: "The more enthusiastic the audience, the more inspired the performance." In informal writing, the comma is generally omitted. (See also **Articles.**)

theater, theatre   *Theater* is now the more common spelling except in proper names of long standing: the Abbey Theatre, the Hampstead Theatre Club, *World Theatre* (a periodical).

The standard pronunciation is /thē′ə tər/; the nonstandard, /thē ā′tər/.

their, theirs   Both are possessive forms of *they. Their* is used before nouns; *theirs* (no apostrophe) is used alone:

We used *their* toboggan.
Theirs is the red brick house.

   The form *theirn* (for *theirs*) is nonstandard English.

theirself, theirselves   Nonstandard for *themselves.*

them   Used only in nonstandard English as a demonstrative adjective and pronoun:

NONSTANDARD: *Them* girls are always picking on me.
STANDARD: *Those* girls are always picking on me.

NONSTANDARD: *Them* are the shoes I gave him.
STANDARD: *Those* are the shoes I gave him.

themselves   See **Reflexive pronouns** and **Intensive pronouns.**

then   When used as a conjunctive adverb, joining the two clauses of a compound sentence, *then* should be preceded by a semicolon:

She stared at us for a moment; then she began to cry.
Sam waited until Mrs. Wiley's back was turned; then he slipped me the note.

If *and then* is used to make a closer connection, a comma separates the clauses:

He talked us all into signing up for the trip, and then at the last minute he decided not to go.

   (See also **than, then.**)

therefore   See **Conjunctive adverbs.**

there is, there are   1 When the subject following the introductory word *there* is singular, a singular verb is used; when the subject is plural, a plural verb is generally used:

There *is* a hair in my soup.
There *were* too many people in the kitchen.
There *were* several cars and one truck in line ahead of us.   [Compound subject.]

When the first part of a compound subject following *there* is singular, a singular verb is sometimes used:

There *was* one truck and several cars in line ahead of us.

257

2 Though the occasional use of sentences beginning with *there is* adds variety, an overuse tends to make writing unemphatic:

UNEMPHATIC: There was a thick, brownish haze hanging over the city every morning.
DIRECT: A thick, brownish haze hung over the city every morning.

UNEMPHATIC: There were several clauses in the contract that were ambiguous or contradictory.
DIRECT: Several clauses in the contract were ambiguous or contradictory.

they   In speech, *they* is often used as an indefinite pronoun (one without a specific antecedent), but this use is not considered appropriate in writing:

COLLOQUIAL: They sell only fresh meat at Shopper's Market
WRITTEN: Shopper's Market sells only fresh meat.

COLLOQUIAL: They have raised the gasoline tax again.
WRITTEN: The gasoline tax has been raised again.
WRITTEN: The state legislature has raised the gasoline tax again.

(See also **Indefinite it.**)

thing   Often deadwood that should be omitted:

WORDY.   My sister thinks that getting a C is a shameful thing.
IMPROVED: My sister thinks that getting a C is shameful.

WORDY: The other thing he also did well was play the piccolo.
IMPROVED: He also played the piccolo well.

this, that   **1** The pronouns *this* and *that* are often used to refer to the whole idea of a preceding group of words:

Dad sent Tim and Donny to their rooms, and *that* ended the fight.

But this use should be avoided if there is any danger that the reader may think the pronoun refers to a particular noun in the group:

AMBIGUOUS: Bill finished first in the cross-country race. *This* was something he had never done before.   [Finished first? Or raced in a cross-country event?]
CLEAR: Bill finished first in the cross-country race — an event he had never entered before.

2 In everyday speech *this* is sometimes used as an emphatic definite article (instead of the usual *the*):

Then *this* bright light shines in my face, and *this* guy yells, "Halt!"

This use is out of place in writing except in quoting conversation.

this here, that there   Used only in nonstandard English for *this* and *that*:

NONSTANDARD: This here bat is mine. That there one is Ken's.
STANDARD: This bat is mine. That one [there] is Ken's.

till, until   Both have the same meaning; choose whichever best fits the rhythm of the sentence. *Until* is more usual at the beginning of sentences:

Until I took physics, I never knew what homework was.
I never knew what homework was *till* (or *until*) I took physics.

Titles of books, articles, etc.   **1 Formal usage.** (a) In most books, in some magazines, and in most school writing, the titles of books, pamphlets, movies, radio and television programs, plays and poems published as separate volumes, and the names of newspapers and magazines are put in italics—underlined in writing:

Book: *In Defense of Liberty*   Newspaper: the Niles *Times*
Pamphlet: *Trip to Nowhere*   Magazine: *Nation's Business*
Movie: *The Lion in Winter*   Long play: *A Man for All Seasons*
TV program: *Sesame Street*   Long poem: *Paradise Lost*

b) The titles of paintings, statues, concertos, operas, ballets, musical comedies are also put in italics:

Painting: Degas's *On the Stage*
Statue: Brancusi's *Bird in Space*
Opera: *The Magic Flute*
Ballet: *Slaughter on Tenth Avenue*

c) Titles of short stories, articles, essays, short poems, and songs are enclosed in quotation marks:

Story: Hesse's "Within and Without"
Article: "Right On!"
Poem: "To Make a Prairie"
Song: "Marching Through Georgia"

2 Informal usage. In some magazines and newspapers the titles of books, movies, magazines, etc., are treated as proper names—capitalized but not italicized or enclosed in quotation marks. In other periodicals the titles are capitalized and put in quotation marks. For your school writing, follow the formal style in italicizing such titles.

together with   A phrase beginning with *together with* (or *along with, as well as, with*) is sometimes added to a singular subject. When the phrase is used in a clearly parenthetical way, it does not affect the number of the verb:

A special drill, together with some extra bits, *is included* in the kit.

259

When the phrase is not intended as a parenthetical addition, usage varies. In informal English, a plural verb is often used, since the singular subject and the phrase are felt to be the same as a compound subject:

The sheriff together with his deputies *were* already on the way.

Formal English sticks to the singular verb or changes the *together with* to *and* and then uses a plural verb:

The sheriff *and* his deputies *were* already on the way.

too See **very, too.**

Topic outline See **Outline form,** section 2.

Topic sentence A statement, in general terms, of the central idea of a paragraph or group of paragraphs. It serves the writer as a guide in determining what details are needed to make the central idea clear to readers, as well as what details are irrelevant.

Though the usual spot for a topic sentence is at the beginning of a paragraph, it may also come at the end. Occasionally if the writer feels that his central idea will be clear to readers without being explicitly stated, he does not include a topic sentence. In narrative writing topic sentences are rare.

toward, towards Both forms are standard, *toward* being more common in the United States and *towards* in England.

Transformational-generative grammar A grammar system intended to account for the production (the "generating") of every possible sentence in a language. According to this system there are in English two kinds of sentences—kernel sentences and transformations, or derived sentences. Kernel sentences are short, report-type statements that fall into a few basic patterns. Transformations—all other sentences—are built, or "derived," from kernel sentences according to a limited set of rules (shifting, deleting, or inserting words and phrases, for example, or combining two or more kernels).

Transitive and intransitive verbs A verb is called *transitive* when it is used with an object to complete its meaning:

We *pushed* the car off the road.
Roger *was taking* a picture of the monkey.

A verb is called *intransitive* when it does not need an object to complete its meaning or when the receiver of the action is not named:

Clorinda *sighed.*
They *have rehearsed* every night for a month.

Linking verbs (those that merely link a predicate noun or pronoun or adjective to the subject) are regarded as intransitive:

His room *was* a mess.
The chickens *looked* healthy to me.

Many verbs are used either transitively or intransitively, usually with different meanings:

TRANSITIVE: A pickpocket *stole* his wallet.
INTRANSITIVE: Robert *stole* out of the room.

Trite expressions   Usually figures of speech that through constant over-use have lost their original effectiveness. They may be expressions that have been around for many years, such as *take a dim view, the worse for wear, dyed in the wool;* or they may be more current expressions that have caught on too quickly and too well, such as *do your thing* or *get down to the nitty-gritty.* The overuse of such expressions marks writing as amateurish.

try and, try to   Although the formal idiom is *try to,* informal English has long used *try and*:

FORMAL: He is going to try to get another assistant.
INFORMAL: He is going to try and get another assistant.

type, type of   In speech, especially in business, *type* is often used as an adjective: the same *type* work, that *type* employee, a special *type* machine. But in formal English and in nonbusiness writing, *type of* is preferred: the same *type of* work, that *type of* employee, a special *type of* machine.

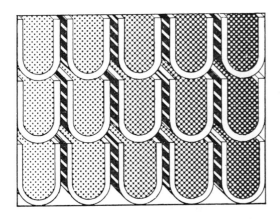

Underlining   Underlining in longhand and typewritten copy corresponds to the use of italic type in printed matter.

1 Titles of books and magazines are underlined:

Crichton's first book was <u>The Andromeda Strain</u>.
She wrote an angry six-page letter to the editor of <u>Newsweek</u>.

(For more details about this use, see **Titles of books, articles, etc.**)

2 Any word that a writer wishes to emphasize may be underlined (ital icized in print), but this kind of emphasis loses its force if used too frequently:

The Morgans don't just <u>belong</u> to society; they <u>are</u> society.
We simply cannot <u>afford</u> any more careless errors.

3 Letters, figures, and words used not for their meaning but as words are generally underlined, especially in books and articles on language:

Don't forget the <u>c</u> in <u>discern</u>.
Bob's <u>33</u> looked more like an <u>88</u>.

4 Foreign words and phrases are underlined:

Karen's <u>joie de vivre</u> is certainly infectious.

Understatement   A figure of speech in which words less strong than expected are used. Understatement generally lends emphasis to an idea:

My father was a bit upset about the fifty-dollar telephone bill.

(See also **Litotes**.)

uninterested   See **disinterested, uninterested.**

unique   In strict formal usage *unique* means "the only one of its kind" and therefore cannot be compared. In informal usage it has become generalized to mean "rare or unusual," and is compared with *more* or *most* or modified by *very* or *rather:*

Andy won the prize for the most unique costume.
I had to admit that his plan was rather unique.

(See also **Comparison of adjectives and adverbs,** section 2.)

United States   As the name of a country *United States* is singular and is preceded by the article *the:*

The United States has produced many distinguished statesmen.

For lack of a better word, *United States* is also used as an adjective, as in *the United States Supreme Court,* although *the Supreme Court of the United States* is preferred as less awkward. (See also **American.**)

until   See **till, until.**

up   Informal English often uses *up* after certain verbs though it adds no new element to the meaning:

During the membership drive, four new students joined [up].
He had left the dog tied [up] to a parking meter.

In formal writing this use of *up* would be avoided.

Usage   Usage—the ways in which words are actually used—determines whether the words are appropriate or inappropriate English. The three main kinds of English usage (formal, informal, and nonstandard) are described in **Levels of English usage.** Most of the other entires also discuss usage.

used to   Though the *d* is not pronounced, it should not be omitted in writing:

Joe *used to* play center for the Panthers.   [Not: Joe *use to.*]

But the negative and interrogative forms are usually made with *did* and *use* (without the *d*):

She *did not use* (or *didn't use*) to be afraid of spiders.   [More formal: She *used not* to be afraid.]
Did you *use* to save baseball cards?

Used to could is a nonstandard idiom:

NONSTANDARD: He can't yodel as well as he used to could.
STANDARD: He can't yodel as well as he once could.   [Or: as well as he used to be able to.]

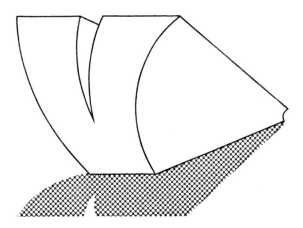

Variant   A different form or spelling of a word. Spellings such as *buses—busses, catalogue—catalog;* pronunciations such as /tə mā′tō/ —/tə mä′tō/,

/ant/ — /änt/; and constructions such as *the student's — of the student, sillier — more silly, was burned — was burnt* are variants.

Though most variant forms are equally good, there may be slight differences in the shade of meaning expressed or in the degree of formality that makes one or another more appropriate. The form *indices*, for example, is preferred in formal English, *indexes* in informal.

Verb   A word or group of words used to "assert" or express action, condition, or being:

Leo *was skating* backward when he *fell.*   [Physical action.]
Janet really *believes* in ghosts.   [Mental action.]
The doughnuts *looked* stale, but I *was* sure they *were* fresh.   [Condition, being.]

The verb may also express a command or request:

Do not *lean* on the guardrail.
Show me your pass, please.

For further discussion and examples, see **Auxiliary verb, Principal parts of verbs, Tenses of verbs,** and **Verb phrases.**

Verb-adverb combinations   In the sentence "She put down her book and turned on the TV," *down* is an adverb. It has the usual adverb use: it modifies the verb *put*, telling *where* she put the book. But in "The Army put down the rebellion," *down* (although technically an adverb) is semantically a part of the verb. *Put* literally means "place," but the combination *put down* means "suppress"; it has nothing to do with placing.

English has many such verb-adverb combinations, two-part verbs that have a meaning different from the literal meaning of their parts.

VERB AND MODIFIER	TWO-PART VERB
Al walked out to the curb.	Have the Teamsters *walked out*?
They ran off to play.	She *ran off* ten copies.
Pull the wire through.	Did the patient *pull through*?
I looked up at them.	I *looked up* the word.

Sometimes the two-part verb is separated, as in "I *looked* the word *up*." But the verb in this example is still *look up* rather than *look* (modified by *up*), as in "I *looked up* at them."

The examples cited and hundreds of other verb-adverb combinations are in common use, especially in informal English. Formal English is likely to prefer single words: *investigate* for *look into*, *require* for *call for*, *persuade* for *win over*, *conclude* for *wrap up*, etc. Informal English prefers the emphatic rhythm of the verb-adverb combinations.

verbal   See **oral, verbal.**

Verbals   Verb forms that are used as nouns (*Seeing* is *believing*), adjectives (a *whining* child), or adverbs (They stopped *to help* us). For further information, see **Gerund, Participle,** and **Infinitive.**

Verb phrases   Verbs that consist of more than one word (also called *phrasal verbs*):

are leaving	will have called	is being served
could keep	might have fallen	will have been caught
has left	did stop	had been sleeping

Some grammarians use the term *verb phrase* to stand for a main verb and any complements and modifiers it may have.

very, too   **1** In formal English *very* and *too* are not used in sentences like "He was very disliked by his neighbors" and "She is too impressed with her own importance," in which *very* and *too* modify a past participle directly. In such sentences formal English uses intensifiers like *very much, too much, greatly, highly, overly,* etc.: "He was *very much* disliked by his neighbors." "She is *overly* impressed with her own importance." Informal English makes no such distinctions.

2 *Very* has been so commonly overused that it has little value as an intensive. Avoid using it unless you are sure that it really adds meaning to your statement:

WEAK: The hotel was very expensive. But our room was big and very comfortable, and the service was very good.

IMPROVED: The hotel was expensive. But our room was big and comfortable, and the service was excellent.

viewpoint   *Viewpoint* is an economical substitute for *point of view* (though some purists object to its use as unidiomatic). In sentences in which *point of view* would be followed by another *of* (from the point of view of the critic), *viewpoint* would perhaps be less clumsy (from the critic's viewpoint, from the viewpoint of the critic).

viz.   Abbreviation of the Latin *videlicet* /və del'ə set/, meaning "that is to say" or "namely." *Viz.* is used only in rather formal documents or reference works. It is usually read "namely."

Voice   See **Active and passive voice.**

vs.   An abbreviation for the Latin *versus*, meaning "against." *Vs.* (sometimes *vs*, without the period) is most often used in headlines and writing about sporting events (Chicago Bears vs. New York Jets). In other writing, the full form — *versus* — is more common.

In law the abbreviation *v.* is used (The State of Ohio v. Richard Roe).

wages   See **salary, wages.**

wait on, wait for   *Wait on* used in the sense of "wait for" is dialectal:

DIALECT: I promised Joe I'd wait on him at the corner.
STANDARD: I promised Joe I'd wait for him at the corner.
STANDARD: The couple Ginny waited on left a ten-cent tip. [Meaning "served."]

want   The use of *want for* (He wants for me to drive) is common in Southern speech and is occasionally heard in other regions. But the *for* is generally omitted in writing:

WRITTEN: We want you to come early and stay late.
SPOKEN: We want for you to come early and stay late.
NONSTANDARD: We want you should come early and stay late.

(See also **like for.**)
   Want is colloquial for *should*, *ought*, or *had better*:

You want to handle an antique carefully.
You want to think before you answer.

   Want meaning "lack" or "need" is formal, and chiefly British usage:

That child wants a little discipline.

want in, off, out, up, etc.   Localisms for *want to come in, want to get off, want to go out*, and so on:

LOCAL: I think the cat wants in.
GENERAL: I think the cat wants to come in.

way, ways   In everyday speech, *ways* is often used instead of *way* in a sense of "distance":

COLLOQUIAL: It is only a short ways from our house to theirs.
WRITTEN: It is only a short way from our house to theirs.   [More formal: a short distance.]

Way is informal in the sense of "condition" or "state":

Bonnie was really in a bad way after the accident.

we   1 *We* is sometimes used as an indefinite pronoun referring to people in general:

We live in a highly industrialized society.
We tend to mistrust what we do not understand.

2 In editorials and other featured columns of newspapers and magazines the writer often refers to himself as *we*, thus suggesting that he speaks also for his newspaper or editorial staff (though he may be speaking for himself alone).

This editorial *we* is sometimes used in familiar and informal writing, especially of a light tone. But used only to keep from using *I*, *we* is conspicuous and is better avoided.

we boys, us boys, etc.   Whether to use the nominative form *we* or the objective form *us* in such expressions depends on the function of the pronoun in the sentence:

Will *we* boys be excused early?   [Subject.]
It was *we* boys who did all the work.   [Predicate complement.]
You can't fool *us* girls.   [Direct object.]
Linda told *us* girls the whole story.   [Indirect object.]
They can come with *us* three.   [Object of preposition.]

well   See **good, well.**

whatever, wherever, whyever   See **ever.**

when, where, in definitions   See **Defining words**, last paragraph.

where   Although in informal speech *where* is sometimes used in place of *that*, it is not appropriate in writing:

I read in yesterday's paper *that* the Bulls have a new coach.   [Not: I read . . . *where* the Bulls have a new coach.]

where . . . at, where . . . to   Though used in certain dialects, the *at* and *to* are generally omitted in standard English. For example:

Where is Linus?   [Not: Where is Linus *at*?]
Where can that hamster have gone?   [Not: have gone *to*.]

whether   See **if, whether.**

which   1 As a relative pronoun, *which* is used for things and for collective nouns referring to people (*team, family, delegation, audience, class*) when the group, not the individuals, is meant:

He said the *Moulton*, which seemed huge to me, was one of the smaller ships in the fleet.
The Hebron team, which hasn't lost a game in two years, is expected to win the tournament.

When the individual members of the group are meant, *who* is used:

Bob's family, who often stay up half the night arguing politics, can't understand his marrying Sara, a political know-nothing.

(See also **that, which.**)
   Which is also used occasionally to refer to the whole idea expressed in a preceding group of words:

Not one of the dogs barked, which seems strange.
No one heard him call for help, which was unfortunate for him.

But this use should be avoided if there is any danger that the reference of *which* will not be clear; that is, if *which* may seem to refer to a particular noun in the group instead of to the group as a whole:

NOT CLEAR: A week later he circulated a second petition, which infuriated the manager.
CLEAR: His circulating a second petition a week later infuriated the manager.

   Whose is often used as the possessive of *which*, instead of the more awkward *of which*:

Down on the beach was an old shack, whose roof had fallen in.

   2 *Which*-clauses are subordinate clauses and should not be carelessly joined to a main statement by *and* or *but*:

CARELESS: It is a complicated and exacting process, and which takes a great deal of time.
BETTER: It is a complicated and exacting process which takes a great deal of time.

CARELESS: He told us there were several cars on the back lot, mostly older models, but which were within our price range.
BETTER: He told us there were several cars on the back lot, mostly older models, which were within our price range.

while 1 *While* is used mainly as a subordinating conjunction introducing adverbial clauses of time:

While he was cleaning the fish, I built a fire.

2 *While* is also used, rather weakly, in the sense of "though" or "but":

While Mickey enjoyed Chicago, he missed his friends in Utah.
John is extremely cautious, while his sister is incurably rash.

3 *While* is used colloquially and in journalese for *and*, a construction avoided in careful writing:

Karl and Andy won cash prizes, while Mark received an honorable mention. [Better: *and* Mark received an honorable mention.]

(See also **awhile, a while.**)

who, whom, whose 1 The pronoun *who* — used both as a relative and as an interrogative — refers to people and sometimes to animals:

The girl who won is a cousin of one of the judges.
Rover, who is well named, ran away again yesterday.

2 When the relative or interrogative pronoun is the subject of the verb, the nominative form *who* is used, even when the subject is separated from its verb by other words:

The woman who the witnesses said had caused the accident is suing the truck driver. [Subject of *had caused.*]
Who does he think did all the work? [Subject of *did.*]

When the interrogative pronoun used as the object of a verb or preposition comes at the beginning of a sentence or clause, informal English generally uses *who*, while formal English uses the objective form *whom*:

FORMAL: Whom did Mr. Sullivan recommend for the promotion?
INFORMAL: Who did Mr. Sullivan recommend for the promotion?

FORMAL: To whom should we address our letters?
INFORMAL: Who should we address our letters to? [Or: To whom should we address our letters?]

FORMAL: I have no idea whom they suspect.
INFORMAL: I have no idea who they suspect.

When the relative pronoun is the object of a verb or preposition, formal English uses the objective form *whom*. In informal English the pronoun object is often omitted or *that* is used:

FORMAL: He was boasting about the pilots whom he had trained.
INFORMAL: He was boasting about the pilots [that] he had trained.

FORMAL: The candidate for whom she had worked was defeated.
INFORMAL: The candidate [that] she had worked for was defeated.

The form you should use in a particular context depends, of course, on the situation. On formal occasions — during an interview, in giving an address or report before a group, in a research paper or other serious expository writing — you should use the forms preferred in formal English. In informal situations — in conversations with friends, in personal letters, in informal narratives — the forms used in informal English are appropriate.

The possessive form *whose* shows ownership:

Whose are the books in the kitchen?
He is the neighbor whose car was stolen.

(For *whose* as the possessive of *which*, see **which,** section 1.)

3 When *who* is the subject of a relative clause, its verb agrees in number with its antecedent:

Sandra Maklin is the only one of the clerks who *likes* filing.   [Antecedent is *one.*]
My brother-in-law is one of those men who *admire* brawn more than brains.   [Antecedent is *men.*]

(For further examples and discussion, see **one of those who.**)

will   See **shall, will.**

without   *Without* used in the sense of "unless" is dialectal:

DIALECT: I won't come without she does.
STANDARD: I won't come unless she does.

woman, lady   See **man, woman.**

wonderful   Used exactly, *wonderful* means "causing wonder; marvelous; remarkable": the *wonderful* majesty of the Taj Mahal. *Wonderful* is also used informally as a counter word of approval: *wonderful* vacation. (See **Counter words.**)

woods   Both *woods* and *wood* are used to refer to a thick growth of trees. Although plural in form, *woods* takes a singular verb when preceded by the noun marker *a*, and usually when a particular woods is named:

A woods *provides* shelter for many small animals.
Whittaker Woods *was destroyed* by fire last year.

When preceded by *the*, *woods* usually takes a plural verb:

The woods near the junction *are* full of Queen Anne's lace.

Wordiness   The use of more words than are needed to express ideas clearly and accurately results in weak, often vague, writing. The commonest types of wordiness are:

1 Circumlocution — using several words or roundabout phrasing to say what migl. be said more directly, in fewer words:

WORDY: With respect to its historical accuracy, the film is sound.
BETTER: The film is historically accurate.

WORDY: Their new living room has a floor that is made of woods of different shades arranged in a geometric pattern.
BETTER: Their new living room has a parquet floor.

WORDY: Owing to the fact that I had handed in my report ten days after the time at which it was due, the grade I received on it was lowered.
BETTER: Because I had handed in my report ten days late, I received a lowered grade.

2 Deadwood — words that add nothing to the meaning:

Carl Sandburg wrote a three-volume biography [about the life] of Abraham Lincoln.
He said that the meeting had been businesslike [in character].
Three of the [five] quintuplets are still quite small [in size].

Word order   In an "inflected" language like Latin, special endings are added to words to show what work they are doing in a sentence. The words in a Latin sentence can be put in almost any order, and the listener or reader can still tell by the endings whether a word is the subject of a sentence, for example, or the verb or the object.

In English, meaning does not depend on inflectional endings. Instead we rely on word order to make clear such things as which word is the subject and which the object. The usual order in English sentences is subject — verb ("Mortimer laughed"; "Mary smiled"), subject — verb — object ("She called Herbie last"), or subject — linking verb — complement ("It was a very silly scheme").

We deviate from this normal word order only (1) to ask a question or (2) to give special emphasis to an object or a complement:

Were you there?   Was Mary smiling?
Herbie she called last.   And a very silly scheme it was.

Words: classes of   A common way to classify, or sort out, the words in the English language is into eight classes (or "parts of speech"): nouns, verbs, adjectives, adverbs, pronouns, prepositions, conjunctions, and interjections. This classification is based on the meaning and use of a word in a sentence, as well as its form.

For further discussion, see the individual entry on each word class and the following word-class chart. Compare also **Form classes.**

WORD CLASS	STRUCTURAL CHARACTERISTICS	SOME TYPICAL DERIVATIONAL ENDINGS
NOUN	Plural form ending in -s or -es or equivalent; possessive forms ending in 's or (s)'	-ance, -dom, -er, -ess, -ism, -ist, -ment, -ness, -or, -ship
VERB	Forms ending in -s, -ed, -ing, or equivalents	-ate, -en, -ify, -ize
ADJECTIVE	Comparative forms ending in -er, -est (or preceded by more, most)	-able, -al, -ful, -ible, -ic, -ious, -ish, -ive, -ous, -y
ADVERB	Comparative forms ending in -er, -est (or preceded by more, most)	-ly, -ward, -wards, -way, -wise
PRONOUN	----	A closed class—no additions possible
PREPOSITION	----	A closed class—no additions possible
CONJUNCTION	----	A closed class—no additions possible

MAIN USES IN SENTENCE	TYPICAL POSITION IN SENTENCE	TRADITIONAL DEFINITION
Subject, direct or indirect object, complement, object of preposition, appositive	Before and after verb; after *a* or *an*, *the*, *this*, *my*, *some*, etc.; after a preposition	A *noun* is a word used as the name of a person, place, thing, quality, action, or idea.
Predicate; as verbal: participle, infinitive, gerund	After subject in statement; often before subject in question	A *verb* is a word or phrase used to assert or express action or being.
Modifier of noun or pronoun	Between *a*, *an*, *the*, etc., and noun; after linking verb	An *adjective* is a word used to modify a noun or pronoun by making its meaning more exact.
Modifier of verb, adjective, adverb	After verb or verb and object; before adjective, adverb, verb; at beginning of sentence	An *adverb* is a word used to modify a verb, adjective, or another adverb.
Subject, direct or indirect object, complement, object of preposition	Before and after verb; after a preposition	A *pronoun* is a word used in place of a noun.
Forming phrase with noun or noun equivalent (to show relationship of object to some other word in sentence)	Before its object (a noun or noun equivalent)	A *preposition* is a word used to show the relationship between its object and some other word in the sentence.
Coordinating: joining two or more words, phrases, clauses, sentences Subordinating: introducing a clause that is used as part of a sentence	----	A *conjunction* is a word used to join words, phrases, clauses, and sentences.

Words: formation of Since its beginning English has been a growing and changing language. It has to be, to keep pace with the growing and changing lives of the English-speaking peoples. Every new event in their lives—every new idea, invention, discovery—creates a need for new words, for an expanded vocabulary.

There are two main ways by which words are added to the language:

1 By borrowing words. The richness of the English vocabulary is due in great part to the freedom with which English-speaking peoples have adopted and adapted foreign words. (For examples of borrowings and discussion of their use, see **Borrowed words.**)

2 By creating new words. One of the simplest ways of creating new words is by combining two existing words to form a compound whose meaning is more than the sum of its parts. The words *freeway, cowboy, egghead, underdog, pushover, skyscraper*, and *fastback* are all products of compounding.

Another, similar way of creating new words is by combining existing word elements. Greek elements, for example, are often used in naming new inventions. The element *-phone*, from a Greek word meaning "sound" or "voice," has been used in such words as *telephone, microphone, phonograph*, and *stereophonic*. The *tele-* in *telescope, television*, and *telephone* is also from a Greek word, meaning "far."

Sometimes words are made from the names of people who have some connection with the thing or process the word refers to. *Dahlia*, for example, derives from the name of Anders Dahl, a Swedish botanist; *mackintosh*, from Charles Macintosh, the inventor; *pasteurize*, from Louis Pasteur, the discoverer of the process; and *shrapnel*, from General Henry Shrapnel. Places and events are also sources. The words *damask, tangerine*, and *milliner* come from the names of cities—Damascus, Tangier, and Milan. The word *tawdry* is derived from St. Audrey's Fair, where cheap lace necklets were sold.

Many times, instead of creating a new word to describe a new thing or idea or situation, an existing word is used in a figurative way. For example, the word *bottleneck* originally meant only "the neck of a bottle." Then someone used *bottleneck* figuratively to mean "something or someone that hinders progress," the way the narrow neck of a bottle slows the flow of liquid. People found this figurative meaning convenient; and they used it so often and so naturally that in time it became just another "regular" meaning. Some other words and phrases with a figurative meaning that became regular are *rat* (a despicable, sneaky person), *gravy* (money acquired through graft), *butter up* (flatter), *small fry* (children or unimportant persons), *nest egg* (money saved or held in reserve for emergencies), *stuffed shirt* (a pompous, inflexible person), *iron curtain* (an imaginary wall or dividing line).

For discussion and examples of several other ways in which new words and meanings are created, see **Acronym, Back formations, Blend, Clipped words, Coining words, Nonce word, Prefix.**

world   Deadwood in such expressions as "in the political world," "in the world of finance." "In politics" or "in finance" is enough.

worthwhile   Now generally written as one word:

The experiment produced no worthwhile results.
Learning to type almost always proves to be worthwhile.

would of   A misspelling of *would've* (*would have*).

would rather   See **had rather, would rather.**

Xmas   Pronounced /kris′məs/, not /eks′məs/. This form is sometimes used in advertising and in headlines. In other writing, *Christmas* is generally spelled out because the shortened form is objectionable to so many people.

X-ray, X ray   Usually written with a capital *x*. When used as a verb or an adjective it is hyphened; when used as a noun it is generally not: to *X-ray* an injury, an *X-ray* technician, a dental *X ray*.

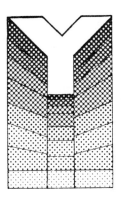

ye, the   The *ye* in such names as *Ye Olde Wayside Inn* is simply the archaic form of *the*. It is correctly pronounced /ᵵHē/, not /yē/. (In Old English writing, the sound /ᴛʜ/ was represented by a single symbol, the letter thorn: þ. Early printers who did not have this symbol substituted the letter *y*, which somewhat resembled the letter thorn.)

yes, no   These adverbs may modify sentences (*Yes*, Hank has a scholarship) or may stand by themselves as complete sentences ("Have you seen my sweater?" "*No*."). Remember that when *yes* or *no* modifies a sentence it is always set off by a comma.

yet   *Yet* is used chiefly as an adverb:

Hasn't he paid the bill yet?   It had not yet rained.

It is also used as a coordinating conjunction, equivalent to *but*. Then it is preceded by a comma:

Jay admitted he had been rude, yet he refused to apologize.

you   In informal speech and writing *you* is commonly used as an indefinite pronoun, referring to people in general:

In Uruguay you can be fined for not voting.
Next you mix the wet and dry ingredients.

In formal English *one* is preferred, or else a different construction:

In Uruguay one can be fined for not voting.
Next the wet and dry ingredients are mixed.

The indefinite *you* should be avoided whenever it might be misunderstood as personal rather than impersonal—especially if the misunderstanding would turn a generalization into an insult, as in the sentence "You should use a mouthwash every morning."

you-all   In Southern American speech *you-all* (often contracted to *y'all*) is widely used as the plural of *you*:

. . Sometimes when the children staggered onto the porch worn out with play, red-cheeked, moist-browed and quarreling, she would say, "Come on, you-all, sit down somewhere or other and I'll tell you a story." —Elizabeth Enright, "When the Bough Breaks," *The Moment Before the Rain*, Harcourt Brace Jovanovich, Inc.

Educated Southerners avoid its use as a singular.

your, you're   Do not confuse the possessive form *your* (your parents) with the contraction *you're* (you are). Remember that an apostrophe is never used in forming the possessives of the personal pronouns.

yourself, yourselves   The reflexive forms of *you*. (See **Reflexive pronouns** and **myself**.)

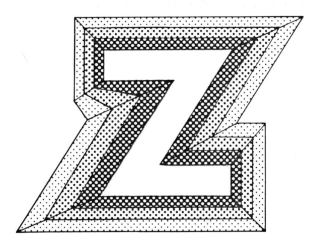

zh   The phonetic symbol representing the sound in *measure* /mezh'ər/, *division* /də vizh'ən/, *seizure* /sē'zhər/, and so on.

zoology   Pronounced /zō ol'ə jē/, not /zü ol'ə jē/. People who mispronounce it are probably confused by the word *zoo* (a shortened form of *zoological garden*).

EXERCISE 1.   Each of the following numbered items contains one or more nonstandard verb forms. Be ready to read the sentences aloud, substituting standard forms for the nonstandard ones.

[In brackets at the end of each exercise in this book, you will find a list of entries to turn to for answers to questions you may have about items in the exercise.]

1. You was right; I should have chose the other one.
2. By the time the bus come, our toes were froze.
3. They begun to suspect that Albert had stole the steaks.
4. We should have took a look at it while we was there.
5. Does anyone know how many people have swam the English Channel?
6. The cashier seen them and rung the alarm.
7. If he hadn't ran, he wouldn't have fell.
8. Winslow wouldn't have drank the iced tea; he don't like it.
9. The sweater had shrank, but the socks hadn't.
10. Mortimer must have wrote that anonymous letter. I'm almost sure he done it.
11. She would have rode with us if she hadn't went with the Custers.
12. I could have swore you was wearing a real fur coat.
13. Herb and Sue have broke up. They haven't spoke to each other in weeks.
14. Has he ever wore the shirt you give him?
15. We seen right away that a man had fell overboard.
16. She had mistook the bill for an ad and had tore it up.
17. When he seen that I needed help, he run over and give me a hand.
18. Don't she know who drunk the iced tea?
19. The wind had rose, and big chunks of ice had began to float down the river.
20. You would have saw it too if you had came with us.
21. He had ate everything in sight, but he could have ate more.
22. I think the coach would have gave us another chance, but Al don't.
23. A rumor had sprang up that a ship had sank in the harbor during the night.
24. I don't think he has ever drove in city traffic before.
25. If she had swam a little faster, she would have came in first.

[be, section 1 / don't, doesn't / Principal parts of verbs]

EXERCISE 2.   Be ready to read the following sentences aloud, using the verb forms in parentheses appropriate in standard English.

1. No, Phil (*saw, seen*) the billfold first.
2. At this point the boy's mother (*began, begun*) to scream.
3. Three years later Sam Kasias (*became, become*) president of the firm.
4. Poor Aunt Louisa had (*sank, sunk*) to the floor in a dead faint.
5. Nora (*drank, drunk*) her milk. Why hasn't Len (*drank, drunk*) his?
6. Had the cashier (*stole, stolen*) the money?

7. Dorothy and Joan must have (*went, gone*) in already.
8. Someone had (*tore, torn*) the coupon from the ad.
9. I could have (*swore, sworn*) it was you.
10. When he (*came, come*) to me, I refused to sign.
11. You should have (*saw, seen*) the look on his face when he (*saw, seen*) them come in.
12. Winslow sent us a very astute criticism that George Newell had (*wrote, written*).
13. Uncle Joe has (*drove, driven*) that same old car for ten years.
14. Now I wish I had (*took, taken*) the big box so I could have (*gave, given*) you some.
15. Mitch had (*fell, fallen*) against the tree and had (*broke, broken*) several ornaments.
16. Terry had (*ate, eaten*) six hot dogs and could have (*ate, eaten*) a couple more.
17. Have you ever (*rode, ridden*) on a funicular?
18. The boys had (*took, taken*) the 10-point questions, and the girls had (*chose, chosen*) the 5-point ones.
19. And she hasn't (*spoke, spoken*) to him since.
20. By the time the bus (*came, come*), we had almost (*froze, frozen*) to death.
21. He must have (*mistook, mistaken*) my coat for his; nobody in his right mind would have (*stole, stolen*) a coat as (*wore, worn*) out as mine.
22. The delivery boy had (*rang, rung*) the wrong doorbell.
23. You shouldn't have (*gave, given*) up so soon
24. Before we had (*went, gone*) three miles, that old jalopy of his (*began, begun*) to sputter
25. Someone had (*broke, broken*) into the safe and had (*stole, stolen*) the Zeeco formula. I wonder who (*did, done*) it.
[Principal parts of verbs]

EXERCISE 3. Be ready to read the following sentences aloud, using the appropriate verbs.

1. Did Barry remember to (*bring, take*) his watch to the jeweler?
2. I (*laid, lay*) awake for hours, worrying about the test.
3. Uncle Ralph was (*learning, teaching*) us how to set traps.
4. When she heard the price, her eyebrows (*rose, raised*).
5. Someone had (*laid, lain*) a muddy shoe on the sofa.
6. Someone with muddy shoes had (*laid, lain*) on the sofa.
7. Who (*learned, taught*) you how to dance?
8. She won't (*leave, let*) anyone (*sit, set*) in that chair.
9. You can (*bring, take*) my radio to the picnic with you, but don't forget to (*bring, take*) it home again.
10. Prices have (*risen, raised*) steadily during the past year.
11. They (*left, let*) the car (*sitting, setting*) in the ditch.
12. They (*left, let*) it (*sit, set*) there for a week.

13. He says he will (*learn, teach*) us how to make a million dollars.
14. After the dough is mixed, (*sit, set*) it in a warm place until it (*rises, raises*).
15. "Whose coat is that (*laying, lying*) there?" "Henry's. He must have (*laid, lain*) it there and forgot it."
16. Dad wouldn't have (*left, let*) them borrow the mower if he'd known they'd (*leave, let*) it (*sitting, setting*) out in the rain.
17. When they returned, seven bottles of sour milk were (*sitting, setting*) on the doorstep.
18. Within an hour the temperature had (*rose, raised, risen*) another twenty degrees.
19. The doctor handed me a prescription and told me to (*bring, take*) it to the drugstore on Fourth Street.
20. It is silly for you to (*leave, let*) them interfere.

[bring, take / lie, lay / learn, teach / leave, let / rise, raise / sit, set]

EXERCISE 4. Be ready to read each of the following sentences aloud, using the verb form in parentheses that agrees with the subject.

1. Many miles of Australia's southwest coast (*are, is*) treeless.
2. The family in the upstairs flat (*have, has*) decided to move.
3. (*Do, Does*) he and his brothers still practice law?
4. A number of students (*have, has*) already won scholarships.
5. (*Have, Has*) the manager or his secretary called yet?
6. One page of the photographs (*were, was*) printed upside down.
7. The assembly hall, as well as some of the classrooms, (*need, needs*) painting.
8. A box of apples or a bag of oranges (*sell, sells*) for eighty cents.
9. Neither the manager nor his secretary (*have, has*) called yet.
10. On the far side of the attic (*were, was*) the trunk and some boxes.
11. The number of students applying for scholarships (*have, has*) grown considerably.
12. He is one of those people who never (*know, knows*) when to quit.
13. Oscar Oda or one of the Kelly twins usually (*mow, mows*) the lawn.
14. Harper's best friend and most valued assistant (*were, was*) Dr. Whitten, a young physicist.
15. Not one of our neighbors (*own, owns*) a dog or a cat.
16. Measles sometimes (*leave, leaves*) serious aftereffects.
17. Neither of the girls (*mind, minds*) coming early.
18. The kind of shoes he wears (*make, makes*) him look taller.
19. (*There are, There's*) usually about one hundred mosquitoes and a hornet in our tent.
20. Every cup, saucer, and plate (*were, was*) wrapped and packed.
21. The directions on the package (*tell, tells*) how much to use.
22. She is the only one of those girls who consistently (*type, types*) more than sixty words a minute.
23. One attraction of the apartments (*are, is*) the new appliances.

24. He reported that the safe, along with its contents, (*were, was*) undamaged.
25. Of course, the size of the pools (*vary, varies*).

[Agreement, section 1]

EXERCISE 5. A. Be ready to read the following sentences aloud, using the pronoun forms in parentheses that are appropriate in formal English.

1. (*He, Him*) and (*I, me*) were the first to sign up.
2. Between you and (*I, me*) it was a very dull party.
3. The milkman told Don and (*she, her*), and they told Harold.
4. Not one dog owner had bought a license for (*his, their*) dog.
5. (*Who, Whom*) substituted for (*who, whom*) in the first half?
6. But it wasn't (*they, them*) who did all the complaining.
7. Don't you remember (*me, my*) telling you about the accident?
8. Ron is taller than (*I, me*), but I weigh more than (*he, him*).
9. He acted as though he didn't trust (*we, us*) boys.
10. Calvin sent Gordon and (*she, her*) postcards from Miami.
11. Everyone has signed the petition except Robin and (*he, him*).
12. Mrs. Grundy said (*he, him*) and (*she, her*) never agreed.
13. Are you sure that was (*she, her*) and her sister on the bus?
14. Everyone was asked to sign (*his, their*) name on the gift card.
15. The Quinns and (*we, us*) used to be neighbors.
16. For (*who, whom*) were his remarks intended?
17. Mr. Higgins never objected to (*our, us*) whistling in the hall.
18. My uncle quit because his boss gave Mrs. Wills a bigger raise than (*he, him*).
19. Couldn't you and (*he, him*) have waited for Stanley and (*I, me*)?
20. Neither of the girls can show (*her, their*) slides today.
21. The editor appointed (*we, us*) two to write the article—Phillip and (*I, me*).
22. (*Who, Whom*) does he think was responsible?
23. Even Mr. Adams did not know (*who, whom*) they were.
24. If anyone wants (*his, their*) money back, (*he, they*) must have (*his, their*) receipt with (*him, them*).
25. I know the reason for (*them, their*) withdrawing.
26. Give (*whoever, whomever*) comes to the door a sample.
27. We play a much faster game than (*they, them*).
28. Someone had taken my raincoat and left (*his, theirs*).
29. (*Who, Whom*) do you suppose Ted saw today?
30. "Did Mr. King ask anyone to help him?" "Yes, Arturo and (*I, me*)."

B. Go over the sentences in Part A again. Of the pronoun forms that you decided were not appropriate in formal English, pick out any that *would* be appropriate in casual conversation or in informal English. Be ready to tell what these forms are and where they would be appropriate.

[Agreement, section 2 / Case, section 1 / who, whom, whose, section 2]

EXERCISE 6. Each of the following sentences contains one or more pronoun forms not appropriate in formal English. Be ready to read the sentences aloud, substituting the appropriate forms.

1. No one volunteered but Angie and I.
2. Him and me did twice as much work as them.
3. Neither of the women would give up their place in the line.
4. Are them the presents she brought for Ellen and I?
5. Well, whom do you think deserved first place?
6. Are you sure it was Roy and him who told Mrs. Lentz?
7. Tell whomever answers that Rob and me will be late.
8. Between you and I, it was us girls who thought of the idea; it wasn't Ken and him.
9. The reporter from the *News* wanted to know whom had invited who to the briefing.
10. Them are the copies that him and me ran off on the mimeograph.
11. Us three winners — Sam, Pete, and me — were asked to pose for a picture with the governor and she.
12. Cal just brushed hisself off and got on the horse again.
13. Without Florence and she the alto section was pretty weak.
14. Wayne turned out to be a better skier than us two old-timers, Bill and me.
15. As usual, him and me ate more spaghetti than Jack and her.
16. Miss Gordon asked Frank and I why we were late.
17. That might be her in the booth at the back.
18. Dad and him were on the night shift then.
19. Sam offered to drive Pat and I home in his new car.
20. The only people who she could depend on in an emergency were Peter and me.

[Agreement, section 2 / Case, section 1 / myself / them / who, whom, whose]

EXERCISE 7. Each of the following sentences contains one or more forms not appropriate in formal English. Be ready to read the sentences aloud, substituting the appropriate forms.

1. I wanted him to take a picture of Anita and myself.
2. If they would put theirself in our place, they would understand.
3. There was little love lost between the Boones and ourselves.
4. Them are the ones I myself would like.
5. We need more hard workers like John and yourself.
6. Mr. Cortez and myself were the only ones who welcomed them.
7. He thinks Rob and I can repair the car ourself.
8. Doctors themselves say them are the worst kind.
9. Are them the tools he bought hisself?
10. They invited Faye and myself to go with them.

[Intensive pronouns / myself / Reflexive pronouns / theirself, theirselves / them]

EXERCISE 8. Be ready to read the following sentences aloud, using the adjective or adverb in parentheses that is appropriate in standard written English.

1. Be sure to stir it (*good, well*).
2. Please pack them (*separate, separately*).
3. Don't feel (*bad, badly*); it wasn't your fault.
4. You'll have to admit that he dresses very (*neat, neatly*).
5. Does he always drive that (*reckless, recklessly*)?
6. Gilbert can't see (*good, well*) without his glasses.
7. Didn't you think the pizza tasted (*peculiar, peculiarly*)?
8. When Mr. Krause heard my excuse, he looked (*skeptical, skeptically*).
9. Then we realized why they had left so (*sudden, suddenly*).
10. Luckily neither was burned (*bad, badly*).
11. Why does she sound her r's so (*strange, strangely*)?
12. Don't talk so (*foolish, foolishly*).
13. He'd be better if he practiced (*regular, regularly*).
14. However (*good, well*) their scheme sounds, I'm sure it won't work out (*good, well*).
15. She eats very (*hearty, heartily*) for someone on a diet.
16. The cheese may smell (*horrible, horribly*), but it tastes (*delicious, deliciously*).
17. Your voice sounds (*different, differently*) over the phone.
18. The engine started (*easy, easily*), but it didn't run (*smooth, smoothly*).
19. He doesn't play (*bad, badly*), but he doesn't play (*good, well*) either.
20. Andy's father expects him to do everything (*perfect, perfectly*).

[Adjective / Adverb / bad, badly / good, well / Linking verb]

EXERCISE 9. Be ready to read the following sentences aloud, using the adjective or adverb in parentheses that is appropriate in standard written English.

1. Doesn't that last verse sound (*strange, strangely*) to you?
2. Well, this time he sounded so (*convincing, convincingly*) that we voted for him.
3. I wouldn't feel (*bad, badly*) about missing the play; the cast didn't do too (*good, well*).
4. I wish you wouldn't talk so (*sarcastic, sarcastically*) to your father, young man.
5. He asked the waitress to bring more butter—some that didn't taste (*rancid, rancidly*).
6. Nothing, he said, smells more (*fragrant, fragrantly*) than his wife's homemade bread.
7. How (*stunning, stunningly*) Sharon looks in that outfit!
8. I can get my report done (*easy, easily*) by noon.
9. No one in the car was hurt (*bad, badly*).

10. She speaks quite (*fluent, fluently*) for a person who has been here only a year.
11. The car door opened (*easy, easily*) enough, but then it wouldn't close.
12. The frightening thing about the accident was how (*sudden, suddenly*) it happened.
13. He writes (*bad, badly*) because he doesn't observe (*close, closely*) or think (*clear, clearly*).
14. No wonder Margaret Ann swims so (*good, well*); she practices (*regular, regularly*).
15. Your father sounded quite (*impatient, impatiently*) when I called the third time.
16. It's funny, but Professor Ramirez sounds every vowel so (*distinct, distinctly*) that he sounds (*strange, strangely*).
17. The jury looked rather (*solemn, solemnly*) when they filed back into the jury box.
18. Doesn't that grapefruit taste too (*sour, sourly*) without sugar?
19. The shop steward warned the men not to act too (*hasty, hastily*).
20. Dick felt (*bitter, bitterly*) about the matter, but he covered up (*beautiful, beautifully*).

[Adjective / Adverb / bad, badly / good, well / Linking verb]

EXERCISE 10. A. Be ready to read the following sentences aloud, supplying the comparative or superlative form of the modifier in parentheses that would be appropriate to use in standard written English.

1. Boyd and I had a weight-lifting contest to see who was (*strong*).
2. Which is (*difficult*) to learn — bridge or pinochle?
3. Which is the (*intelligent*) — an ape, a dog, or an elephant?
4. Last night's game between the Mets and the Astros proves that the (*good*) team does not always win.
5. Why not check the prices of both brands and see which is (*cheap*)?
6. That was the (*bad*) joke he has ever told.
7. All three can do the stunt, but Carl does it (*well*).
8. Elaine, the (*old*) of his two sisters, is the (*attractive*) by far.
9. Both dogs are timid, but I think Woof is the (*cowardly*).
10. Who lives (*far*) from school — Inez or the twins?

B. Each of the following sentences contains a faulty comparison. Rewrite the sentences, making whatever changes or additions are necessary.

1. His parents like jazz more than any type of music.
2. The fables of La Fontaine are just as entertaining as Aesop.
3. The paint spots on my face were harder to remove than my arms.
4. Is it true that Chicago's crime rate is higher than New York?
5. I like *The Brothers Karamazov* better than any novel by Dostoevski.
6. This year's fashions are more ridiculous than last year.

7. Madame Perrino has the best-trained voice of all the other sopranos in the opera company.
8. Robert Breen, the sports-page editor, has done more to make the paper a success than anyone on the staff.

[Comparison of adjectives and adverbs / Faulty comparisons]

EXERCISE 11. Each of the following sentences contains one or more forms that are not appropriate in standard written English. Be ready to read the sentences aloud, substituting the appropriate forms.

1. There wasn't scarcely enough space for the trombone.
2. Most all of his remarks were beside the point.
3. I kind of expected Basil to know better than to try them tricks on Mr. Dispart.
4. Obviously he hadn't learned nothing about Irish history.
5. John's writing is careless; he never dots a *i* or crosses a *t*.
6. If this here boy will stand out of the way, I'll show you how to weld them rods.
7. Not many people buy these sort of grapes.
8. That is a honor they don't hardly deserve.
9. I don't care much for that kind of a movie.
10. He said those kind of plants won't grow in this here climate.
11. Most of the contestants seemed sort of confused.
12. Didn't neither of the boys want the job?
13. I noticed most all of the girls were wearing them kind of shoes.
14. Is that there the sort of a coat you're looking for?
15. Mr. Smock can't hardly move his arm, yet he won't let nobody help him.

[a, an / Double negative / kind, sort / kind of, sort of / kind of a, sort of a / most, almost / them / this here, that there]

EXERCISE 12. Each of the following sentences contains a dangling modifier or a misplaced modifier. Rewrite the sentences so that the danglers have a word to modify and the misplaced modifiers clearly modify the words they are intended to modify.

1. Browsing in the library, a book on mastodons caught my eye.
2. The chairman appointed a committee of three to count the ballots before the voting began.
3. Perched on the iron railing, we saw a scarlet tanager.
4. Having turned off her hearing aid, the children could not be heard by Grandmother.
5. If left alone with nothing to do, parents can't expect children to stay out of mischief.
6. Yesterday there was a debate on the bill to provide financial aid to displaced persons in the Senate.

7. Swimming out toward the raft, an overturned rowboat was spotted by the lifeguard.
8. The king left all his personal records and papers to the state after he abdicated for the benefit of future historians.
9. At the age of six Margaret's father retired from the Army and opened a bakery.
10. Uncle Quentin would tell us exciting stories about the oil wells he had drilled whenever he had nothing else to do.
11. While bicycling through the New England states, our neighbors watered our plants and took in our mail.
12. In getting off the escalator, Marge's heel caught in the last tread.
13. Trying to get through the barbed-wire fence, Paul's shirt tore across the back.
14. At last, battered and torn but still readable, she found the book.
15. Ambrose agreed to take the children to the department store that was staging a puppet show to humor his mother-in-law.
16. She told me not to burn the toast three times.
17. Being allergic to eggs, the omelet was turned down by Nancy.
18. Although twice my size, his threats didn't frighten me.
19. We could see two men busily uncrating some color TV sets through a crack in the door.
20. A corsage was given to every girl made of pink rosebuds.
[Dangling modifiers / Misplaced modifiers]

EXERCISE 13. Decide which of the following sentences are run together and which are correctly punctuated. Then rewrite the run-together sentences, correcting them in one of the four ways explained in the entry **Run-together sentence.** You should use each of the four ways at least once.

1. The English horn is not a true horn, it is a woodwind instrument of the oboe family.
2. The steaks were all right, the vegetables were overdone.
3. Along the top of the aqueduct lay a flume, this carried the water across the valley from one mountain to the other.
4. Arthur remembered to bring his report, mine was at home on my desk.
5. In his own time Wyatt Earp was better known as a gambler than as the marshal of Dodge City and Tombstone, in fact, he was never a regularly commissioned U.S. marshal in any city.
6. Major Baker was informed, therefore, that the test had to be postponed a second time.
7. By sundown the temperature was zero, the drafty old cabin was bitterly cold.
8. Ethan didn't show up for rehearsal until it was half over, then he asked to be excused early.
9. At first many farmers refused to use iron plows, they thought that the iron would poison the soil.

10. Stop the engine of the motorboat before attempting to rescue a drowning swimmer, the spinning propeller may injure the victim.
11. According to legend, Zeus instigated the Trojan War, he wanted to rid the world of excess population.
12. The cynic, who thrives on sour grapes, is a great bore, the Pollyanna, who fares on sweet lemons, is equally tiring.
13. Celine was not elected unanimously, there were two votes for Roy.
14. If Mr. Crommie has the original, then yours must be a copy.
15. We hurried over to the biology lab, there he was, busy with an experiment.
16. Tom Paine was a revolutionist, he fought for freedom wherever it was being suppressed.
17. Even though we had sold most of the farm animals, there were still two horses and a henhouse full of chickens to be disposed of.
18. Reporters predict that the match will last for more than ten rounds, this will give the younger fighter an advantage.
19. Mrs. Kinny said she always tried to keep her words soft and sweet, she never knew when she might have to eat them.
20. The government started a program of soil conservation, it was to teach farmers how to keep valuable topsoil from eroding.

[Comma, section 1 / Run-together sentence / Semicolon, sections 1 and 2]

EXERCISE 14. Be ready to point out the major sentences, the minor sentences, and the sentence fragments in the following numbered items. Be prepared also to tell how you would correct each of the fragments.

1. Melissa leaned forward to speak and then suddenly drew back. Silenced by Casey's warning glance.
2. "What was Mary Lou doing in Dr. Brady's office yesterday?" "Having her eyes examined."
3. Mr. Santo sent Mary Lou to Dr. Brady's office yesterday. To have her eyes examined.
4. No one knows where Simon went. After resigning his job, he just disappeared.
5. Gene turned on his heel and stormed out of the room. Without realizing that Ted's remark had been meant as a joke.
6. How ridiculous! Randy couldn't have lifted that heavy stone.
7. The coach didn't give Elmo a chance to play until the last game of the season. When he sent him in for two minutes in the last quarter.
8. I have invited the Karts too. The more, the merrier.
9. Dr. Finch was an Egyptologist. A scientist who studies the monuments, history, and language of Egypt.
10. The investigation demanded by two of our council members is certainly a good idea. But what about the expense?
11. Mrs. Perkins refused to sell the candlesticks for less than twenty-five dollars. Which was about twice their value.

12. For eighteen months Geronimo held off five thousand United States troops and five hundred Indian auxiliaries. With a force of only thirty-five men, eight boys, and one hundred women.
13. Mr. Novak spent ten minutes reading the menu. And then gave his usual order of tea and toast.
14. Why was Lincoln elected President for a second term in 1864, when high officials actively opposed him, and not a single senator in the country campaigned for him? Because the people had faith in him.
15. We felt sure that Christine would get the lead in the operetta. Because she could dance and act as well as sing.
16. Aztec jewelers used gold more often than silver. Because silver rarely occurs pure in nature, it was harder for them to get.
17. We finally found the car keys in the ignition. Right where Mom had left them the day before.
18. And where did we finally find the car keys? In the ignition, right where Mom had left them the day before.
19. Andrew was there. But standing in the shadows where he couldn't be seen easily.
20. Andrew was there. But standing in the shadows, he couldn't be seen easily.

[Sentence fragment / Sentences: major and minor types]

EXERCISE 15. All but two of the following sentences contain shifted constructions. Rewrite each of the faulty sentences, correcting the shifted construction by using parallel forms.

1. Many gases are invisible, odorless, and they have no taste.
2. For Rocco's part we need a boy with some acting experience and who has a pleasant singing voice.
3. The instructor told me to hold on to the edge of the pool, to put my head under water, and that I should kick as hard as I could.
4. The ant is an industrious insect, and they live in highly organized communities.
5. Each year many Hindus visit Benares and Allahabad to bathe in the Ganges and to take home some of its holy water.
6. He let us choose between reading another novel or we could put on a play for another class.
7. The thin ice cracked under Don's skates, and the next minute he plunges into the water.
8. Though I was trying to do a good job, the E-Z-Kleen mixture kept oozing out of the sponge, dribbling down the walls, and left streaks that were hard to remove.
9. The old man was hated by his tenants, shunned by his neighbors, but the children at the Leonard School idolized him.
10. The book tells about Hansen's disease—how it affects the patient, what effect it has on the patient's family, and its treatment.

11. The book was written in India, translated in Germany, and a company in London published it.
12. Anyone can learn to aquaplane, if you practice a little.
13. The smaller car is more practical because it uses less gas and because of its greater ease of parking.
14. I neither found his bongo playing nor his glockenspiel practice objectionable.
15. The man at the nursery gave us written instructions telling when, where, and how to plant the rosebushes.
16. Anyone who is as overweight as June is and with her small feet is bound to have trouble finding a comfortable pair of shoes.
17. At first Elias Howe's sewing machine was thought to be too expensive and that it was too complicated for general use.
18. After removing the old paint, clean the surface with turpentine, or you can use a paint thinner.
19. Thousands of years ago the Chinese obtained natural gas from deep wells, sending it through bamboo pipes, and it was used to evaporate brine for making salt.
20. The guild would not allow a member to work at night or on Sundays or holidays, even if they wanted to.

[Correlative conjunctions / Shifted constructions]

EXERCISE 16. Rewrite each of the following sentences, expressing the same details without using *and* or *so* to join main clauses.

1. Matt wanted to make all decisions by himself, and this was his main fault as committee chairman.
2. Cypress trees grow between the bayous and the lakes, and the trees are draped with Spanish moss.
3. He had been champion for more than four years, so it took a while for him to get adjusted to his defeat.
4. Bruce Leavitt was a young apprentice magician, and he was practicing near their tent, and he overheard the whole argument.
5. The early pioneers lived in small groups, and these groups were isolated from others, and so contagious diseases were not a major problem to them.
6. Gilbert Stuart painted William Grant skating on a pond, and in this way he first won fame as an artist.
7. Della's father had died before she was born and her family was poor, so she had to work her way through school.
8. The next dealer offered Mrs. Starkey even more for the painting, so it obviously had some value she was not aware of, so then she began to be really curious.
9. The attic was an enormous room, and it was cluttered with a hundred years' accumulation of trunks and boxes and furniture, and it was always a wonderful place for us to explore on rainy days.

10. The crofters had been unsuccessful in gaining the reforms they needed, so they organized their own political party, and the organization became the first independent Labour Party in the history of Parliament.
11. Cliff did not want to wake his parents, so he climbed upstairs in his stocking feet.
12. Their house is a red-brick house that has white shutters, and it is three stories high, so it is the biggest house on the block.
13. For an hour I sat outside in the car, and I tried desperately to think of a plausible excuse.
14. Sam and Ken had been rummaging around in the city dump as usual, and they had found a tennis racket there, and it had a perfectly good frame.
15. The only clock in the cottage was a rickety old Big Ben, and it didn't have a minute hand, so it proved more confusing than helpful.
16. Tom was annoyed by Mrs. Lane's prying questions, so he reminded her that curiosity had killed the cat.
17. Fred Alispaw was the trainer, and he fought with the crazed elephant for an hour, and he was armed only with an elephant hook.
18. The twins were sitting at the counter, and they were eating hamburgers and French fries, so they didn't see Julie come into the restaurant.
19. Les Slocum was the referee at the game with Donner Academy, and he seemed to have it in for our team.
20. The New York police had only one clue, and it was a piece of cord from a Venetian blind, so they began their investigation by interviewing all the cord wholesalers in the city.

[and, section 2 / so, section 2]

EXERCISE 17. Read the following sentences and decide where commas are needed (to set off introductory clauses and verbal phrases, interrupting elements, appositives, contrasting expressions, etc.). On a sheet of paper, write the number of each sentence. After it, write any word or words that should be followed by a comma. After each of these words, place the comma. If no punctuation is needed, write "None." Be ready to explain why you have punctuated as you have.

1. Most of Grandpa's good advice however fell on deaf ears.
2. As soon as the pond freezes Harry is going to teach me to ice-skate.
3. Yes I think Mr. Martin will be reelected.
4. Mr. Martin will be reelected I think.
5. Those who left left between the third and fourth acts.
6. Sidney Fortrender the producer of the program was not available for comment however.
7. The day after Beverly apologized.
8. In fact we found letters dating from as early as July 15 1887 from relatives long since dead.
9. Gilbert's parents spoke German at home; Juan's Spanish.

10. But in the campaign of 1840 it was the Whigs not the Democrats who thought up the catchy slogan.
11. Well to tell the truth Mother you are not the only parent who disapproves of the idea.
12. The newspaper I was quite sure had said that the performance would be given on Sunday November 10 at McCormick Place.
13. By exercising and starving Linda managed to lose ten pounds.
14. He called again and again the line was busy.
15. When Claude Deerfield comes to bat the left fielder automatically moves back.
16. Thinking that Lester had spent the summer in London England rather than London Ontario Marcia asked him whether he had seen the changing of the guard at Buckingham Palace.
17. After all there is only one course open to us now isn't there?
18. He came back the day after Beverly apologized.
19. After calling his mother Melvin spent the night at our house.
20. In *All the King's Men* Robert Penn Warren tells the story of Willie Stark a demagogue and dictator from the point of view of Jack Burden one of his assistants.
21. To make them produce more hens have been provided with everything from vitamins to stereophonic music.
22. Not until after he had hung up did he realize poor fellow that he had made a date not with Sarah but with Susan her twin sister.
23. Outside the heat waves rising from the desert were actually visible.
24. They usually cut thick slices of bread and butter them while they are still warm.
25. Because the tunes were pleasing and simple people remembered them.

[Comma, sections 2, 4, 6, 7b, 8, 9]

EXERCISE 18. Read the sentences and decide where punctuation marks — commas or semicolons — are needed to separate items in a series. On a sheet of paper, write the number of each sentence. After it, write any word or words that should be followed by a punctuation mark. After each of these words, place the appropriate mark. Three of the sentences also need marks to set off various sentence elements. Be sure to include these marks in your answers. If no punctuation is needed, write "None."

1. Don measured the fish shook his head in disbelief and then measured once more.
2. Slowly cautiously noiselessly Fulton crept toward the sentry.
3. Walters immediately sent samples to the laboratories in New York Kansas City San Francisco and Orlando.
4. Portia had always liked the rambling comfortably old-fashioned house.
5. Madeira is famous for its embroideries its wicker baskets and furniture and its wines.
6. For three whole days it rained and rained and rained.

7. In the office on the bus and at home Phil mulled over how best to present his idea.
8. I have also exchanged duplicate stamps with pen pals in Brisbane Australia Dunedin New Zealand and Nicosia Cyprus.
9. At the inn they were given a small dark stuffy room with a single grimy window facing a fish market.
10. Thackeray considered New York vigorous and exhilarating Boston rather stolid and settled and Charleston gracious and cosmopolitan.
11. Often snakes spiders scorpions and centipedes were as much of a hazard to the jungle patrols as the snipers were.
12. Within fifteen minutes we had cleared the table washed and dried the dishes put the cat out and were ready to go.
13. Mr. Lasky was a tall tough-looking old man with a bald head and a black handlebar mustache.
14. Into the gully near the big billboard people had dumped four empty beer bottles a dented and rusty box and a car seat with a gash in the upholstery.
15. Because the early typewriters were expensive because they had many defects and because few people were trained to use them businessmen considered them impractical.
16. Mrs. Barlow knew how many people lived in each of her apartments where each adult worked and approximately how much he earned.
17. During his student days in Vienna his best friends were Anton Mattesich an Austrian Casimir Drwiega a Pole and Hedwig Zintl a German.
18. She said she had no idea who the man was or why he had called.
19. In a typical week Sammy traded his Monopoly set for a stamp collection the stamps for ten model rockets the rockets for a catcher's mitt and the mitt for a pair of roller skates.
20. Last week the class elected Virginia Murillo president Maureen Evans vice-president Geraldine Smith secretary and Victor Swanson treasurer.

[Comma, sections 3, 10e, 10f / Semicolon, section 3]

EXERCISE 19. Decide which of the phrases and clauses in the following numbered items are nonrestrictive and should be set off by commas. On a sheet of paper, write the number of each sentence. After it, write any word or words that should be followed by a comma. After each of these words, place the comma. Write "None" after the number of any sentence in which commas are not needed. Be ready to explain why you punctuated the sentences as you did.

1. Mr. Berkowitz simply put on his coat and walked out leaving us to draw our own conclusions.
2. The deadline had to be met no matter how late they would have to work.
3. If anything happened to his hands which are insured for a hundred thousand dollars his career as a concert pianist would be finished.

4. Down the aisle came Mr. Natwick his clothes reeking of stale tobacco.
5. An hour later when we needed him most he was gone.
6. The new dietitian accustomed to planning meals for resort hotels had a hard time adjusting to a school-cafeteria budget.
7. Every woman coming into the store on opening day was given a red rose.
8. The people in the next apartment complain if we have our TV on after ten o'clock
9. She'll be the first to complain if I know Helen.
10. All the gifts wrapped in green and gold are for the girls; the others wrapped in red and silver are for the boys.
11. Mr. Torrence who felt neither old nor incompetent resented having to retire just because he was fifty-five.
12. Within ten minutes as Stan well knew his paper would be collected whether he had completed the test or not.
13. Many artists whose works were ridiculed ten or twenty years ago are now praised for having developed a completely new concept of painting.
14. She was very much interested in politics especially at the local level.
15. For centuries man has enjoyed inventing and listening to stories which scare him out of his wits.
16. During the winter Thackeray stayed in New York where he met and fell in love with Sally Baxter.
17. The car was hopelessly stuck; the back wheels sunk above the hubcaps in mud just dug in deeper each time I accelerated.
18. The following day the dock where the prize fish had been caught was mobbed with eager anglers.
19. The librarian refused to let me take the book until I returned the magazines I had borrowed.
20. During her freshman year Lucy had a crush on her English professor and her fencing instructor. She soon lost interest in the professor who had a wife and two children; but the fencing instructor who had no wife and had fought in the Hungarian Revolution was more romantic daydream material.

[Comma, section 5 / Restrictive and nonrestrictive]

EXERCISE 20. The italicized modifiers in these sentences could be punctuated as either restrictive or nonrestrictive, depending on the meaning the writer intended in a particular context. Be ready to explain the difference in meaning when the modifiers are not set off and when they are.

1. The gray metal box *in which he kept his bonds* had disappeared.
2. The kindergarten children *seated in the last three rows* could neither see nor hear.
3. Yesterday Mr. Zellner assigned only one problem *which I could not do.*
4. The boys *who had volunteered to help decorate the gym* came early.

5. The next day Kay discovered another cigarette burn *on the table.*
6. Many people praised the costumes *which the art class had designed.*
7. The guards *posted at the west gate* could not hear his shouts.
8. Why don't you sign your name *as you were told to do?*
9. If I had been there, I would have bought one of the polyester suits *which were on sale.*
10. The owner of the restaurant glared at the waitress *who had dropped the tray.*

[Comma, section 5 / Restrictive and nonrestrictive]

EXERCISE 21. Copy the following sentences, adding quotation marks, capital letters, and all other punctuation that is needed.

1. Pointing her finger sternly at Norman Mrs. Bridges said there is absolutely no excuse for such behavior young man
2. Wasn't it Will Rogers who used to say all I know is just what I read in the papers
3. What a clever idea Jill exclaimed do you really think it will work
4. As a clincher Max quoted Murphy's Law if anything can go wrong it will
5. Shaking his head with finality Mr. Bowman said no you cannot take the test over
6. How would you like to have to recite all the stanzas of The Highwayman asked Lawrence
7. Coach Tate was really angry he threatened to bench the whole first string Eric reported looking very worried
8. Do you know what you are he shouted you're a jinx
9. The other article Mr. Sanchez assigned Early Man in the Andes is in this month's *Scientific American* Gerald said
10. Why aren't you laughing where's your sense of humor Dan asked
11. What a surprise it was to hear someone like him say I haven't got none
12. Did you notice Sylvia asked indignantly how those two girls kept talking and giggling all the while Ellen was auditioning it was disgusting
13. In his address to the United States Senate on January 22 1917 Woodrow Wilson stated I am seeking only to face realities and to face them without soft concealments
14. Bob told me he had no idea who turned on the hose but I don't believe him Jane said wringing out her dripping skirt
15. Well what would you do Leo asked if someone pointed a gun at you and said this is a holdup
16. He asked Agnes if she would play Stardust and Begin the Beguine those are the only tunes I really like he explained gravely
17. I will she replied if you'll hum a few bars for me I've forgotten how they go
18. Whatever you do the guard warned us don't stray from the group

[Quotation marks]

295

EXERCISE 22. Each of the following sentences contains one or more punctuation marks that are misleading or are not essential to the meaning. Be ready to tell what these marks are and to explain why it would be better to omit them (or substitute other marks).

1. Lars did his best, but, not even he could move the heavy log.
2. Coleridge never did finish the poem, "Kubla Khan," which he had begun writing, after awakening from a dream.
3. Following the fire engines in the parade were: the Girl Scouts; the Eagles; a high-school band; and a group of riders, from a local dude ranch.
4. He asked me "if I had finished my report?"
5. When Laura flashed her diamond ring,—but you can probably guess the excitement at the office then!!!
6. Soon the fiddlers were playing, "Turkey in the Straw."
7. Shoes, which are too short, should not be worn.
8. Once more the lights, the crowds, the noise of the city, exhilarated him.
9. She patiently, and accurately transferred the pattern to the white, linen, cloth.
10. Jerry was so stunned at hearing his number called, that he just sat there, and stared at the ticket in his hand.
11. I asked myself "what I would have done if I had been Ted?"
12. The woman who claimed to be her best (?) friend, was the very one, who had spread all the rumors.
13. Because the guarantee on our TV set had run out the day before it went out of commission; it cost us over a hundred dollars for repairs, and we missed, seeing our favorite programs for three weeks in a row.
14. Louise, Ginny, and Marie both called, and volunteered to help.
15. The only thing we could do was: to pay the fine.

[Colon / Comma / Dash / Exclamation mark / Period / Question mark / Quotation marks / Semicolon]

EXERCISE 23. Decide which words in each of the following sentences should be capitalized. After the number of the sentence, write these words, supplying the necessary capital letters.

1. in andrew jackson's time alabama, kentucky, tennessee, and mississippi were considered part of the west, not the south.
2. yesterday professor vandermeer and his wife sailed for holland on the *nieuw amsterdam.*
3. no, uncle mike, walnut street is one block south of lincoln avenue.
4. during the summer don wears only arrow drip-dry shirts.
5. now there are busts of both orville and wilbur wright in the hall of fame on the campus of new york university.
6. the buckingham memorial fountain in chicago's grant park is made of georgia marble.

7. at rockefeller center the japanese tourists especially enjoyed radio city music hall and the studios of the national broadcasting company.
8. before labor day the board of education hired a young man from michigan to teach biology 2, english, and social studies.
9. in 1836 the democrats nominated martin van buren; the whigs, william henry harrison.
10. but oh, how i dreaded giving that five-minute talk in french!
11. on june 15, 1215, english noblemen at runnymede forced king john to sign the magna charta guaranteeing civil and political rights to the people of england.
12. he also appeared last year at the stratford festival at stratford, ontario, as the clown in shakespeare's *as you like it* and as sir benjamin backbite in sheridan's *school for scandal*.
13. yes, thanksgiving always comes on a thursday; easter, on a sunday.
14. tom kent is president of the senior class and vice-president of the spanish club at our high school.
15. the campers from stone lodge walked indian file through the woods.
16. the story about david and goliath is in the old testament, maurice, not the new testament.
17. you haven't met bill's mother yet, have you, mom?
18. every sunday arlene, a roman catholic, goes to st. patrick's cathedral; peggy, a methodist, to kelvyn park community church.
19. "when the mayor arrives — oh, there you are, mayor!"
20. dad turned first to the article entitled "why the cost of living keeps creeping up."

[Capital letters]

EXERCISE 24. In each of the following sentences, one of the noun forms in italics is incorrect. The noun is misspelled, the apostrophe is in the wrong place, or there should be no apostrophe. Read each sentence carefully to be sure you understand the intended meaning. Then on a sheet of paper, copy each sentence, substituting a correct form for the incorrect one. Circle the form that you substituted.

1. Ed offered to drive the *Harris's* home from the *Elsons'* party.
2. The *Harris's* house is three miles from the *Elsons'* house.
3. We made *pig's* of ourselves, eating all those pickled *pigs'* feet.
4. It wasn't *Bob's* fault that *Charle's* hamster got out of the cage.
5. Does the *mens'* league or the *ladies'* league bowl on Tuesday?
6. Never open other *people's letter's* without their permission.
7. A special committee of *instructor's* counted the *students'* votes.
8. *Gary's* bicycle was lying in the middle of the *Dooley's* drive.
9. The *man's* jokes about the high price of *women's* clothing did not amuse the *saleslady's*.
10. His two *son-in-laws* aren't much interested in *sports*.

[Plurals of nouns / Possessive case, section 1]

7 8 9 10 11 12 13 14 15 16 17 18 19 20 21 22 23 24 25   80 79 78 77 76 75 74